Financial Report
of the
United States

Financial Report of the United States

NELSON CURRENT

A Subsidiary of Thomas Nelson, Inc.

This edition is based on the *2005 Financial Report of the U.S. Government (Financial Report)* published by the Department of the Treasury on December 15, 2005.

Published in Nashville, Tennessee, by Nelson Current, a division of a wholly-owned subsidiary (Nelson Communications, Inc.) of Thomas Nelson, Inc.

Nelson Current books may be purchased in bulk for educational, business, fundraising, or sales promotional use. For information, please e-mail SpecialMarkets@ThomasNelson.com.

Library of Congress Cataloging-in-Publication Data

United States. Dept. of the Treasury.
    Financial report of the United States / intro by Jim Cooper.
      p. cm.
    Includes bibliographical references and index.
    ISBN 1-59555-080-1 (alk. paper)
    ISBN: 978-1-59555-080-4
    1. Finance, Public--United States--Accounting. 2. Financial statements,
Consolidated—United States. 3. Financial statements—United States. I. Title.
    HJ257.U55 2006
    336.73—dc22

                                                        2006021079

Printed in the United States of America
06 07 08 09 10 RRD 5 4 3 2 1

JIM COOPER represents the people of the Nashville, Tennessee, area in Congress and teaches graduate business students at the Owen School of Management, Vanderbilt University. In Congress, Jim serves on the Budget Committee and Armed Services Committee, and is Policy Co-Chair of the Blue Dog Coalition, a group of 37 fiscally-conservative Democrats. A former attorney and investment banker, Jim has been chairman of the audit committees of three public companies. Jim is a graduate of Harvard Law School, Oxford University (Rhodes Scholar), and the University of North Carolina-Chapel Hill (Morehead Scholar).

To my wife, Martha,
and our children: Mary, Jamie, and Hayes

Foreword

Why This Report Matters to You

The White House does *not* want you to read this book. Although federal law compels U.S. Treasury officials to publish the information in this Financial Report, they hope you will not see it. That's why they issued this shocking news just before a major holiday without a press conference or even a press release. They succeeded. There was no media coverage.

The Bush Administration had a similar reaction to the *9/11 Commission Report*. But that document, compiled by an able independent group, became a national bestseller anyway. People demand the truth.

Apparently, the White House does not think that you can handle the truth about the various financial threats facing America. I think the White House is underestimating you. Your future—and your family's future—depends on what you do with this information. I think you can handle it.

This book is the "annual report" for America, using the format and accounting methods familiar to the shareholders of all stock-exchange companies. Sadly, very few people in government know this Financial Report even exists, much less what it contains, although it can be said to complement the U.S. Constitution itself. That magnificent document is the charter of the world's only superpower; this Report tells you how America is doing financially 219 years later. The Constitution is about governance; this Report is about operations. Isn't it time you got the facts?

You already get your favorite company's annual report, why not your favorite country's? While you've been pledging allegiance, politicians have been pledging your assets. So, let's salute the flag and scrutinize the financials. You are citizen-shareholders because, as President Lincoln said, our government is "of the people, by the people, and for the people." You also pick up the tab when your elected leaders pledge the "full faith and credit" of the United States.

Your most important investment occurs when you pay your taxes every year. We live in the greatest nation on earth, but we must work hard to keep it that way. This Report is the best way to check on your investment, just as reading Warren Buffet's famous annual report is the best way to keep up with Berkshire Hathaway.

This Financial Report for America is full of surprises. WARNING: it flatly contradicts most of the speeches that Washington politicians make. For example, according to the federal government's own financial statements for 2005,

- The "true" 2005 **deficit was $760 billion,** not the $318.5 billion that is usually reported—a whopping $441.5 billion difference

- The deficit is not 2.6% of Gross Domestic Product (GDP) and shrinking, as we are frequently told, but **6.2% of GDP and growing rapidly**

- **President Bush's promise** to cut the deficit in half in five years **did not refer to this "true" deficit**

- The news is **much worse if you count the unfunded commitments of Social Security and Medicare**

- America's debts and commitments do not total $8.3 trillion, as commonly reported, but **$49 trillion**

- In 2000, our total **debts and commitments** totaled $20 trillion, but they have more than **doubled in the last five years**

- The 2003 Medicare **drug bill** alone added over $8 trillion in unfunded commitments to American taxpayers

- **Giant tax loopholes,** or tax expenditures, are also at fault

- America's **top auditor is unable to give an opinion** about our nation's finances due to, in his words, **"material weaknesses"** and America's **"broken business model"**

- The federal agency that keeps **the worst books** is the Department of Defense; and

- This Report **doesn't even cover problems with Fannie Mae, Freddie Mac,** or other government-sponsored enterprises with widely reported financial problems

Economists politely call many of these trends "unsustainable." I call them the road to ruin. And the following information is not a partisan attack; this is *an official document of the U.S. Government issued by the Bush Administration itself.*

It's not all bad news. The Report also gives you interesting information about your birthright as an American.

- **How much gold** do we own in Fort Knox or elsewhere, and how is it valued?

- How many items are in the **Smithsonian Museum?**

- How much **government land** is there, and how much is still forested?

This is the *only* book that gives you the answers you need to your questions about America's financial position. Non-government reports often lack credibility; other government reports are inadequate. This is the only government-wide report that uses modern accounting to tell how America is doing. And yet, the Bush Administration does not want you to read it.

Don't take my word for it. This year, the Budget Committee of the U.S. House of Representatives voted unanimously to require this Report to be used in next year's presidential and congressional budget process. Although Democrats and Republicans usually agree on very little, they agreed that we should be using the numbers in this Report to help guide our nation. But don't get your hopes up. The White House and congressional leaders will figure out a way to dodge the requirement. You'll have to watch closely this year to see who kills the proposal and with what weapon.

- - - - -

What about the President's Budget that we hear so much about? Doesn't it contain the same information? Can't the average citizen learn about government finances from it? Not really. The Budget that receives all the political and media attention every year is comprised of several volumes, four inches thick, and costs $285 from the Government Printing Office. It is hand-delivered to every office on Capitol Hill. The Report you hold in your hands now is far more accessible: it doesn't weigh as much as a stack of phone books, costs less than fifteen dollars, is more comprehensive although less detailed, and is distributed wherever books are sold.

But inaccessibility isn't the only problem with the President's Budget. Standing alone, the Budget is also grossly misleading. Look at how much it differs from the Financial Report. It's hard to believe that the two documents are describing the same nation in the same year. Does the column on the right look like America, or Argentina?

	President's Budget	Financial Report
2005 Deficit:	$318.5 Billion	$760 Billion
National Debt & Commitments:	$8.3 Trillion	$49 Trillion
Your Share:	$28,000	$156,000

Again, remember, the Financial Report is an official U.S. government document. When historical, official numbers are this far apart, it is difficult to have a realistic debate about the future—particularly if you talk, as Congress does, only about the smaller numbers. No wonder budget debates in Washington are so confusing and unrealistic. If you don't know where you are, how can you know where you are going?

According to the Budget, every man, woman, and child in America is already obligated to pay $28,000, that is, if we ever plan to reduce our national debt. But it's really much worse than that. The Financial Report indicates that each citizen "owes" $156,000. For every *working* American, the total is a whopping $375,000. And this assumes that Congress stops making promises!

It's not surprising that the Administration is covering up the fact that, as a working American, your personal share of federal debt and obligations is so huge. It's tough to tell you that you already owe your government the equivalent of a luxury home—only you don't get to live in it. You just get the mortgage. And that's on top of the mortgage you are already paying on the home you live in, in addition to all your other living expenses.

During the five years of the Bush Administration, your share of the government's liabilities and commitments has *more than doubled*, from $165,000 in 2000 to $375,000 today. It took 214 years of American history (from George Washington through Bill Clinton) for our elected officials to burden you with $165,000 in government obligations, but only five years of the George W. Bush Administration to double that number. At this rate, you and your family will soon "owe" well over a million dollars to the U.S. Government.

Of course, the most painful part of any debt is making the monthly interest and principal payments. In order to service a $375,000 debt, you must pay $1,400 a month in interest *forever* even at the low government interest rate of 4.5%. To make typical 30-year, level principal-and-interest payments in order to pay down the debt, your monthly payments would be $1,900. Where are you going to get that kind of money? Most Americans are already stretched financially. The national savings rate has recently declined to below zero. We are spending more than we earn. That cannot last.

Our government paid $327 billion in interest in 2005 just to carry the debts we already have, without making any effort to reduce them. This was money that could not be spent on schools, parks, roads, or homeland security because it had to satisfy our creditors. As our debts mount, our interest costs are predicted to rise higher than $400 billion annually—more money than is spent by Congress on all of our normal domestic needs (i.e. what is technically called "non-defense, non-homeland-security, domestic discretionary spending"). *In a few years, it will be a better financial deal to be a creditor of America than a citizen.* Even that might not be much of a problem if we had borrowed the money from our own citizens, because we would be paying the interest to ourselves. But the low national savings rate means that we have had to turn to foreign lenders.

Today, America is borrowing more money from foreigners than ever before, resulting in more and more interest payments to Japanese, Chinese, British, and other lenders. During the last five years, President Bush has borrowed more money abroad than all previous American presidents *combined.* Many of these countries are not close allies. China holds roughly $300 billion of our debt. Russia, Iran, and Venezuela are becoming major creditors. And remember, interest payments to these nations are given priority over all other government spending, even national defense.

If you had been able to read a book like this earlier, you might have been able to help slow our massive borrowing and reduce our dependence on foreign capital. But it's not too late to stop the government from sinking deeper into debt.

- - - - -

Every businessman and woman in America knows the importance of keeping honest books. If they budgeted the way the U.S. Government does, they'd be in jail.

Wharton School Professor Kent Smetters testified to Congress that "current federal budgetary practices would be illegal in the private sector." Another expert has said that "the size of this accounting distortion makes Enron look like a minor accounting error."

- - - - -

How could the President's Budget and the Financial Report be so different? The answer is different yardsticks. The Budget measures government by looking at cash and obligations, i.e. primarily when dollars are received and spent. The Financial Report, on the other hand, uses the same measuring method that all large American businesses are required to use—"accrual" accounting. Both ways of measuring are important, if you want a clear understanding of your financial position.

Although the word accrual may be unfamiliar to some readers, it should not be confused with the word *cruel* (which is an easy mistake to make when looking at such negative numbers). Not only is it spelled differently, it is different. Accrual accounting means recognizing income when it is *earned* and expenses when they are *incurred*, not just when cash changes hands. This is a vital distinction. Not only is accrual accounting not cruel, you could say that it is, in many circumstances, the kindest form of accounting because it remembers your loved ones. It helps you better understand the bills that you have committed your children and grandchildren to pay.

In our credit-card world, we need to make forward-looking measurements such as are possible with accrual accounting. This is particularly important in the budgeting process for our nation. Ironically, budgeting is the one area where Congress has *not* been using accrual techniques.

As **Alan Greenspan,** former Chairman of the Federal Reserve Board, testified,

> Scoring the budget on an accrual basis—the private sector norm and, I believe, a sensible direction for federal budget accounting—would better underscore the tradeoffs we face. Under accrual accounting, benefits would be counted as they are earned by workers rather than when they are paid out by the government.

Don't you want to know how America looks under both cash and accrual measurements so that you can get a better perspective? Isn't it important to see both a current financial snapshot and the long-term picture? A nation that is 219-years-old needs to use bifocals: reading glasses for counting cash, and different lenses to see our long-term obligations—the same way any corporation or business views its own finances.

- - - - -

Why didn't you know about this Report before now? Why doesn't your Congressman or Senator know about it? True, the numbers have been hidden, but Congress has not been looking very hard. It's been a game of hide and *no seek*.

Beginning in the mid-1990s, the U.S. Treasury was required by federal law to prepare consolidated financial statements for the U.S. Government. These Reports have been gradually improving in their presentation, content, and methodology. Fortunately, due to the excellent work of the Financial Accounting Standards Advisory Board (FASAB), we are now able to measure government activity much more fairly and more completely than before, although more work remains to be done.

The Report is also increasingly important because its bottom line has begun to diverge significantly from the Budget's. The graph on the following page shows the relationship between the Report's bottom line and the Budget's for the last nine years.

Trends like these are causing the leading bond-rating agency, Standard & Poor's, to project that the United States could lose its AAA credit rating by 2012, and fall "below investment grade" by 2025. Today's policies are literally destroying America's credit.

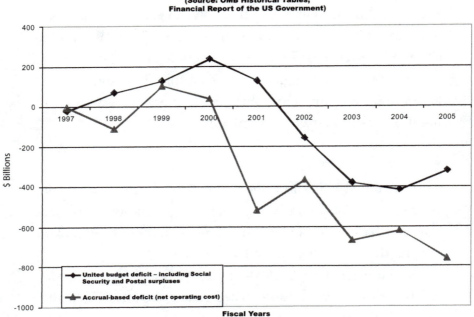

Surpluses and Deficits
(Source: OMB Historical Tables;
Financial Report of the US Government)

Notice the last year on the chart: 2005. Not only is the "net operating cost"—the technical term for the accrual deficit—over twice as large as the Budget deficit, it seems to be growing larger, not smaller, as the Bush Administration claims. Growth in veterans' benefits and civil service retirement obligations has caused this divergence. Notice also that the "net operating cost" varies more than the cash deficit numbers because assumptions can change about accrued expenses. The trends in the accrual numbers are undeniably worse than the cash deficits, although both trends have turned negative since 2001.

- - - - -

Critics of the Financial Report will use a variety of arguments to downplay its importance. Their main objection is not to accrual budgeting itself, at least when considered parallel to cash budgeting, but to the size of the deficits it reveals. These critics don't believe that you will react responsibly to the higher deficit figures, so they prefer to keep you in the dark about the existence of this Report. They feel that their favorite programs may be threatened if government tightens or rearranges spending. They may be right. But those programs are living on borrowed time anyway because, whether measured in cash or by accrual, eventually the government has to pay its bills. I would argue that the best way to save deserving programs is to recognize their true costs now so that we can prepare to fund their needs.

Some critics will raise technical objections, criticizing or at least obscuring the trustworthiness of accrual accounting.

Is accrual easier to manipulate due to the assumptions that must be made regarding interest rates, life expectancy, health costs, and retirement expenses? I don't think so. With transparency and supervision, we can keep the numbers honest. Cash accounting is also easy to manipulate.

Are the time horizons too long for accuracy when you are estimating 75 years out? It is difficult to estimate, but we must try. The alternative is to send children born today into an even more uncertain financial future. Given longer life expectancy, 75 years is often not long enough.

Finally, is it fair to apply accrual accounting to government, which is non-profit? Certain modifications have been made in order to estimate, for example, the value of our military equipment and its depreciation. But with such adjustments, the method is fair and very revealing.

The most common objection that I've heard from colleagues is that "I've made so many speeches using the President's Budget numbers, I don't want to change now." Old habits die hard. All I advocate is adding a new habit to your old one: keep one eye on your cash accounts and the other on your accruals.

- - - - -

When you read the Financial Report, you will be surprised to see that it describes all of the federal government in only five pages of financial statements. This condensed view of our massive $2.8 trillion government is a remarkable technical accomplishment, especially since it was compiled within 75 days after the end of the fiscal year. It is a veritable Rosetta Stone, enabling us to translate how agencies ranging from the Department of Defense to the U.S. Postal Service do their jobs. Together with the Notes describing line items, these five pages give the most complete and concise view available anywhere of America's finances. And it is presented in a language that the average small businessman or woman understands.

To make the five pages of financials easier to digest, they are preceded by "Management Discussion and Analysis," just as you would find in any corporation's annual report. This explanation tends to be a bit self-serving, but is helpful in placing the numbers in context. For example, a crucial paragraph on page 22, entitled "Other Responsibilities," helps us begin to understand how Social Security and Medicare could fit into the accrual budget.

When you look at the Balance Sheets for America, don't be alarmed because it shows a negative "Net Position" of $7.7 trillion. Although such a huge liability on the net equity line of a corporate balance sheet would bankrupt any corporation in the world, nations can live quite well with large negative net positions.

America is obviously a going concern. Our assets are probably worth far more than the financials indicate, and the government's ability to raise revenue is considerable.

It would be interesting, and probably scary, if the federal government were required to include the "Risk Factors" section that is required of all publicly-traded companies. Then, Americans could see, in plain English, the threats that each administration fears. Even Stephen King and Wes Craven might shudder at some of the lurking dangers.

An unaudited section on "Stewardship" of national assets and responsibilities helps readers begin to quantify the gigantic out-year promises that have been made, but not funded, using our national credit card. These obligations are not accrued into our financials the way veteran's benefits and civil service retirement benefits are, because they are not legally binding obligations of the U.S. Government. They are "scheduled" in the bureaucratic parlance of Washington and must be better understood. Here the Financial Report borrows heavily from the Social Security and Medicare Trustees Report, which projects 10-year, 75-year, and even "infinite" outlooks for the benefits of each program.

Finally, the Financial Report contains letters from America's top auditor, David M. Walker, the Comptroller General of the United States, and head of the U.S. Government Accountability Office (GAO). One letter is only six pages long, the other twelve. They, with their supporting documents, contain some of the most devastating analyses of America's current financial position, including his conclusion that America has a "broken business model."

Walker points out how many agencies with giant budgets simply cannot account for the taxpayer money they receive.

The Pentagon is the worst offender, even during peacetime. But most agencies have significant accounting problems. We know, for example, that the government made $38 billion in improper payments in 2005, and that over $20 billion cannot be properly accounted for. **So, we've paid $38 billion to the wrong people, and completely lost another $20 billion!** It's time that more taxpayers knew about this abuse and forced their government to do something about it.

- - - - -

What about *your* Social Security benefits? What about *your* Medicare benefits? Almost all seniors feel strongly that Washington should not tamper with Social Security or Medicare. So do workers paying their part of today's 12.4% and 2.9% payroll taxes. This Financial Report gives a much clearer picture of those benefits than is available from a cash budget, or is available from the Social Security Trustees (although the Trustees have begun quietly including some more helpful information in their reports).

You will see that for all the President's efforts to reform Social Security in 2005, Medicare is in much worse shape. You will also see that unless reform efforts on both programs are undertaken very soon, experts estimate that (a) benefits will have to be cut in half, (b) payroll taxes doubled, or (c) some combination of the two. All of these choices are unacceptable to voters. Therefore, structural reforms of both programs are necessary, *right now*. President Bush called for a high-level entitlement reform commission in his January 2006 State of the Union Address, but as of June, had yet to appoint a single commissioner.

Foreign policy expert Michael Mandelbaum has written in

his new book, *The Case for Goliath: How America Acts as the World's Government in the 21st Century,* that the greatest single long-term threat America faces is not from terrorists, a belligerent China, or a resurgent Russia, but from our own Medicare program.

One of the chief sources of confusion is the large amount of money that the Bush Administration (and every president since Reagan) borrows from Social Security every year. In 2005, the Bush Administration borrowed $173 billion from Social Security. In 2006, it will borrow another $180 billion. This does not mean that anyone misappropriated any money owed to beneficiaries. But it does mean that we are misleading ourselves when we reduce the publicly reported deficit by that amount. Under current law, the U.S. Government is able to borrow this money from Social Security because buying Treasury bonds (i.e. lending money to Uncle Sam) or other U.S. Government-backed securities is the only investment allowed to the Social Security Trustees. The result is that the true size of the federal budget deficit is downplayed, even within the guidelines of cash budgeting.

In 2005, the federal budget deficit was reported as $318.5 billion, but the government borrowed $570 billion that year from lenders here and around the world, and from our own trust funds. Our net cash deficit was $318.5 billion, but the gross deficit was $570 billion. Why is the larger number rarely reported? Because Uncle Sam has its own captive lender in Social Security. Many economists believe that, because "the government is borrowing from itself," you don't have to report the gross figure. My view is that if you believe that you must repay Social Security just as faithfully as you do foreign lenders, you should report the larger figure. Both are strict obligations of the U.S.

Government. Having a captive lender does not reduce the amount of the borrowing.

Under accrual accounting, the government must keep track of every expense it incurs, including the retirement costs of those government workers who are paying into a legally-binding retirement fund. Here is where many of our nation's seniors—including federal employees hired after 1984—are in for a nasty surprise. Veterans and older federal employees are earning such benefits, but Social Security, Medicare, and younger federal employee beneficiaries are not, because theirs are not considered to be contractual benefits. Under the 1960 U.S. Supreme Court ruling in *Fleming v. Nestor*, these seniors can have their future benefits reduced by Congress at any time without recourse in the courts.

Every living politician has made countless speeches about "the nation's commitment to seniors" or "our sacred obligation" to them. As an employee, you get an annual statement from the Social Security Administration listing the payroll taxes you have paid along with your expected benefits. Yet, this statement includes the warning that the Social Security trust funds lack the money to pay all these benefits. Legally, the benefits you expect are only "scheduled," not contractual—but who reads the fine print? As such, they are not included in accrual accounting.

Fortunately, the Report details the government's responsibility for these benefits in the "Stewardship" section, almost as if they were legally-binding obligations. Here, the Report goes beyond accrual accounting to give us a clearer picture of our nation's promises, which total $49 trillion, not the $8.3 trillion commonly reported. The $49 trillion is a present-value number, meaning that we need to find $49 trillion today and invest it wisely, in order to have enough money to pay the Social Security and Medicare bills of babies born today. Forty-nine trillion dollars is roughly the annual earnings of everyone and every company on earth. In other words, if we confiscated all wages, salaries, and profits worldwide for one year, we might have enough money, if it were invested prudently, to cover the shortfall in America's two major entitlement programs.

These staggering out-year commitments are hard for anyone to comprehend, so it may be helpful to see five different definitions of the single-year 2005 deficit so that you can pick your favorite and understand its size.

"True" 2005 Deficit?	Definition of Deficit	Size Comparison
$318.5 Billion (cash accounting)	"Unified," After Borrowing $173 Billion from Social Security & Postal Service	Austria's Gross National Product
$494 Billion (cash accounting)	"On Budget," Excluding Social Security & Postal Service Surpluses	Switzerland's and Israel's GNP
$760 Billion (accrual accounting)	"Net Operating Cost" of Federal Government, Not counting Social Security or Medicare Promises	Russia's GNP
$2.2 Trillion ("accrual+" accounting)	"Net Operating Cost," plus 2005 Increase in Social Security Promises	United Kingdom's GNP
$3.3 Trillion ("accrual+" accounting)	"Net Operating Cost," plus 2005 Increase in Social Security and Medicare Promises	China's and India's GNP

The last two deficit numbers, which include Social Security and then both Social Security and Medicare, I owe to Professor Howell Jackson of Harvard Law School. He estimated the annual increments of our two largest entitlement programs, then added them to the $760 billion accrual deficit, in order to show how rapidly our fiscal gap is widening. The result is harrowing.

These larger deficit numbers are startling because they mean that the real deficit is probably *10 times larger than you have been told*, even if you are the most diligent watcher of C-SPAN, or work in the White House. They also mean that, unless we radically change our deficit calculations, we are not preparing to honor the commitments we have made to American workers.

Another reason these numbers are shocking is that the cost of one year's delay in addressing these problems is over $3 trillion. Costs are mounting at $347 million an hour, or $95,000 a second.

In Washington, the common assumption is that Congress will work less in 2006 because of the upcoming elections in November. Congress is scheduled to work fewer days than any time since 1948, or fewer than 90 days. President Truman called the 1948 Congress the "Do Nothing Congress." Such a short schedule allows little time for solving our fiscal problems, but lots of time for campaigning. We don't know who will win the election, but we do know that when Congress returns to its duties in January, 2007, our obligations will be $3 trillion larger than they are today. Time is of the essence.

History will not be kind to officeholders who persist in believing, despite the availability of modern accounting techniques, that their annual deficits are only one-tenth their true

size. Voters should not be kind either. You should make the numbers in this Report a major issue in the coming election.

- - - - -

It is not too late for our nation's first president with an MBA
degree to champion equal consideration of accrual numbers. If
you want government to be run more like a business, you have to
use business-like budgeting. The House Budget Committee's
unanimous March, 2006, vote to require inclusion of accrual
budgeting is a sign that bipartisan pressure may be building for
modern budgeting techniques in government.

A more radical thought is to require congressmen and sena-
tors to sign our country's financial statements just as corporate
executives must sign their annual reports, on penalty of personal
criminal liability. That would ensure that Congress members do
not ignore our nation's accounts.

At a minimum, it is time for the White House and U.S. Treasury
Department to stop hiding this crucial information in plain sight. It
is also time for federal candidates to declare whether they believe
America should budget using both cash and accrual numbers.

Here is a simple test: If they say the "true" deficit for 2005 was

1. $318.5 billion, then they favor the *status quo* (using cash
   budgeting only and hiding our borrowing from Social
   Security)

2. $760 billion, then they favor real change (using accrual
   budgeting as well as cash budgeting), but if they say

3. $3.3 trillion, then you might actually get real change,
   instead of a nice speech

We need a new generation of leaders to face the facts and make wise choices. This book empowers you to do a better job of choosing those leaders. If not you, who? If not now, when?

Jim Cooper
Nashville, June 2006

Acknowledgments

As Co-Chair for Policy of the fiscally conservative Blue Dog Coalition in Congress, I have benefited greatly from the wisdom of former Rep. Charlie Stenholm (D-TX) and the fellowship of all thirty-seven Blue Dogs. This centrist group may well hold the balance of power in the next Congress. I have benefited as well from the deep insight of Rep. John Spratt, the ranking member of the House Budget Committee, and his able staff, particularly Tom Kahn and Kimberly Overbeek. Across the aisle, members like Chris Chocola (R-IN), Frank Wolf (R-VA), Jeff Flake (R-AZ), and Jeb Hensarling (R-TX) have shown courage in facing up to budget facts.

I would like to thank David Walker, the Comptroller General of the U.S., for his tireless championing of better government accounting practices and greater fiscal responsibility. His testimony in the House Budget Committee first tipped me off to the elusive Financial Report of the United States. Under David's leadership, and with the able assistance of Sue Irving, the Government Accountability Office has published numerous materials to help us understand our fiscal predicament, particularly "21st Century Challenges: Reexamining the Base of the Federal Government," and "Understanding the Primary Components of the Annual Financial Report of the United States Government."

Howell E. Jackson, the James S. Reid, Jr. Professor of Law at Harvard Law School, deserves praise for his pioneering accrual analysis. Jagadeesh Gokhale and Kent Smetters of the Cato Institute and the Wharton School of the University of Pennsylvania have changed the way everyone understands our two most important entitlement programs: Social Security and Medicare. Isabel Sawhill and Peter Orszag of the Brookings Institution, Bob Greenstein, Jim Horney, and Richard Kogan of the Center for Budget and Policy Priorities, Gene Steuerle of the Urban Institute, and the *National Journal's* budget columnist Stan Collender, have helped many in Congress better understand budget issues.

Several congressmen merit praise for focusing particularly on the accrual issue. Todd Platts (R-PA) has held hearings every year on the Financial Report, even when Ed Towns (D-NY) was the only attendee.

A wide variety of advocacy groups have been advocating better budgeting for years, although not necessarily accrual budgeting. The Concord Coalition, the Committee for a Responsible Federal Budget, CED, Centrists.Org, Citizens Against Government Waste, National Taxpayers Union, and Institute for Truth in Accounting, have been working hard on these issues for many years.

My friend Robert Davidson is my favorite accountant. He and his firm of Davidson, Golden & Lundy in Nashville, Tennessee, have taught me more about number crunching than I ever learned in "Accounting for Lawyers" at Harvard Law School.

My brother John Cooper has long had the idea of creating "An Owner's Manual to Government," a handy paperback that would teach people much more effectively than civics textbooks tend to do about the way government really works, with an emphasis on your rights and responsibilities as a citizen. This book fulfills only a portion of my brother's dream but every journey begins with a single step.

A final thank you to my outstanding congressional staff, particularly my Chief of Staff, Greg Hinote, who gave up a business career to serve his country. Tom Emswiler and Cicely Simpson have been a big help to me in my Budget Committee work.

Whatever errors or omissions are in the Foreword are mine, and mine alone.

"[O]ne of the most secretive documents in Washington—the official Financial Report of the United States Government."

David Broder,

Washington Post,

13 April 2006

The following pages are an exact word-for-word, chart-for-chart, and graph-for-graph copy of an official U.S. Government Document entitled "2005 Financial Report of the United States Government" that was issued by the U.S. Treasury Department on December 15, 2005. The only changes made to the document involve reformatting the original pages to standard paperback dimensions. This Report became a collector's item the day it was published because the Government Printing Office only printed 2,100 copies.

Contents

Notes to the Financial Statements

List of Social Insurance Charts

A MESSAGE FROM THE
SECRETARY OF THE TREASURY

Our objective in preparing the fiscal year *2005 Financial Report of the U.S. Government* is to give the Congress and the American people a timely and useful report on the cost of the Federal Government's operations, the sources used to fund them, and the implications of our long-term financial commitments and obligations.

As Treasury and the Office of Management and Budget reported in October in our 2005 fiscal-year-end budget report, the growing economy brought 2005 revenues to a level of $2.2 trillion. This increase of almost $275 billion over 2004 revenues was nearly a 15 percent increase and was also the largest year-over-year percentage increase in receipts in over 20 years. These increased revenues resulted in a much lower-than-expected 2005 budget deficit. While deficits are never welcome, the 2005 deficit of $319 billion, when expressed as a percent of Gross Domestic Product, was lower than the deficits in 16 of the last 25 years.

In comparison with the October budget report, the *Financial Report* presents the government's accrual-based net operating cost, which was $760 billion in 2005. There is a difference in the amounts reported for the budget deficit and the net operating cost because of the distinct methods of accounting used. This year, the difference of $441 billion is due principally to a $198 billion increase in Veterans

Affairs' actuarial costs, mainly a reflection of changes in interest rate assumptions.

In addition to looking at the financial results of this past year, this report looks toward our nation's fiscal future. An important measure of the government's fiscal position is the cost of its responsibilities for social insurance programs such as Social Security and Medicare. Including these future financial responsibilities in this report gives a more complete and long-range look at the government's finances.

These government-wide financial statements reflect the Treasury Department's long-standing responsibility and commitment to report on the Nation's finances and our desire to inform and support the financial decision making that is critical to the nation's fiscal future.

John W. Snow

MANAGEMENT'S DISCUSSION AND ANALYSIS

Introduction

The accompanying *2005 Financial Report of the United States Government (Financial Report)* provides the President, Congress, and the American people information about the financial results and position of the Federal Government. It provides, on an accrual basis of accounting as prescribed by U. S. generally accepted accounting principles (GAAP) for Federal entities, a broad, comprehensive view of the Federal Government's finances. This report states the Government's financial position and condition, its revenues and costs, assets and liabilities, and other obligations and commitments. Finally, it discusses important financial issues and significant conditions that may affect future operations.

The *Financial Report,* required by 31 U.S.C. § 331(e)(1), is to be submitted to Congress by March 31 and is subject to audit by the Government Accountability Office (GAO). The Office of Management and Budget (OMB) accelerated its issue date to December 15 beginning with fiscal year 2004. Material deficiencies in financial reporting (which also represent material weaknesses in internal control) and other limitations on the scope of its work resulted in conditions that continued to prevent GAO from forming and expressing an opinion on the U.S. Government's consolidated financial statements for the fiscal years ended September 30, 2005 and 2004. See GAO's disclaimer of opinion on pages 233–263 for a full explanation of this and other material weaknesses that relate to this report.

Some of the significant agencies included in the *Financial*

Report received unqualified opinions on their fiscal year 2005 financial statements. For example, the Department of the Treasury (Treasury), which accounts for substantially all of the Federal Government's revenues and Federal debt, received an unqualified audit opinion on its fiscal year 2005 financial statements. Moreover, the Department of Veterans Affairs (VA), the Office of Personnel Management (OPM), and the Department of Defense's (DOD) Military Retirement Fund, which account for significant amounts included in this report for employee and veteran benefits, all received unqualified audit opinions on their fiscal year 2005 financial statements. Lastly, the *Financial Report's* Statements of Social Insurance include disclosed amounts subject to considerable scrutiny by the process used by the Trustees to prepare the numbers. These amounts will be audited for the first time starting for fiscal year 2006.

The *Financial Report* consists of Management's Discussion and Analysis, Statements of Net Cost, Statements of Operations and Changes in Net Position, Reconciliations of Net Operating Cost and Unified Budget Deficit, Statements of Changes in Cash Balance from Unified Budget and Other Activities, Balance Sheets, Stewardship Information, Notes to the Financial Statements, Supplemental Information, and Auditor's Report. The *Financial Report's* five financial statements are interrelated and work together. Chart A, on page 9, provides an overview of the statements and how selected parts of them tie together.

Management's Discussion and Analysis (MD&A) provides management's perspectives on the information presented in the Federal Government's financial statements and social insurance responsibilities. Table 1 is the table of contents for this MD&A.

Table 1: MD&A's Table of Contents
(Fiscal Year 2005)

Section	Page Number
Introduction	3-9
Executive Summary	10-12
Financial Results & Social Insurance Responsibilities	12-28
Economy, Federal Budget, & Federal Debt	28-33
U.S. Government's Mission & Organizational Structure	33-36
Significant Performance Accomplishments	37-46
Systems, Controls, & Legal Compliance	47-49
History of the Report & Additional Information	50-51

Accrual-Based Results and Basis of Accounting

Each year, the Administration issues two reports that detail financial results for the Federal Government: the President's Budget on the cash basis and the *Financial Report* on the accrual basis. The two reports complement each other. The budget report contains mainly cash receipt and outlay information and compares the results to the appropriations for the current fiscal year. The *Financial Report* uses those transactions as its base and also contains noncash-based revenues and expenses. For example, revenue accruals produce accounts receivable balances and the expense accruals produce liabilities for items such as pensions for Government workers, accounts payable, and environmental cleanup costs. As a result, this *Financial Report* is intended to provide the results of the Federal Government's financial operations, its financial condition, its revenues and costs, assets and liabilities, and other obligations and commitments. As such, it can be used with the budget as a planning and control tool not only for the current fiscal year but with a longer term focus as well.

The information in the financial statements (pages 69–73) was prepared based on U.S. GAAP standards developed by the Federal

Accounting Standards Advisory Board (FASAB). GAAP for the Federal Government is tailored to the U.S. Government's unique characteristics and special needs. For example, the Stewardship Information section of this report contains important information about diverse subjects such as land set aside for the use and enjoyment of present and future generations, heritage assets, and social insurance programs such as Social Security and Medicare.

Limitations of the Financial Statements

The principal financial statements have been prepared to report the financial position and results of operations of the Federal Government, pursuant to the requirements of 31 U.S.C. § 331(e)(1). While the statements have been prepared from the books and records of the entity in accordance with U.S. GAAP for Federal entities and the formats prescribed by OMB, the statements are in addition to the financial reports used to monitor and control budgetary resources which are prepared from the same books and records.

It must be noted that the audit opinions of several significant agencies are disclaimed. This means that the data could not be satisfactorily audited and may be incorrect, perhaps materially so. This report includes the balances provided by all agencies including those with disclaimed opinions. However, 18 of the 24 major Chief Financial Officers Act (CFO) agencies that are consolidated in this report received unqualified audit opinions.

Reporting Entity

These financial statements cover the three branches of the U.S. Federal Government. A list of the significant entities included in these financial statements is in the Appendix. Information from the judicial branch is limited to budgetary activity because its entities are not required by law to submit and do not submit comprehensive financial statement information to the Treasury. Even though the legislative branch is not required by law to submit comprehensive financial statement information to the Treasury, parts of it do so voluntarily while the information for other parts is limited to budgetary activity. The Federal Reserve System is excluded because it is an independent entity having both public purposes and private aspects. The Federal Retirement Thrift Investment Board is excluded because it is fiduciary in nature. Moreover, Government-sponsored but privately-owned enterprises (e.g., the Federal Home Loan Banks, the Federal National Mortgage Association, and the Federal Home Loan Mortgage Corporation) are also excluded.

How the Federal Government's Financial Statements are Related to Each Other

Federal accrual accounting has many similarities with accrual accounting used by virtually any entity, both private and public throughout the globe. On page nine, Chart A depicts how the Government's statements interrelate with each other and how each statement supports the next.

The Government uses several statements the average reader may not be familiar with. For example, items normally found on a private corporation's income statement are shown on two different statements. Expenses are shown on the Government's Statements of Net Cost (net of programmatic revenues), and general governmental revenues are shown on the Statements of Operations and Changes in Net Position. The Reconciliation of Net Operating Revenue (or Cost) and Unified Budget Surplus (or Deficit) statement and the Statements of Changes in Cash Balance from Unified Budget and Other Activities are both unique to the Federal Government. They are extremely important because they show how the budget deficit was funded and how it varies from the accrual results. In the private sector, when costs exceed revenues it is called a loss; in the Federal accrual world, we call this the Net Operating Cost. On the next page, Chart A shows how the statements fit together and which numbers are shown on more than one statement.

Chart A: How the Federal Government's Financial Statements are Related to Each Other

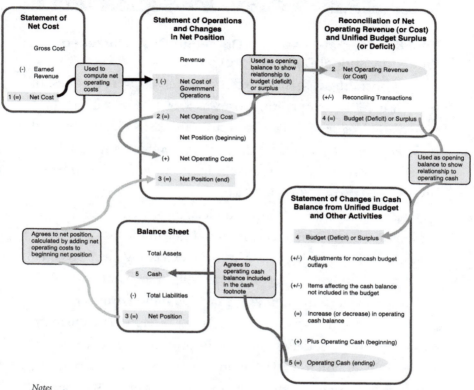

Notes

1 The total operating expense, called Net Cost, presented in the Statement of Net Cost is used in the Statement of Operations and Changes in Net Position to determine whether the Federal Government's financial operations (revenue less expenses) resulted in net operating cost or net operating revenue for the year.

2 The operating result from the Statement of Operations and Changes in Net Position explains the change in the Federal Government's net position. It is also the beginning balance in the Reconciliation of Net Operating Revenue (or Cost) and Unified Budget Surplus (or Deficit).

3 The Net Position from the Statement of Operations and Changes in Net Position agrees to the Net Position on the Balance Sheet, which is based on the difference between the Federal Government's reported assets and liabilities.

4 The unified budget result is used in the Reconciliation of Net Operating Revenue (or Cost) and Unified Budget Surplus (or Deficit) and the Statement of Changes in Cash Balance from Unified Budget and Other Activities to show how the Federal Government's financial operations and changes in operating cash are connected to the unified budget results.

5 The Federal Government's ending operating cash balance from the Statement of Changes in Cash Balance from Unified Budget and Other Activities is the same as the operating cash component of the "Cash and other monetary assets" line on the Balance Sheet. The operating cash amount can be found in the Balance Sheet note for Cash and other monetary assets.

Source: Government Accountability Office.

Executive Summary

Why the Accrual-Based Net Operating Cost Worsened While the Budget Deficit Improved

Net operating cost is the excess of expenses over revenues. In fiscal year 2005, net operating cost was $760 billion, which represented an *increase* of $144 billion from the $616 billion reported in fiscal year 2004. As was the case in 2004, most of the variability in net cost was driven by the change in the noncash veteran benefits actuarial costs at the VA.

Fiscal year 2005's budget deficit improved. The budget deficit, or the cash-based cost required to run the Government's operations, is a result of cash outlays exceeding cash receipts. The Federal budget deficit was $319 billion in fiscal year 2005, which represented an *improvement* of $93 billion, from the $412 billion reported in fiscal year 2004. Larger receipts were the main reason the budget deficit picture improved. Receipts rose by almost $274 billion to $2,153 billion, an increase of 14.6 percent, which more than offset the increase in outlays of $179 billion to $2,473 billion, or 7.9 percent.

As seen in Table 2, most of this year's net operating cost increase was caused by the significant increase in actuarial costs at the VA. The $228 billion increase in these costs explains why the net operating cost worsened while the budget results were significantly improved. These costs have experienced wide fluctuations over the past 6 years. For example, this noncash cost decreased by $52 billion in 2003, decreased by another $136 billion in 2004, and then increased by $228 billion this year.

Table 2: VA Actuarial Cost Impact on Net Operating Cost in Fiscal Year 2005
(In billions of dollars)

Impact on Net Operating Cost	$ Change
Budget Deficit Decline ($412-319)	$ 93
VA Actuarial Cost Increases	(228)
Other Net Cost Increases, Net	(9)
Net Operating Cost Increase ($616-760)	($144)

Social Insurance Responsibilities

In fiscal year 2005, the President began a discussion with the American people and Congress about reforming the 70-year-old Social Security Program. For 2005, the trustees again concluded that they "do not believe the currently projected long run growth rates of Social Security and Medicare are sustainable under current financing arrangements." Go to pages 24–28 to get a better understanding of what the trust funds are and the trustees short- and long-range outlooks for them. A summary of the trustees' 2005 Annual Reports may be found at www.social security.gov/OACT/TRSUM/trsummary.html.

Federal Hurricane Relief Effort

In response to the catastrophe of the Gulf Coast region caused by the hurricanes, Congress appropriated a little over $62 billion. Congress also temporarily increased the Federal Emergency Management Agency's (FEMA) National Flood Insurance Fund borrowing authority by $17.0 billion to a total of $18.5 billion.

For fiscal year 2005, FEMA's Disaster Relief Fund expended $3.5 billion related to Hurricanes Katrina and Rita. In addition, FEMA has accrued just over $23 billion this year related to the

hurricanes, including a major increase in its flood insurance liability. The final Federal amount that will be required to restore the
Gulf Coast region has not yet been determined.

Financial Results & Social Insurance Responsibilities

Statement of Net Cost Summary

The purpose of the Statement of Net Cost is to show how
much it costs to operate the Federal Government by Federal
agency and department, and in total. It provides costs on an
accrual basis, which recognizes expenses when they happen,
regardless of when the cash is paid. As a result, it provides
cost information for the accounting period that can be related to
the goods produced, services rendered, and the outcomes of the
Federal Government's agencies and departments for the same
period.

For fiscal year 2005, the Government reported a total gross
cost of $3,174.6 billion. This was an increase of $442.6 billion or
16.2 percent over last year's reported gross cost. An important
concept of the Statement of Net Cost is that the revenue earned
by Federal components from their operations, such as admis-
sions to national parks and fees paid for postal services and
stamps, is subtracted from their gross cost of operations to get to
the components' Net Cost. In fiscal year 2005, the Government
earned $224.8 billion from this type of revenue. This compares to
$207.1 billion earned in fiscal year 2004 for an increase of $17.7
billion (or 8.5 percent). The $3,174.6 billion gross cost minus the

$224.8 billion in earned revenue resulted in a total net cost of $2,949.8 billion in 2005 compared to the $2,524.9 billion net cost reported in fiscal year 2004. Net cost is the amount to be financed from tax revenue and, as needed, borrowing. Net cost is also impacted by the variability of the costs that result from the change in actuarial liabilities.

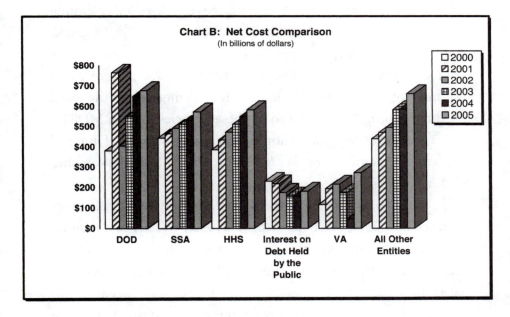

Chart B compares the major net cost elements over the past 6 fiscal years. Along with interest on debt held by the public, the source of over three-quarters of the Government's net cost comes from four Federal entities. For fiscal year 2005, the Government's total net cost increased by $424.9 billion over fiscal year 2004. And once again, these five major elements accounted for more than three-quarters or $2,289.3 billion of the Government's total $2,949.8 billion net cost.

In all fiscal years, except 2000 and 2002, DOD incurred the highest net cost. Most of DOD's net cost increases have been due to increases in the continued global war on terror and the actuarial liabilities related to its Military Retirement Fund and Military Retirement Health Benefits.

The total costs at the Department of Health and Human Services (HHS) and the Social Security Administration (SSA) together make up 39.3 percent or $1,157.9 billion of the Government's total net cost and continued their upward trend during fiscal year 2005. These increased net costs were mainly due to increases in benefit payments, operating expenses, and the number of beneficiaries. Some of the increases in operating expenses were related to the Medicare Prescription Drug Program. At SSA, its disability program experienced the most growth in its net cost (19.1 percent), benefit payments (19.4 percent), and number of beneficiaries (5 percent). To read more about the social insurance programs managed by these agencies, see the MD&A's Social Insurance Responsibilities section and the *Financial Report's* Statements of Social Insurance in the Stewardship Information section.

The VA again incurred the most variability in its year-over-year change in reported net costs. This year, VA's net cost grew by $225.3 billion, mainly due to an increase in the noncash actuarial cost of future veteran compensation and burial benefits as seen in Table 3. The changes in these costs have been due to assumption changes to VA's actuarial model used to calculate the related liability. Examples of the assumptions that impact the amount of the liability include: the number of veterans and dependents receiving payments, discount rates, cost of living adjustments, and life expectancy.

Table 3: The Change in VA's Total Actuarial Cost from 1999 to 2005
(In billions of dollars)

Year	Total Actuarial Cost	$ Change from Prior Year
1999	($95)	–
2000	$69	$164
2001	$139	$70
2002	$157	$18
2003	$106	($52)
2004	($30)	($136)
2005	$198	$228

Note: Table 3's data is from VA's 2000 to 2005 net cost statements and Treasury's analysis of them. Also, totals may not add due to rounding.

Also in fiscal year 2005, costs at the Department of Homeland Security (DHS), the Department of Agriculture (USDA), the Department of Education, and the Department of Energy experienced growth that increased net cost by $76.6 billion toward the reported $424.9 billion total increase in net cost. Among other things, these cost increases were related to the disasters caused by the hurricanes, protecting the homeland, the enhancement of post secondary and adult education, and changes in unfunded environmental liability estimates. However, these increases were somewhat offset by decreases in other areas.

Statement of Operations and Changes in Net Position Summary

Because the Government traditionally has been viewed from a budget perspective, and because many of the terms used to describe financial events have different meanings when describing budget outcomes, a conscious effort has been made to refer to budget-based amounts by using the term "budget" in order to eliminate any possible confusion. Net operating revenue (cost) is the term used to represent accrual-based operating results and equates to revenue less net cost of Government operations.

Similar to a corporation's income statement, the Statement of Operations and Changes in Net Position shows the financial results of the Federal Government's annual operations. This equals revenue less net cost. It also shows the impact—improvement or deterioration—these results had on the Government's net financial position.

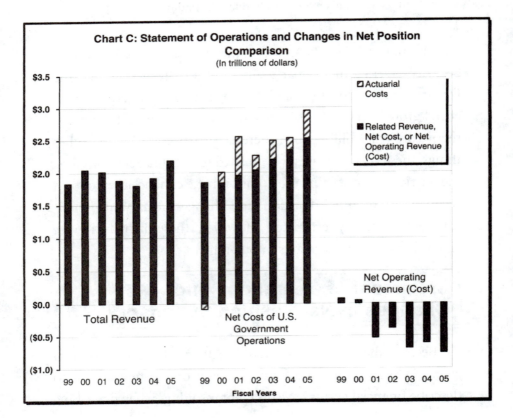

Chart C: Statement of Operations and Changes in Net Position Comparison
(In trillions of dollars)

Chart C shows the Government's total revenue (its net operating cost, including the amount attributable to actuarial costs), and its resulting net operating revenue (cost) for the past 7 years. In fiscal years 1999 and 2000, the Government's total revenue exceeded its net cost and resulted in net operating revenue of $101.3 billion and $39.6 billion for these years, respectively. However, in fiscal years 2001 through 2005, the Government's net cost exceeded its revenue and resulted in net operating costs of $514.8 billion, $364.9 billion, $667.6 billion, $615.6 billion, and $760.0 billion, respectively.

This chart also shows that, absent the actuarially computed accruals, total costs have increased steadily throughout the period. The large variability in actuarial costs, as discussed previously, is largely attributed to assumption changes at the VA.

The Statements of Operations and Changes in Net Position also shows how much tax revenue the Government generated in total and from its various categories of taxes and the extent to which this tax revenue covered the Government's net cost. Fiscal year 2005's total revenues of $2.2 trillion were 14.3 percent higher than in 2004, the highest increase in revenues in over 20 years. Tax revenue increased in all categories, mainly due to large increases in both personal income and corporate profits.

Chart D shows the amount of individual income and withholding taxes the Government has collected over the past 7 years. During this time, individual income and withholding collections ranged between $1.46 trillion to $1.66 trillion. However, this year they experienced their highest collection amount to $1.69 trillion.

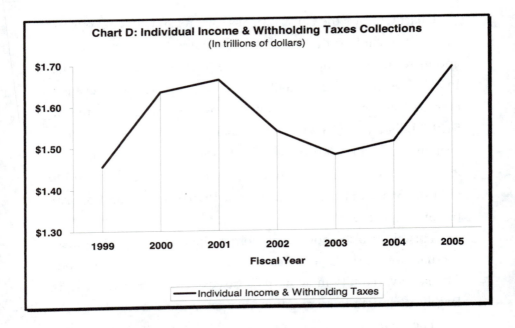

Chart D: Individual Income & Withholding Taxes Collections
(In trillions of dollars)

Reconciliation of Net Operating Cost and Budget Deficit Summary

The purpose of this statement is to reconcile the accrual-based net operating cost to the more widely-known budget deficit. The main components of the net operating cost that are not included in the budget deficit are the changes in accrued expenses related to employee and veteran benefits. The main component of the budget deficit that is not included in the net operating cost is the amount related to purchases of capitalized fixed assets. Table 4 is a condensed version of the Reconciliations of Net Operating Cost and Budget Deficit for fiscal years 2005 and 2004.

and Budget Deficits for 2005 and 2004
(In billions of dollars)

	2005	2004
Net Operating Cost	($760)	($616)
+/- Employee Benefits	+232	+212
+/- Veterans Benefits	+198	-30
+/- Other, Net	+11	+22
Budget Deficit	($319)	($412)

Statement of Changes in Cash Balance from Budget and Other Activities Summary

The primary purpose of the Statements of Changes in Cash Balance from Unified Budget and Other Activities is to report how the annual unified budget surplus or deficit relates to the Federal Government's borrowing and changes in operating cash. It explains how a budget surplus or deficit normally affects changes in debt balances.

For fiscal years 2005 and 2004, the Federal Government reported that it increased net borrowings from the public by $296.7 billion and $379.7 billion to help finance the $319 billion and $412 billion budget deficits, respectively. As can be seen, debt increases financed over 90 percent of the deficits in these years; however, the debt operations of the Federal Government are much more complex than this would imply. That is, each year trillions of dollars of debt matures and new debt takes its place. For example, in fiscal year 2005, new borrowings were $4.6 trillion and maturing debts were $4.3 trillion.

Balance Sheet Summary

The balance sheet shows an end-of-year view of the Federal Government's overall financial position, its assets, liabilities, and the difference between the two. This difference is called net position. It is important to note that the balance sheet excludes the Government's sovereign powers to tax, regulate commerce, and set monetary policy. It also excludes its control over nonoperational resources, including national and natural resources, over which the Government is a steward. Moreover, the Government's responsibilities are broader than the liabilities presented on the balance sheet, including the Government's future Social Insurance Responsibilities (e.g., Social Security and Medicare), as well as other programs and contingencies. These responsibilities are discussed in this section's Social Insurance Responsibilities and the *Financial Report's* Stewardship section.

Assets

The Government's total assets increased from $1,397.3 billion as of the end of fiscal year 2004 to $1,456.1 billion as of the end of fiscal year 2005. This increase was due to increases in all of the Government's assets except its cash and other monetary assets, which declined slightly. Representing almost 50 percent of total assets this fiscal year, net property, plant, and equipment has been the Government's largest asset over the past 7 fiscal years. In fact, the reported value of these assets increased substantially in fiscal year 2003 as a result of a change in Federal accounting standards.

This change resulted in the recognition of a net book value of $325.1 billion in military equipment being presented on the balance sheet for the first time.

Liabilities

Chart E is a 7-year comparison of the major components of liabilities, or what the Government owes, reported on the balance sheets as of September 30, for fiscal years 1999 through 2005. At the end of fiscal year 2005, the U.S. Government's liabilities increased 8.9 percent from $9,107.1 billion to $9,914.8 billion.

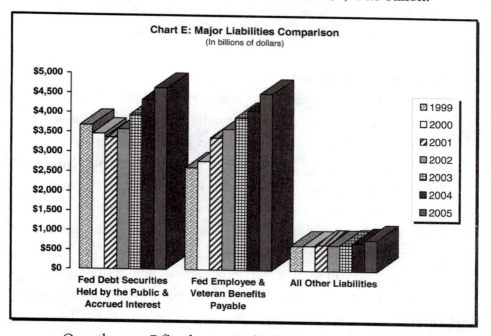

Over the past 7 fiscal years, Federal debt securities held by the public and accrued interest have tended to vary with the budget results. In years with budget surpluses, there have been reductions and in years with budget deficits, there have been corresponding increases. By contrast, Federal employee and veteran benefits payable have been increasing dramatically. From $2,600.7 billion as of the end of fiscal year 1999, this amount stands at $4,491.8 billion as of 2005. Together these amounts make up over 90 percent of the Government's total reported liabilities.

Increases in other liabilities were mainly due to the increases in insurance programs. In fact, the liability related to the National Flood Insurance Program that DHS' FEMA administers increased by $22 billion, from $1.4 billion in 2004 to $23.4 billion in 2005. This sharp rise was due to the disasters caused by the hurricanes. Other liabilities also increased as a result of the increase in pension benefit liabilities at the Pension Benefit Guaranty Corporation. This liability went from $60.8 billion in 2004 to $69.8 billion in 2005 (see Note 14 on page 185 for additional details).

Other Responsibilities

The 2005 balance sheet shows liabilities of $9,915 billion. In addition, the Government's responsibilities to make future payments for social insurance and certain other programs are not shown as liabilities according to Federal accounting standards; however, they are measured in other contexts. These programmatic commitments remain Federal responsibilities and as currently structured will have a significant claim on budgetary resources in the future.

The net present value for all of the responsibilities (for current participants over a 75-year period) is $49,403 billion, including Medicare and Social Security payments, pensions and benefits for Federal employees and veterans, and other financial responsibilities. The $49,403 billion includes amounts disclosed in the Statements of Social Insurance for the Social Security, Medicare, and Railroad Retirement programs on pages 75–78 (these amounts do not include future participants), as well as amounts disclosed in Notes 19 (Contingencies) and 20 (Commitments) that are not presented on the balance sheet.

Featured Balance Sheet Item: Civilian Federal Employee Benefits Payable

This section of the balance sheet summary is meant to feature one of the many items the U.S. Government owns or is responsible for. This year's featured item is civilian Federal employee benefits payable. Civilian Federal employee benefits payable is actually one part of Federal employee and veteran benefits payable (see Note 11 on pages 170–171) that made up almost 50 percent of all the Government's reported liabilities in fiscal years 2005 and 2004. This is about twice as much, percentage-wise, when compared to the U.S. Government's northern neighbor, the Canadian Government.

The OPM administers the largest civilian pension plan. It covers about 90 percent of all Federal civilian employees and includes two components of defined benefits: the Civil Service Retirement System (CSRS) and the Federal Employees' Retirement System (FERS). The CSRS is a defined benefit plan that covers employees hired before 1984, and the FERS is a combined defined benefit-defined contribution plan that covers mainly employees hired after 1983. The CSRS covers 664,000 current employees and 2.2 million annuitants and the FERS covers 1.9 million current employees and 241,000 annuitants. The basic benefit components of both plans are paid by the Civil Service Retirement and Disability Fund (CSRDF). Funding sources for the CSRDF include: 1) Federal civilian employees' contributions, 2) agencies' contributions on behalf of employees, 3) appropriations, and 4) interest earned on investments in Treasury securities.

In addition to the basic benefit components of both plans, the Government also offers the Thrift Savings Plan (TSP) as an especially important element of the FERS plan. FERS employees may contribute up to 15 percent of their base pay and the Government matches up to 5 percent. CSRS employees may contribute up to 10 percent of their base pay with no Government match. Both FERS and CSRS contributions are capped by IRS limits (generally $14,000 for 2005). The Federal Retirement Thrift Investment Board, an independent Government agency, administers the TSP. These financial statements exclude the TSP because the CSRS and FERS employees own its assets and the program is fully funded from its investment income.

Not only does the Government offer pensions to its civilian employees, it also offers post-retirement health and other benefits. At the end of fiscal year 2005, civilian Federal employee benefits payable was $1,613.0 billion or 35.9 percent of total Federal employee and veteran benefits payable. This was a 4.0 percent increase over fiscal year 2004. The $1,613.0 billion liability included $1,273.8 billion of pensions, $290.7 billion of health, and $48.5 billion of other benefits.

Social Insurance Responsibilities

Social Insurance Trust Funds

The Social Insurance trust funds were created to account for all related program income and disbursements. Social Security and Medicare taxes, premiums, and other income are credited to the funds. Benefit payments and program administrative costs are the only purposes for which disbursements from the funds can be made. Program revenues not needed in the current year to pay

benefits and administrative costs are invested in special nonnego-
tiable securities of the U.S. Government on which a market rate of
interest is credited. Thus, the trust funds represent the accumulated value, including interest, of all prior program annual surpluses and provide automatic authority to pay benefits.

There are four separate trust funds. For Social Security, the
Old-Age and Survivors Insurance (OASI) Trust Fund pays retirement and survivors benefits, and the Disability Insurance (DI)
Trust Fund pays disability benefits. (The combined trust funds are
described as OASDI.) For Medicare, the Hospital Insurance (HI)
Trust Fund pays for inpatient hospital and related care. The
Supplementary Medical Insurance (SMI) Trust Fund is composed
of Part B, which pays for physician and outpatient services, and
effective in 2004, Part D, which provides a prescription drug benefit. Medicare benefits are provided to most people age 65 and over
and to most workers who are receiving Social Security disability
benefits.

Trustees Report on the Trust Funds

Each year the six trustees of the Social Security and Medicare
Trust Funds—the Secretary of the Treasury, the Secretary of Labor,
the Secretary of Health and Human Services, the Commissioner
of Social Security, and two members appointed by the President
and confirmed by the Senate to represent the public—report on
the current status and projected condition of the funds over the
next 75 years and the indefinite future. That is, short-range (10-
year), long-range (75-year), and indefinite future estimates are
reported for all funds. The estimates are based on current law and
assumptions about all of the factors that affect the income and
outgo of each trust fund. Assumptions include economic growth,

wages, inflation, unemployment, fertility, immigration, and mortality, as well as factors relating to disability incidence and the cost of hospital, medical, and prescription drug services.

Because the future is uncertain, three sets of economic and demographic assumptions are used to show a range of possibilities. The intermediate assumptions reflect the trustees' best estimate of future experience. The low-cost assumptions are more optimistic for trust fund financing, and the high-cost assumptions more pessimistic; they show trust fund projections for more and less favorable economic and demographic conditions for trust fund financing than the best estimate. The assumptions are reexamined each year in light of recent experience and new information about future trends, and are revised as needed. In general, greater confidence can be placed in the assumptions and estimates for near-term projection years than for years in the distant future.

Trustees Short-Range Outlook (2005-2014)

The adequacy of the OASI, DI, and HI Trust Funds is measured by comparing their assets at the beginning of a year to projected costs for that year (the "trust fund ratio"). A trust fund ratio of 100 percent or more—that is, assets at least equal to projected benefit payments for a year—is considered a good indicator of a fund's short-term adequacy. This level of projected assets for any year means that even if expenditures exceed income, the trust fund reserves combined with annual tax revenues would be sufficient to pay full benefits for several years, allowing time for legislative action to restore financial adequacy.

By this measure, the OASI and DI funds are considered financially adequate throughout the short range because the assets of each fund are projected to exceed the 100 percent level through the year 2014. The HI fund does not meet the short-range test of financial adequacy because its assets fell below the 100 percent level of one year's outgo during 2014. For SMI, a less stringent annual "contingency reserve" asset test applies to both Part B and Part D because the financing of each of those accounts is provided by beneficiary premiums and Federal general fund revenue payments automatically adjusted each year to meet expected costs. Thus, under current law both SMI accounts are fully financed throughout the 75-year projection period no matter what the costs may be.

Trustees Long-Range Outlook (2005-2079)

Costs for Social Security and Medicare increase steeply between 2010 and 2030 because the number of people receiving benefits will increase rapidly as the large baby-boom generation retires. Thereafter, Social Security costs grow slowly primarily due to projected increasing life expectancy. Medicare costs continue to grow rapidly due to expected increases in the use and cost of health care. In particular, the continued development of new technology is expected to cause per capita health care expenditures to continue to grow faster in the long term, than the economy as a whole.

Thus, a good way to view the projected cost of Social Security and Medicare is in relation to gross domestic product (GDP), the most frequently used measure of the total U.S. economy. Medicare's cost is projected to exceed Social Security's in 2024. Social Security outgo amounted to 4.3 percent of GDP in 2004 and is projected to increase to 6.4 percent of GDP in 2079. Medicare's cost amounted to 2.6 percent of GDP in 2004 and is projected to grow more than fivefold to 13.6 percent of GDP in 2079. The two together, absent reform, will almost triple as a percentage of the U.S. economy, from just under 7 percent last year to 20 percent by 2079.

Economy, Federal Budget, & Federal Debt

Growth in the U.S. economy remained favorable and well balanced through fiscal year 2005. Real GDP increased throughout the fiscal year, led by steady growth in personal consumption expenditures and business fixed investment. Productivity growth continued and real hourly compensation increased. Job creation was robust during most of the fiscal year and the unemployment rate fell to a 4-year low. Federal outlays for the continuing costs of operations in Iraq and Afghanistan and hurricane relief are expected to raise the budget deficit in the short term, affecting budget results in fiscal year 2006. In the medium to long term, the additional burden of the deficit from defense operations and the storm damage is not expected to undermine efforts at deficit reduction. Long-term efforts at deficit reduction will be shaped by the actions taken to address the actuarial imbalances in Social Security and Medicare noted in the *Financial Report's* Stewardship Information section.

Economy

Real GDP increased 3.7 percent over the four quarters of fiscal year 2005, a little less than the 3.8 percent increase over the four quarters of fiscal year 2004. Growth was led by a 3.9 percent increase in real personal consumption expenditures over the year and by a year-over-year gain of 10.6 percent in real equipment and software investment. Corporate profits and cash flow rose during the fiscal year, helping to support the growth in business investment. Labor markets improved substantially in fiscal year 2005, with more than 2.2 million new payroll jobs created. The unemployment rate fell from 5.4 percent at the start of the fiscal year to 5.1 percent in the final month, and the 5.0 percent average for the last quarter of the fiscal year was the lowest quarterly rate in 4 years. The overall consumer price index (CPI) rose 4.7 percent over the year, well above the 2.5 percent increase during fiscal year 2004 as energy prices increased significantly in fiscal year 2005. The "core" CPI (which excludes food and energy prices) remained benign, up just 2.0 percent over the 12 months of fiscal year 2005.

Federal Budget

The Federal budget deficit declined to $319 billion in fiscal year 2005, from $412 billion in fiscal year 2004. The deficit in the latest fiscal year represented 2.6 percent of nominal GDP, smaller than the percentages of the deficits in relation

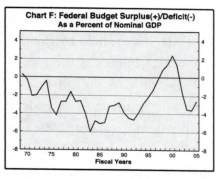

Chart F: Federal Budget Surplus(+)/Deficit(-) As a Percent of Nominal GDP

to GDP in 16 of the last 25 years. Stronger receipts are the main reason the deficit picture has improved. In fiscal year 2005, actual tax collections have come in higher than expected as both individual income and corporate profits have strengthened. Receipts rose by 14.6 percent and outlays rose by 7.9 percent.

Federal outlays for the continuing costs of operations in Iraq and Afghanistan and hurricane relief are expected to raise the deficit in the short term, affecting budget results in fiscal year 2006. In the medium to long term, the additional burden of the deficit from defense operations and the storm damage is not expected to undermine efforts at deficit reduction. Long-term efforts at deficit reduction will be shaped by the actions taken to address the actuarial imbalances in Social Security and Medicare noted in the *Financial Report's* Stewardship Information section.

Debt held by the public, not including accrued interest of $35 billion, rose by $293 billion or 6.8 percent in fiscal year 2005. Publicly held debt, not including accrued interest, represented a relatively moderate 37.6 percent of GDP. That compares to the average 44.5 percent share that prevailed from the late 1980s through most of the 1990s.

Federal Debt

Currently, the largest liability for the Federal Government is the Federal debt held by the public and accrued interest, which was $4,624 billion at the end of 2005. This was an increase of $295 billion over the 2004 debt of $4,329 billion. However, this $295 billion increase in Federal debt was actually 23 percent smaller than fiscal year 2004's reported increase of $385 billion. The Government borrowed a smaller amount of cash from the public this year to finance its operations because of the sharp increase in tax revenues that helped to offset somewhat the increase in its costs.

Composition of the Federal Debt

There are two kinds of Federal debt: debt held by the public and the debt the Government owes to itself. At the end of fiscal year 2005, the total of these two kinds of debt were $7,970 billion.

The first kind of Federal debt is debt held by (or owed to) the public. It includes all Treasury securities (bills, notes, bonds, inflation-protected, and other securities) held by individuals, corporations, Federal Reserve banks, foreign governments, and other entities outside the U.S. Government. This debt is included as a liability on the balance sheet. The second kind is debt the Government owes to itself (intra-governmental debt), primarily in the form of special nonmarketable securities held by various parts of the Government. The laws establishing Government trust funds generally require the excess receipts of the trust funds to be invested in these special securities. This debt is not included on the balance sheet because these payments are claims of one part of the Government against another and are eliminated for consolidation purposes (see Note 10 on page 167).

Federal debt is subject to a statutory ceiling that is known as the debt limit. Prior to 1917, the Congress approved each issuance of debt. In 1917, to facilitate planning in World War I, the law established a dollar ceiling for Federal borrowing, which has been periodically increased over the years. On November 19, 2004, legislation became effective raising the current limit to $8,184 billion from the previous $7,384 billion limit. The gross debt, excluding some adjustments, is the measure that is subject to the Federal debt limit. At the end of fiscal year 2005, the amount of debt subject to the limit was $7,871 billion. As a result, $313 billion of the $8,184 billion remained as the amount the Government could borrow to finance its operations.

How the Federal Budget is related to the Federal Debt

The budget surplus or deficit is the difference between total Federal spending and revenue in a given year. To finance a budget deficit, the Government borrows from the public. On the other hand, a budget surplus happens when the Government accumulates excess funds that are used to reduce debt held by the public. In other words, deficits or surpluses are related to the annual net change in the amount of debt held by the public, while the debt held by the public generally represents the total of all cash-based deficits minus all cash-based surpluses built up over time.

Federal Debt Held by the Public as a Percentage of GDP

The Federal debt held by the public as a share of GDP is a useful measure because it reflects how much of the Nation's wealth is absorbed by the Federal Government to finance its obligations. Chart G shows debt held by the public as a share of GDP from 1980 through 2004. Starting in the late 1970s, increasing budget deficits spurred a corresponding increase in debt held by the public, which essentially doubled as a share of GDP over a 15-year period throughout the mid-1990s and reached about 50 percent in 1993. The budget controls instituted by the Congress and the President, together with economic growth, contributed to the budget surpluses at the end of the 1990s. These surpluses led to a decline in the debt held by the public, and from fiscal years 1998 through 2001, the debt-to-GDP measure declined from about 43 percent to about 33 percent.

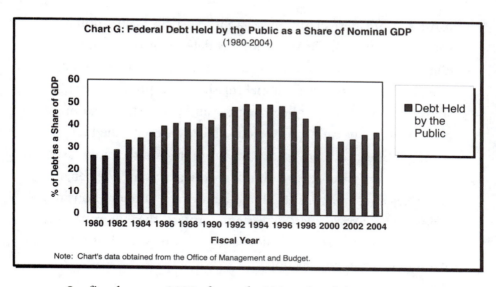

Chart G: Federal Debt Held by the Public as a Share of Nominal GDP (1980-2004)

Note: Chart's data obtained from the Office of Management and Budget.

In fiscal years 2002 through 2004, the debt-to-GDP ratio started to rise slightly. This increase was due to many factors, including increased spending for homeland security and defense commitments, the decline in receipts owing to the recession and lower stock market value, as well as tax cuts, and the expiration of the budget controls that once helped instill spending discipline. By the end of fiscal year 2004, the debt-to-GDP ratio had risen to about 37 percent. This is still lower, however, than the roughly 50 percent of GDP reached in the mid-1990s.

U.S. Government's Mission & Organizational Structure

Mission & Organization

Today, the U.S. Government's most visible mission of managing the security of the Nation, homeland, and economy is still derived from the original mission in the Constitution: ". . . to form a more perfect union, establish justice, insure domestic tranquility, provide for the common defense, promote the general welfare and secure the blessings of liberty to ourselves and our posterity." Since the original mission's inception, other missions have developed as the Congress authorized the creation of other agencies to carry out various objectives established by law. Some of these objectives are to promote health care, foster income security, boost agricultural productivity, provide benefits and services to veterans, facilitate commerce, support housing, support the transportation system, protect the environment, contribute to the security of energy resources, and assist the States in providing education.

U.S. Government's Organization

The fundamental organization of the U.S. Government is established by the Constitution. Article I vested legislative powers in a Congress consisting of a Senate and a House of Representatives; Article II vested executive powers in a President and Vice President; and Article III vested judicial power in a Supreme Court and lower courts to be established by the Congress. To get a sense of how the U.S. Government is organized, even though not all-inclusive, a U.S. Government organization chart follows.

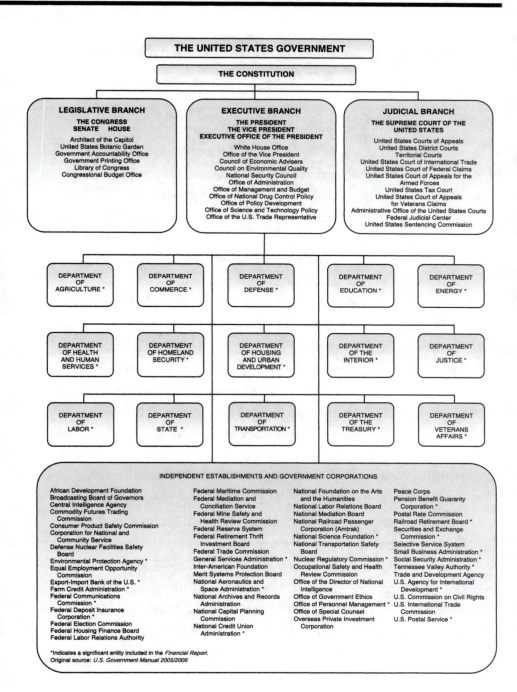

Featured Agency: The U.S. Department of Agriculture

Representing 3.1 percent of the Government's net cost in 2005, the USDA's mission is to provide leadership on food, agriculture, natural resources, and related issues based on sound public policy, the best-available science, and efficient management. The USDA achieves its mission through its more than 100,000 employees who deliver in excess of $75 billion in public services through approximately 300 USDA worldwide programs.

The USDA was originally founded in 1862 to help farmers who needed good seeds and information to grow their crops. Today, the USDA remains committed to helping American farmers and ranchers and does so mainly through its Farm and Foreign Agricultural Services. The USDA also helps all Americans through its other six mission areas: 1) Natural Resources and Environment, 2) Rural Development, 3) Food Safety, 4) Research, Education, and Economics, 5) Marketing, and Regulatory Programs, and 6) Food, Nutrition, and Consumer Services.

As part of the Food, Nutrition, and Consumer Services mission area, the Center for Nutrition Policy and Promotion (CNPP) was established in 1994 to improve the nutrition and well-being of Americans. One of the tools the CNNP developed to improve the nutrition and well-being of Americans was the "Food Pyramid." This past April, the CNNP transformed the Food Pyramid into Mypyramid.gov (see above right). To learn more about the USDA and its seven mission areas, including Mypyramid.gov, visit www. usda.gov and www.mypyramid.gov, respectively.

Significant Performance Accomplishments

The President's Management Agenda: Managing for Results

Fiscal responsibility requires the sound stewardship of taxpayer money. This means that once the Congress and the President decide on overall spending levels, taxpayer dollars should be managed to maximize results. The President's Management Agenda (PMA) is creating a results-oriented Government where each agency and program is managed professionally and efficiently and achieves the results expected by the Congress and the American people.

The PMA, launched in August 2001 with the broad goal of making the Government more results-oriented, focuses on achievement, efficiency, and accountability. It emphasizes improving how the Government operates by setting clear goals and action plans, and then following through on those plans. Agencies continue to manage for and achieve better results.

Strategic Management of Human Capital

The Strategic Management of Human Capital Initiative recognizes that the men and women employed by the Government represent more than mere entries on a balance sheet. Rather, it focuses Government's efforts on maximizing the value of its most important resource, its workforce.

The demographics of the Federal workforce are changing, requiring agencies to identify successful succession management systems and strategies to ensure continuity of service and mission.

Agencies are working to pinpoint pending competency gaps in mission critical occupations and develop and implement successful strategies to close them.

Agencies have made significant progress in establishing and implementing personnel management practices to better achieve their missions. They are deploying and improving performance management systems which better link individual performance to agency mission and results. The establishment of strong performance management systems will provide the foundations for establishing new compensation systems that reward performance instead of time on the job.

Federal executives can play a key role as change agents when it comes to enhancing or replacing performance management systems. Over the past year, agencies have improved their senior executive service performance plans, particularly in the way performance measures are established. These programs aim not only to ensure that potential future managers are waiting in the wings, but that those individuals have the proper skills to work in today's changing work environment.

An ultimate goal of the initiative is to "imbed" the strategic management of human capital into an agency's daily management operations. To accomplish this, agencies must transition to a system of strong self-accountability whereby agency leaders will use human capital results in strategic decision making.

Competitive Sourcing

The Government is conducting studies to determine whether commercial goods and services are best provided by Federal employees or by the private sector. These competitions help agencies reduce costs, improve performance, and achieve a better alignment between its mission and workforce through the redirection of resources to fill mission critical skill gaps. In fiscal year 2004, the PMA agencies completed 217 competitions involving approximately 12,500 jobs. These competitions are expected to generate $22,000 in annualized net savings for every job examined, or a reduction in costs of about 27 percent, regardless of who won the competition. Federal employees won approximately 91 percent of the work competed in fiscal year 2004. Savings were greatest when there was robust participation in the competition, demonstrating that the combination of competition and reengineering, rather than reengineering alone, is the key driver of savings.

Improved Financial Performance

The ultimate goal of the Improved Financial Performance initiative of the PMA is that managers have access to timely and accurate financial information for decision-making. Audited financial statements provide assurance that agencies are accounting for the taxpayers' money in a reliable manner. This year, all of the 24 major Federal agencies issued their Performance and Accountability Reports, including financial statements on or before November 15. This marks a significant milestone in Federal financial management since only a few years ago agencies took up to 5 months to produce similar information. Meeting this goal required agencies to implement new financial management controls and processes, which are the foundation for more reliable information to support day-to-day management.

By establishing greater financial discipline, agencies are producing financial reports faster and with greater reliability. Since the beginning of 2001, the number of auditor-reported material weaknesses Governmentwide has decreased. Fewer material weaknesses translate to greater confidence that financial information is correct. As agencies improve their financial business practices and install new financial management systems and reporting tools, data timeliness and reliability will continue to improve.

Under the PMA, agencies are increasingly focused on using timely and accurate financial information to make decisions about program management. To be rated 'Yellow' under the Improving Financial Performance Scorecard, agencies must have an unqualified audit, meet reporting deadlines, have no material weaknesses, and be in substantial compliance with financial system requirements. To be rated 'Green' agencies must demonstrate how they use financial information in daily decision making and also have a plan to expand the use of financial information to additional areas. By using timely financial information for decision making and program management, agencies are taking steps toward improving their financial performance and overall management of Federal dollars.

Expanded Electronic Government

The Expanded Electronic Government initiative focuses on two key areas—strengthening agencies' management of their information technology (IT) resources and using the Internet to simplify and enhance service delivery to the citizen. The Government must capitalize on its approximate $65 billion annual investment in IT.

Most agencies have improved their IT management since fiscal year 2003. Over 62 percent of major systems now include measurable program objectives in their justifications, a 29 percent increase. Also, 77 percent of agency IT systems have been certified and accredited, up from 62 percent the previous year. In addition, currently about 96 percent of agencies have an effective enterprise architecture, an integral part of ensuring their IT investments support overall agency goals and do not duplicate Governmentwide IT investments; last year it was only 20 percent. Such improvements are central ingredients in developing a more focused and results-oriented approach to IT investment across agencies.

Specific improvements in service delivery are being achieved through the E-Gov Initiatives. For instance, Grants.gov makes it easier for potential recipients to obtain information about Federal grants by creating a single, online site to find and apply for all Federal grants. Also, e-Travel, the new Governmentwide travel management service, may allow the Government to save nearly $300 million over the next 10 years on travel-related activities.

Centers of Excellence are being launched under the Financial Management Line of Business (FMLOB) initiative. The FMLOB Initiative will replace the department/agency-centered model with Centers of Excellence hosting financial systems. Centers of Excellence are expected to improve the quality and integrity of financial information through standardized business process and data definitions, and integrated core financial and subsidiary systems. Moreover, establishing Centers of Excellence could save the Federal Government $4 billion over 10 years by reducing system redundancy and lowering system development, maintenance, and enhancement costs. Currently, four agencies—the General Services Administration and the Departments of Interior, Transportation, and the Treasury—have attained the Center of Excellence designation.

The Government is investing significant resources in IT to assist it in achieving its mission and better serving the American taxpayer. Agencies are making improvements towards ensuring these investments are well managed, more secure, and providing services to the American people more efficiently and effectively.

Budget and Performance Integration

Executive departments and agencies are using meaningful program performance information to inform their budget and management decisions. They are asking whether their programs are working and, if not, they are taking steps to improve them. Assessments of programs using the Program Assessment Rating Tool (PART) have helped focus agency efforts to improve program results. OMB and agencies have now assessed the performance of more than 800 Federal programs, representing almost $1.5 trillion dollars in Federal spending. Summaries of PART findings for each program assessed, as well as the detailed PART analyses for those programs, can be found at the OMB website. The Administration will also launch a new website, ExpectMore.gov, to provide greater public access to information about what programs work, which ones don't, but what all are doing to improve.

The Administration is also using the PART to compare the performance and management of similar programs across Government so that lessons about how to improve program performance can be shared among those programs. These analyses will tell us what steps we need to take to improve program performance for similar programs across Government.

The PART is a vehicle for improving program performance. As more and more program assessments are conducted, the Administration will have better program performance information to use when making budget and management decisions. Agencies will be better able to describe to the taxpayer what they

are getting for their investment and what improvements in efficiency and results can be documented every year.

Eliminating Improper Payments

During fiscal year 2005, the Federal Government made substantial progress in meeting the President's goal to eliminate
improper payments. Most notably, the Governmentwide
improper payments total reported last year decreased by approximately $7.5 billion due to dramatic improvements implemented
by HHS in the stewardship of Medicare funds. In addition, agencies demonstrated improved error detection and measurement,
providing improper payment data on programs for which no
improper payment statistics had been available in the past.

Despite their best efforts, certain agencies have not been able
to establish a baseline improper payment measurement for some
of their risk susceptible programs. These programs are very large
and complex, providing agencies with significant challenges in
their efforts to obtain baseline and annual rates. However, OMB
continues to work with these agencies to ensure that the required
measurements will be produced within the next few years.

Much of this success can be attributed to the PMA initiative
to eliminate improper payments, which established an effective
accountability framework for ensuring that Federal agencies ini-
tiate all necessary financial management improvements for
addressing this critical problem area. With agencies working to
deploy more innovative and sophisticated approaches for
addressing improper payments, the prospects for additional and
significant improper payments reductions in the coming years
are promising. The Chief Financial Officers' Council continues to
play a critical role in these efforts by ensuring that agency best

practices (such as those employed by HHS in the Medicare Program) are disseminated and employed at other agencies.

Asset Management

Agencies continue to make significant progress in implementing both the requirements of Executive Order (EO) 13327, Federal Real Property Asset Management signed February 4, 2004, and the PMA Program initiative that was established in the 3rd quarter of fiscal year 2004. The goal of the initiative is to develop and implement the necessary tools (e.g. planning, inventory, performance measures) to improve management decision-making so that property inventories are maintained at the right size, cost, and condition to support agency mission and objectives.

In fiscal year 2005, the Federal Real Property Council, established under EO 13327, issued guidance to all Federal agencies on the required components to be addressed in each agency asset management plan and identified 23 data elements, including 4 performance measures, to be reported to a Governmentwide database. Agencies have completed or are in the process of drafting their asset management plans and are gathering complete and accurate asset level data inventory and performance measure data for reporting fiscal year 2005 data to the Governmentwide database in early fiscal year 2006. Through the PMA, the Administration is holding agencies accountable to use improved planning and data gathering to implement specific rightsizing activities that will reduce surplus assets, improve the condition of mission critical assets, and ensure that assets are managed at the right cost.

Executive Branch Management Scorecard

The PMA is used to measure agencies' progress and overall achievement in meeting the overall goals of the PMA. These overall goals, known as standards for success, are specified for each initiative and available at www.whitehouse.gov/results/agenda/standards.pdf. A copy of the Scorecard follows.

	Explanation of Status Scores
Green	Agency meets all of the standards for success.
Yellow	Agency has achieved intermediate levels of performance in all the criteria.
Red	Agency has any of a number of serious flaws.
	Explanation of Progress Scores
Green	Implementation is proceeding according to plans.
Yellow	Slippage in implementation schedule, quality of deliverables, or other issues requiring adjustments by agency in order to achieve initiative on a timely basis.
Red	Initiative in serious jeopardy. Unlikely to realize objectives without significant management intervention.

The Scorecard

NOTE: The fourth quarter scorecard presents the agencies' ratings as of September 30, 2005. These ratings were prior to the publication of the fiscal year 2005 audited financial statements. The status and progress ratings in the first quarter scorecard, as of December 31, 2005, will reflect auditors' findings from the fiscal year 2005 financial statement audit. For example, several agency audit opinions and internal controls declined during fiscal year 2005. OMB will review these changes and update the status and progress ratings reflecting the fiscal year 2005 results during the Quarter 1 PMA assessment process.

Executive Branch Management Scorecard										
	Current Status as of September 30, 2005					Progress in Implementing the President's Management Agenda				
	Human Capital	Competitive Sourcing	Financial Perf.	E-Gov	Budget/ Perf. Integration	Human Capital	Competitive Sourcing	Financial Perf.	E-Gov	Budget/ Perf. Integration
AGRICULTURE	Y	Y	R	Y	Y	G	G	G	G	G
COMMERCE	Y↓	Y	G	Y	Y	G	G	G	G	G
DEFENSE	Y	R	R	R	Y	G	R	Y	R	G
EDUCATION	Y	G↑	G	Y	Y	G	G	G	G	G
ENERGY	G	Y↓	G	Y	G	G	Y	Y	G	G
EPA	Y	Y	G	Y↓	Y	Y	Y	G	Y	G
HHS	G	G	R	Y	Y	G	G	G	G	G
HOMELAND	Y	Y	R	R	Y	G	Y	Y	R	G
HUD	Y	Y	R	Y	Y	Y	G	G	G	G
INTERIOR	G↑	G	R	R↓	Y	G	G	G	R	G
JUSTICE	G↑	Y	R	R↓	Y	G	Y	Y	R	G
LABOR	G	G	G	G	G	G	G	G	G	G
STATE	G	Y	G	Y↓	G	G	G	G	G	G
DOT	G	G	R	G	G	G	G	G	G	G
TREASURY	Y	G	R	R	Y	G	G	Y	G	G
VA	Y	R	R	R	R	G	R	Y	G	G
USAID	Y	R	R	R↓	Y	G	G	G	Y	G
CORPS OF ENGINEERS	G	Y	R	R	R	G	G	Y	R	R
GSA	Y	G	G↑	Y	Y	G	Y	G	G	G
NASA	G	G	R	Y↓	G	Y	G	R	Y	Y
NSF	G	R	G	G	G	G	Y	G	G	G
OMB	Y	R	R	Y	R	G	G	G	G	Y
OPM	G	G	R	Y	Y	G	G	G	G	G
SBA	Y	G↑	R	G	G	G	G	G	G	G
SMITHSONIAN	Y↑	R	R	R	Y	G	R	G	G	G
SSA	G	Y	G	Y	G	G	G	G	G	G

Legend: **R** = Red   **Y** = Yellow   **G** = Green
↑↓ Arrows indicate change in status since evaluation on June 30, 2005.

Systems, Controls, & Legal Compliance

Systems

Improving agency investment decisions in financial system solutions is one of the President's top management priorities. As a first critical step in addressing this challenge, the Federal financial community developed a common set of core system requirements and a software certification process based on those requirements. As a result, most major agencies have purchased (and many have completed) the implementation of certified commercial-off-the-shelf financial management systems. This advance has helped ensure that purchased software solutions contain the necessary functionality to meet agency business needs. Nevertheless, agency auditors' Federal Financial Management Improvement Act (FFMIA) reviews have indicated that a majority of CFO Act agencies experience challenges with their financial management systems.

In fiscal year 2004, OMB launched the FMLOB initiative to decrease the overall cost of financial system solutions. Specifically, the FMLOB established a "Centers of Excellence" concept, that provided for cross-servicing of multiple financial systems, achieving cost and quality economies and providing a competitive alternative to stand alone solutions. The Centers of Excellence may be operated by public agencies, private firms, or public/private partnerships. Several agencies were selected in fiscal year 2005 to operate as Centers of Excellence, and several agencies are working toward migrating to this shared service environment.

FFMIA reporting shows that many agencies do not comply

with one or more of three requirements. OMB and the Chief Financial Officers' Council are working together to disseminate best practices on financial system implementations. Through forums and other means, the Federal financial community is working to ensure that mistakes of the past are not repeated and that agencies initiating complex modernization efforts have a clear understanding of significant risks and appropriate mitigation strategies.

Controls

Internal Control

Federal managers have a fundamental responsibility to develop and maintain effective internal control. Effective internal control helps to ensure that programs are managed with integrity and resources are used efficiently and effectively. As the Federal financial management community strives to provide more timely and reliable financial information, managers are increasingly reliant upon a strong foundation of internal control. While progress is being made in reducing internal control weaknesses, agencies continue to face challenges in this area and GAO issued an adverse opinion on internal control at the Governmentwide level.

Recognizing the importance of effective internal control within federal agencies, OMB continues to emphasize the expectations for management accountability and responsibility in maintaining effective internal control. In December 2004, OMB revised Circular A-123, *Management's Responsibility for Internal Control* (A-123). The revisions to A-123 provide agencies with a framework for assessing and managing financial reporting risks more strategically and effectively.

Beginning in fiscal year 2006, the strengthened management requirements for assessing the effectiveness of internal control over financial reporting will be implemented. Appendix A of the A-123 requires management to undertake a more rigorous assessment process and for agency heads to provide a separate management assurance on the internal control over financial reporting. Over the next several months, agencies will complete risk assessments, identify key processes and controls and test these controls to determine their effectiveness. This effort will culminate in the agencies' first management assurance statement for internal control over financial reporting as of June 30, 2006. Key milestones from the plans will also be incorporated into the Improved Financial Performance initiative scorecard under the PMA to ensure agencies are accountable for meeting their goals.

Legal Compliance

Federal agencies are required to comply with a wide range of laws and regulations, including appropriations, employment, health and safety, and others. Responsibility for compliance primarily rests with agency management. Compliance is addressed as part of agency financial statement audits. Agency auditors test for compliance with selected laws and regulations related to financial reporting. As a result of their testing, auditors found no instances of material noncompliance that affected the Governmentwide financial statements. Certain individual agency audit reports contain instances of noncompliance. None of these instances were material to the Governmentwide financial statements. However, GAO reported that its work on compliance with laws and regulations was limited in scope.

History of the Report & Additional Information

History of the Financial Reports of the United States Government

Treasury has prepared a prototype financial report for many years beginning in 1976. The earliest reports were accrual-based and included a balance sheet and statement of operations and were not audited, though Treasury hired private sector firms to conduct independent reviews of source data and collection procedures. The Government Management Reform Act of 1994 (GMRA) required audited financial statements from the 24 CFO Act Federal departments and agencies beginning for fiscal year 1996. GMRA also required the U.S. Government to submit consolidated financial statements audited by GAO beginning with fiscal year 1997's *Financial Report of the United States Government*. A Memorandum of Understanding between Treasury, OMB, and GAO created FASAB to develop formal Federal accounting standards and concepts for these audited financial statements. In 1999, the American Institute of Certified Public Accountants recognized FASAB as the promulgator of GAAP for the Federal Government. See the timeline on the next page to get a sense of not only the *Financial Report's* history but also the significant dates and milestones that led to the issuance of financial reports for the Federal Government that have been subject to audit. Also visit http://www.treas.gov/offices/economic-policy/financial_report_hist.pdf for a more complete discussion of the history of the *Financial Report*.

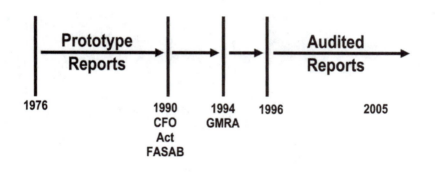

Additional Information

The Appendix contains a list of the significant Government entities included in the *Financial Report's* financial statements, along with their respective web sites. Details about the information contained in the *Financial Report* can be found in the financial statements of these entities in their individual Performance and Accountability Reports. In addition, related U.S. Government publications, such as the *Budget of the United States Government*, the *Treasury Bulletin*, the *Monthly Treasury Statement of Receipts and Outlays of the United States Government*, the *Monthly Statement of the Public Debt of the United States*, the *Economic Report of the President*, and the Trustees' Reports for the Social Security and Medicare Programs may be of interest and accessed from the respective White House, including the OMB and the Council of Economic Advisors; Treasury; SSA; and HHS web sites listed in the Appendix.

G A O
Accountability · Integrity · Reliability

United States Government Accountability Office
Washington, DC 20548

**Comptroller General
of the United States**

December 14, 2005

The President
The President of the Senate
The Speaker of the House of Representatives

Our report on the U.S. government's consolidated financial statements for fiscal years 2005 and 2004 is enclosed. In summary, we found the following:

- Material deficiencies in financial reporting (which also represent material weaknesses[1]) and other limitations on the scope of our work resulted in conditions that, for the ninth consecutive year, prevented us from expressing an opinion on the federal government's consolidated financial statements. Auditors for 4 of the 24 Chief Financial Officers (CFO) Act agencies issued disclaimers of opinion on their agencies' fiscal year 2005 financial statements.[2]

---

[1] A material weakness is a condition that precludes the entity's internal control from providing reasonable assurance that misstatements, losses, or noncompliance material in relation to the financial statements or to stewardship information would be prevented or detected on a timely basis.

[2] The four agencies that received disclaimers of opinion on their fiscal year 2005 financial statements were the National Aeronautics and Space Administration, the Department of Defense, the Department of Energy, and the Department of Homeland Security (DHS). For fiscal year 2005, only DHS's consolidated balance sheet was subjected to audit. The auditor was unable to express an opinion on DHS's consolidated balance sheet as of September 30, 2005, and on the department's consolidated financial statements as of and for the year ended September 30, 2004.

These agencies represent about $848 billion, or 58 percent, of the federal government's reported total assets as of September 30, 2005, and approximately $751 billion, or 25 percent, of the federal government's reported net cost for fiscal year 2005. Furthermore, several CFO Act agencies had to restate certain of their fiscal year 2004 financial statements.

- The federal government did not maintain effective internal control over financial reporting (including safeguarding assets) and compliance with significant laws and regulations as of September 30, 2005.

- Our work to determine compliance with selected provisions of significant laws and regulations in fiscal year 2005 was limited by the material weaknesses discussed in our report.

Three major impediments to our ability to render an opinion on the consolidated financial statements continued to be (1) serious financial management problems at the Department of Defense, (2) the federal government's inability to adequately account for and reconcile intragovernmental activity and balances between federal agencies, and (3) the federal government's ineffective process for preparing the consolidated financial statements. Moreover, as a result of the material deficiencies we found, readers are cautioned that amounts reported in the consolidated financial statements and related notes, certain information contained in the accompanying Management's Discussion and Analysis, and other financial management information that is taken from the same data sources as the consolidated financial statements, may not be reliable. Until the problems discussed in our audit report are adequately addressed, they will continue to have adverse implications for the federal government and the tax-payers, which are outlined in our report.

More troubling still, the federal government's financial condition and long-term fiscal outlook is continuing to deteriorate. While the fiscal year 2005 budget deficit was lower than 2004, it was still very high, especially given the impending retirement of the "baby boom" generation and rising health care costs. Importantly, the federal government's accrual based net operating cost increased to $760 billion in fiscal year 2005 from $616 billion in fiscal year 2004. GAO's fiscal policy simulations illustrate that without significant changes on the spending and revenue sides of the budget, long-term deficits will encumber a growing share of federal resources and test the capacity of current and future generations to afford both today's and tomorrow's commitments.

The current financial reporting model does not clearly and transparently show the wide range of responsibilities, programs, and activities that may either obligate the federal government to future spending or create an expectation for such spending. Thus, it provides a potentially unrealistic and misleading picture of the federal government's overall performance, financial condition, and future fiscal outlook. The federal government's gross debt[3] in the consolidated financial statements was about $8 trillion as of September 30, 2005. This number excludes such items as the gap

---

[3] The federal government's gross debt consists of debt held by the public and intragovernmental debt holdings.

between the present value of future promised and funded Social Security and Medicare benefits, veterans' health care, and a range of other liabilities (e.g., federal employee and veteran benefits payable), commitments, and contingencies that the federal government has pledged to support. Including these items, the federal government's fiscal exposures now total more than $46 trillion, up from about $20 trillion in 2000. This translates into a burden of about $156,000 per American or approximately $375,000 per full-time worker, up from $72,000 and $165,000 respectively, in 2000. These amounts do not include future costs resulting from Hurricane Katrina or the conflicts in Iraq and Afghanistan. Continuing on this unsustainable path will gradually erode, if not suddenly damage, our economy, our standard of living, and ultimately our national security.

Additionally, tax expenditure amounts are not required to be disclosed, nor are they disclosed, in agency or the U.S. government's consolidated financial statements. Tax expenditures are reductions in tax revenues that result from preferential provisions, such as tax exclusions, credits, and deductions. These revenue losses reduce the resources available to fund other programs or they require higher tax rates to raise a given amount of revenue. As we reported in September 2005, the number of tax expenditures more than doubled since 1974, and the sum of tax expenditure revenue loss estimates tripled in real terms to nearly $730 billion in 2004.[4] Enhanced reporting on tax expenditures would ensure

[4] The sum of individual tax expenditure estimates is useful for gauging the general magnitude of the revenue involved, but does not take into account possible interactions between individual provisions. For additional information, see GAO, *Government Performance and Accountability: Tax Expenditures Represent a Substantial Federal Commitment and Need to Be Reexamined*, GAO-05-690 (Washington, D.C.: September 2005).

greater transparency and accountability for revenue forgone by the federal government and provide a more cohesive picture of the federal government's policies and fiscal position.

Addressing the nation's long-term fiscal imbalance constitutes a major transformational challenge that may take a generation or more to resolve. Given the size of the projected deficit, the U.S. government will not be able to grow its way out of this problem— tough choices are required. Traditional incremental approaches to budgeting will need to give way to more fundamental and comprehensive reexaminations of the base of government. Our report, *21st Century Challenges: Reexamining the Base of the Federal Government,*[5] is intended to support the Congress in identifying issues and options that could help address these fiscal pressures. New reporting approaches, as well as enhanced budget processes and control mechanisms are needed to better understand, monitor, and manage the impact of spending and tax policies over the long term. In addition, a set of key outcome-based metrics would inform strategic planning, enhance performance and accountability reporting, and help to assess the impact of various spending programs and tax policies.

- - - - -

We appreciate the cooperation and assistance of the Department of the Treasury and the Office of Management and Budget officials, as well as the federal agencies' chief financial officers and inspectors general, in carrying out our statutory responsibility to

---

[5] GAO, *21st Century Challenges: Reexamining the Base of the Federal Government,* GAO-05-325SP (Washington, D.C.: February 2005).

report on the U.S. government's consolidated financial statements. We look forward to continuing to work with these officials and the Congress to achieve the goals and objectives of financial management reform.

Our audit report begins on page 233. We recently issued a guide[6] to the *Financial Report of the United States Government* to help those who seek to obtain a better understanding of the Financial Report. This guide and other GAO reports noted above are available on GAO's Web site at www.gao.gov.

Our report was prepared under the direction of Jeffrey C. Steinhoff, Managing Director, and Gary T. Engel, Director, Financial Management and Assurance. If you have any questions, please contact me at (202) 512-5500 or them at (202) 512-2600.

David M. Walker
Comptroller General
of the United States
cc: The Majority Leader of the Senate
    The Minority Leader of the Senate
    The Majority Leader of the House
    The Minority Leader of the House

---

[6] GAO, *Understanding the Primary Components of the Annual Financial Report of the United States Government*, GAO-05-958SP (Washington, D.C.: September 2005).

Financial Statements of the United States Government for the Years Ended September 30, 2005, and September 30, 2004

Statements of Net Cost

These statements present the net cost of fiscal years 2005 and 2004 Government operations. For the purposes of this document, "Government" refers to the United States Government. It categorizes costs by Chief Financial Officer Act entities and other significant entities. Costs and earned revenues are presented by department on an accrual basis, while the budget presents costs and revenues by obligations and outlays on a cash basis. In the Statements of Net Cost, the costs and earned revenues are divided between the corresponding departments and entities mentioned above, providing greater accountability by showing the relationship of the agencies' net cost to the Governmentwide net cost. The focus of the budget of the United States is by agency. Budgets are prepared, defended, and monitored by agency. In reporting by agency, we are assisting the external users in assessing the budget integrity, operating performance, stewardship, and systems and control of the Federal Government.

These statements contain the following three components:

- Gross cost—This is the full cost of all the departments and entities. These costs are assigned on a cause-and-effect basis, or reasonably allocated to the corresponding departments and entities.

- Earned revenue—This is revenue the Government earned by providing goods and services to the public at a price.

- Net cost—This is computed by subtracting earned revenue from gross cost.

Net cost for Governmentwide reporting purposes includes the General Services Administration (GSA) and the Office of Personnel Management (OPM) agency allocations, and is net of intragovernmental eliminations. For this reason, individual agency net cost amounts will not agree with the agency's financial statements. Because of their specific functions, most of the costs originally associated with GSA and OPM have been allocated to and reflected in the costs of their user agencies. The remaining costs for GSA and OPM on the Statements of Net Cost are the administrative operating costs, the expenses from prior and past costs from health and pension plan amendments, and the actuarial gains and losses for these agencies. Health and pension benefits that are not reported in the individual agency statements have been allocated out of OPM to the agencies. The interest on Department of the Treasury (Treasury) securities held by the public is part of Treasury's responsibilities, but because of its importance, and the dollar amounts, it is reported separately in these statements.

Statements of Operations and Changes in Net Position

These statements report the results of Government operations. They include unearned revenues that are generated principally by the Government's sovereign power to tax, levy duties, and assess fines and penalties. These statements also cover the cost of Government operations, net of revenue earned from the sale of goods and services to the public (earned revenues). They further include any adjustments and unreconciled transactions that affect the net position.

Revenue

Individual income tax and tax withholdings includes Federal Insurance Contributions Act (FICA)/Self-Employment Contributions Act (SECA) taxes and other taxes including payroll taxes collected from other agencies.

Excise taxes consist of taxes collected for various items, such as airline tickets, gasoline products, distilled spirits and imported liquor, tobacco, firearms, and others.

Miscellaneous earned revenues consist of earned revenues received from the public with virtually no associated cost. This category includes revenues generated by the Federal Communications Commission from the sale of spectrum licenses to promote open-air communication services to the public (spectrum auctions). It also includes rents and royalties on the Outer Continental Shelf Lands resulting from the leasing and development of mineral resources on public lands.

Net Cost of Government Operations

The net cost of Government operations (which is gross cost less earned revenue) flows through from the Statements of Net Cost.

Unreconciled Transactions Affecting the Change in Net Position

Unreconciled transactions are adjustments needed to bring the change in net position into balance due to unreconciled and unaccounted for differences in the consolidated financial statements. Refer to Note 17—Unreconciled Transactions Affecting the Change in Net Position for detailed information.

Net Position, Beginning of Period

The net position, beginning of period reflects the net position reported on the prior year's balance sheet as of the end of that fiscal year.

Prior Period Adjustments

Prior period adjustments are revisions to adjust the beginning net position and balances presented on the prior year financial statements. Refer to Note 1B—Basis of Accounting and Revenue Recognition, and Note 18—Change in Accounting Principle and Prior Period Adjustments for detailed information.

Net Position, End of Period

The net position, end of period amount reflects the net position as of the end of the fiscal year.

Reconciliations of Net Operating Cost and Unified Budget Deficit

The purpose of the reconciliation is to report how the proprietary net operating cost and the unified budget deficit relate to each other. The premise of the reconciliation is that the accrual and budgetary accounting basis share transaction data.

These statements report the reconciliation of the results of operations (net operating cost) on the Statements of Operations and Changes in Net Position to the unified budget deficit in the President's budget.

Receipts and outlays in the President's budget are measured primarily on a cash basis and differ from the basis of accounting measures used in the *Financial Report*. These statements begin with the net results of operations (net operating cost), where operating revenues are reported on a modified cash basis of accounting and the net cost of Government operations on an accrual basis of accounting. Reconciling items to (1) operating revenues include net accrual related to taxes receivable, and (2) net cost of Government operations include items such as changes in liabilities for military, veteran and civilian benefits, as well as depreciation expenses on fixed assets and changes in environmental liabilities.

Components of Net Operating Cost Not Part of the Budget Deficit

This information includes the operating components, such as the changes of benefits payable for veterans, military and civilian employees, and the environmental liabilities and depreciation expense not included in the budget results.

Components of the Budget Deficit Not Part of Net Operating Cost

This information includes the budget components, such as capitalized fixed assets, changes in accounts receivable, and increases in other assets not included in the operating results. These items are typically part of the balance sheets only, and are not part of the operating results.

Statements of Changes in Cash Balance from Unified Budget and Other Activities

The primary purpose of these statements is to report how the annual unified budget deficit relates to the change in the Government's operating cash balance and debt held by the public. It explains why the unified budget deficit normally would not result in an equivalent change in the Government's operating cash balance.

These statements reconcile the unified budget deficit to the change in operating cash during the fiscal year, and explain how the budget deficits (fiscal years 2005 and 2004) are financed. A budget deficit is the result of expenditures exceeding receipts (revenue) during a particular fiscal year.

In depicting how the unified budget deficits were financed, these statements show that in fiscal years 2005 and 2004, the greatest amounts were net new borrowings from the public. Other transactions also required cash disbursements and are not part of the repayments of the debt. These other transactions, such as the payment of interest on debt held by the public, required cash payments and contributed to the use of cash. These statements show the differences between accrual and cash budgetary basis, mainly because of timing differences in the financial statements.

Balance Sheets

The balance sheets show the Government's assets and liabilities. When combined with stewardship information, this information presents a more comprehensive understanding of the Government's financial position. All of the line items on the balance sheets are described in the Notes to the Financial Statements.

Assets

Assets included on the balance sheets are resources of the Government that remain available to meet future needs. The most significant assets that are reported on the balance sheets are property, plant, and equipment; inventories; and loans receivable. There are, however, other significant resources available to the Government that extend beyond the assets presented in these financial statements. Those resources include stewardship assets, including natural resources (see Stewardship Information section), and the Government's sovereign powers to tax, regulate commerce, and set monetary policy.

Selected assets are highlighted in the Stewardship Information section of this report to demonstrate the Government's accountability for these assets. Stewardship assets include stewardship land and heritage assets.

Liabilities and Net Position

Liabilities are obligations of the Government resulting from prior actions that will require financial resources. The most significant liabilities reported on the balance sheets are Federal debt securities held by the public and accrued interest and Federal employee and veteran benefits payable. Liabilities also include social insurance benefits due and payable as of the reporting date.

As with reported assets, the Government's responsibilities, policy commitments, and contingencies are much broader than these reported balance sheet liabilities. They include the social insurance programs disclosed in the Statements of Social Insurance in the Stewardship Information section and a wide range of other programs under which the Government provides benefits and services to the people of this Nation, as well as certain future loss contingencies.

The magnitude and complexity of social insurance programs, coupled with the extreme sensitivity of projections relating to the many assumptions of the programs, produce a wide range of possible results. The Stewardship Responsibilities section describes the social insurance programs, reports long-range estimates that can be used to assess the financial condition of the programs, and explains some of the factors that impact the various programs. Using this information, readers can apply their own judgment as to the condition and sustainability of the individual programs.

Each of the social insurance programs has an associated trust fund to account for its activity. The taxes collected for specific use are credited to the corresponding trust fund that will use these funds to meet a particular Government purpose. If the collections

from taxes and other sources exceed the payments to the beneficiaries, the excess collections are invested in Treasury securities or
"loaned" to the Treasury's General Fund; therefore, the trust fund
balances do not represent cash. An explanation of the trust funds
for social insurance and many of the other large trust funds is
included in Note 21—Dedicated Collections. That note also contains information about trust fund receipts, disbursements, and
assets.

The Government has entered into contractual commitments
requiring the future use of financial resources and has unresolved
contingencies where existing conditions, situations, or circumstances create uncertainty about future losses. Commitments as
well as contingencies that do not meet the criteria for recognition
as liabilities on the balance sheets, but for which there is at least a
reasonable possibility that losses have been incurred, are disclosed
in Note 19—Contingencies and Note 20—Commitments.

Because of its sovereign power to tax and borrow, and the
country's wide economic base, the Government has unique access
to financial resources through generating tax revenues and issuing
Federal debt securities. This provides the Government with the
ability to meet present obligations and those that are anticipated
from future operations and are not reflected in net position.

United States Government
Statements of Net Cost
for the Years Ended September 30, 2005, and September 30, 2004

	Gross Cost	Earned Revenue	Net Cost	Gross Cost	Earned Revenue	Net Cost
(In billions of dollars)	2005			2004		
Department of Defense	703.9	26.9	677.0	672.1	22.3	649.8
Department of Health & Human Services....	623.4	39.6	583.8	583.9	33.4	550.5
Social Security Administration	572.1	(2.0)	574.1	534.9	2.6	532.3
Department of Veterans Affairs	276.6	3.4	273.2	51.1	3.2	47.9
Interest on Treasury Securities held by the public	181.2	-	181.2	158.3	-	158.3
Department of Agriculture	112.6	19.9	92.7	84.1	7.6	76.5
Department of the Treasury	82.3	3.1	79.2	79.2	4.0	75.2
Department of Education	75.6	4.7	70.9	63.9	4.8	59.1
Department of Homeland Security	74.6	6.7	67.9	45.7	5.7	40.0
Department of Transportation	62.4	0.6	61.8	56.7	0.6	56.1
Department of Labor	50.0	-	50.0	58.6	-	58.6
Department of Energy	46.8	3.7	43.1	27.3	4.9	22.4
Department of Housing and Urban Development	43.6	1.3	42.3	41.8	1.3	40.5
Department of Justice	27.3	0.8	26.5	35.4	0.8	34.6
Office of Personnel Management	33.1	14.4	18.7	22.3	13.9	8.4
National Aeronautics and Space Administration	16.5	0.1	16.4	17.3	0.1	17.2
Department of the Interior	19.5	3.2	16.3	18.8	2.2	16.6
Department of State	15.6	2.0	13.6	13.9	1.3	12.6
Agency for International Development	13.0	0.2	12.8	10.7	0.1	10.6
Railroad Retirement Board	9.5	-	9.5	9.3	-	9.3
Environmental Protection Agency	9.3	0.4	8.9	9.5	0.3	9.2
Department of Commerce	9.2	1.5	7.7	9.1	1.4	7.7
Federal Communications Commission	7.2	0.6	6.6	7.6	0.8	6.8
National Science Foundation	5.5	-	5.5	5.2	-	5.2
Federal Deposit Insurance Corporation	1.4	0.2	1.2	0.8	0.2	0.6
Small Business Administration	1.4	0.4	1.0	2.1	0.5	1.6
Pension Benefit Guaranty Corporation	5.1	4.3	0.8	16.9	3.9	13.0
U.S. Nuclear Regulatory Commission	0.9	0.5	0.4	0.8	0.5	0.3
Tennessee Valley Authority	8.6	8.7	(0.1)	8.6	8.3	0.3
National Credit Union Administration	0.1	0.2	(0.1)	0.2	0.1	0.1
General Services Administration	0.2	0.4	(0.2)	-	0.5	(0.5)
Export-Import Bank of the United States	(0.2)	2.5	(2.7)	1.3	2.7	(1.4)
U.S. Postal Service	56.0	68.9	(12.9)	54.0	68.0	(14.0)
All other entities	30.3	7.6	22.7	30.6	11.1	19.5
Total	3,174.6	224.8	2,949.8	2,732.0	207.1	2,524.9

The accompanying notes are an integral part of these financial statements.

United States Government
Statements of Operations and Changes in Net Position
for the Years Ended September 30, 2005, and September 30, 2004

(In billions of dollars)	2005	2004
Revenue:		
Individual income tax and tax withholdings	1,690.1	1,512.3
Corporation income taxes	271.8	183.8
Unemployment taxes	40.0	36.8
Excise taxes	71.0	72.5
Estate and gift taxes	24.7	24.8
Customs duties	22.0	21.0
Other taxes and receipts	46.7	47.7
Miscellaneous earned revenues	19.2	13.8
Total revenue	2,185.5	1,912.7
Less net cost of Government operations	2,949.8	2,524.9
Unreconciled transactions affecting the change in net position (Note 17)	4.3	(3.4)
Net operating cost	(760.0)	(615.6)
Net position, beginning of period	(7,709.8)	(7,094.2)
Change in accounting principle (Note 18)	3.6	-
Prior period adjustments (Note 18)	7.5	-
Net operating cost	(760.0)	(615.6)
Net position, end of period	(8,458.7)	(7,709.8)

The accompanying notes are an integral part of these financial statements.

United States Government
Reconciliations of Net Operating Cost and Unified Budget Deficit
for the Years Ended September 30, 2005, and September 30, 2004

(In billions of dollars)	2005	2004
Net operating cost	(760.0)	(615.6)
Components of Net Operating Cost Not Part of the Budget Deficit:		
Increase in Liability for Military Employee Benefits (Note 11):		
Increase in military pension liabilities	57.7	98.7
Increase in military health liabilities	108.6	42.3
Increase in other military benefits	3.3	2.4
Increase in liability for military employee benefits	169.6	143.4
Increase/(Decrease) in Liability for Veterans Compensation (Note 11):		
Increase/(decrease) in liabilities for veterans	150.1	(39.7)
Increase in liabilities for survivors	47.2	9.6
Increase in liabilities for burial benefits	0.5	0.1
Increase/(decrease) in liability for veteran's compensation	197.8	(30.0)
Increase in Liabilities for Civilian Employee Benefits (Note 11):		
Increase in civilian pension liabilities	43.6	39.8
Increase in civilian health liabilities	24.6	21.7
(Decrease)/increase in other civilian benefits	(5.9)	7.2
Increase in liabilities for civilian employee benefits	62.3	68.7
Increase/(Decrease) in Environmental Liabilities (Note 12):		
Increase/(decrease) in Energy's environmental liabilities	8.1	(1.7)
Increase in all others' environmental liabilities	2.5	1.0
Increase/(decrease) in environmental liabilities	10.6	(0.7)
Depreciation expense	79.7	89.9
Property, plant, and equipment disposals and revaluations	47.8	0.2
Increase in benefits due and payable	14.1	2.9
Increase in insurance programs	31.0	37.0
Increase/(decrease) in other liabilities	15.1	(4.7)
Seigniorage and sale of gold	(0.8)	(0.7)
Increase/(decrease) in accounts payable	7.8	(2.1)
(Increase)/decrease in accounts and taxes receivable	(9.7)	0.3
Components of the Budget Deficit Not Part of Net Operating Cost:		
Capitalized Fixed Assets:		
Department of Defense	(110.2)	(83.2)
Civilian agencies	(36.4)	(28.9)
Total capitalized fixed assets	(146.6)	(112.1)
Increase in inventory	(10.5)	(8.8)
Increase in securities and investments	(18.2)	-
Increase in other assets	(5.0)	(11.7)
Principal repayments of precredit reform loans	9.7	8.5
Net amount of all other differences	(13.2)	23.2
Unified budget deficit	(318.5)	(412.3)

The accompanying notes are an integral part of these financial statements.

United States Government
Statements of Changes in Cash Balance from Unified Budget and Other Activities
for the Years Ended September 30, 2005, and September 30, 2004

(In billions of dollars)	2005		2004	
Unified budget deficit		(318.5)		(412.3)
Adjustments for Noncash Outlays Included in the Budget:				
Interest accrued by Treasury on debt held				
by the public..		(154.4)		(145.6)
Subsidy expense (Note 4)		14.4		6.6
Items Affecting the Cash Balance Not Included in the Budget:				
Net Transactions from Financing Activity:				
Repayment of debt held by the public....	4,317.4		4,379.5	
Borrowings from the public...................	(4,614.1)		(4,759.2)	
Total...		(296.7)		(379.7)
Net Transactions from Monetary Activity:				
(Decrease)/increase in special				
drawing rights	(4.5)		0.7	
Decrease in other monetary assets	(0.1)		(1.3)	
Decrease in loans to the IMF......................	(6.2)		(4.6)	
Total...		(10.8)		(5.2)
Net Transactions from Other Activities:				
Net direct loan activity..........................	-		5.5	
Interest paid by Treasury on debt				
held by the public	152.2		144.7	
Net guaranteed loan activity	(20.1)		(16.7)	
Increase in miscellaneous assets	0.3		0.5	
Decrease/(increase) in allocations of				
special drawing rights.........................	0.1		(0.2)	
Increase in deposit fund balances	(2.0)		(2.9)	
(Increase)/decrease in miscellaneous				
liabilities	-		(1.2)	
Seigniorage and other equity..............	(0.9)		(0.7)	
Reclassification of aged unreconciled				
accounts	-		-	
NRRIT non-Federal securities[1]	2.1		2.4	
Total...	131.7		131.4	
Disposition of deficit...............................		(315.8)		(392.5)
Decrease in operating cash balance		(2.7)		(19.8)
Operating Cash: (Note 2)				
Operating cash balance beginning of				
period		31.0		50.8
Operating cash balance end of period ...		28.3		31.0

[1] For more information, see Railroad Retirement in the Stewardship Information section (page 116).

The accompanying notes are an integral part of these financial statements.

United States Government
Balance Sheets
as of September 30, 2005, and September 30, 2004

(In billions of dollars)	2005	2004
Assets:		
Cash and other monetary assets (Note 2)	85.8	97.0
Accounts and taxes receivable, net (Note 3)	66.1	56.4
Loans receivable, net (Note 4)	221.8	220.9
Inventories and related property, net (Note 5)	272.0	261.5
Property, plant, and equipment, net (Note 6)	678.4	652.7
Securities and investments (Note 7)	75.3	57.1
Other assets (Note 8)	56.7	51.7
Total assets	1,456.1	1,397.3
Liabilities:		
Accounts payable (Note 9)	67.9	60.1
Federal debt securities held by the public and accrued interest (Note 10)	4,624.2	4,329.4
Federal employee and veteran benefits payable (Note 11)	4,491.8	4,062.1
Environmental and disposal liabilities (Note 12)	259.8	249.2
Benefits due and payable (Note 13)	117.0	102.9
Insurance program liabilities (Note 14)	93.2	62.2
Loan guarantee liabilities (Note 4)	47.7	43.1
Other liabilities (Note 15)	213.2	198.1
Total liabilities	9,914.8	9,107.1
Contingencies (Note 19) and Commitments (Note 20)		
Net position	(8,458.7)	(7,709.8)
Total liabilities and net position	1,456.1	1,397.3

The accompanying notes are an integral part of these financial statements.

United States Government Stewardship Information (Unaudited) for the Years Ended September 30, 2005, and September 30, 2004

Stewardship Responsibilities

The social insurance programs were developed to provide income security and health care coverage to citizens under specific circumstances as a responsibility of the Government. Because taxpayers rely on these programs in their long-term planning, stewardship information should indicate whether they are sustainable under current law, as well as what their effect will be on the Government's financial condition. The resources needed to run these programs are raised through taxes and fees. Eligibility for benefits rests in part on earnings and time worked by the individuals. Social Security benefits are generally redistributed intentionally toward lower-wage workers (i.e., benefits are progressive). In addition, each social insurance program has a uniform set of entitling events and schedules that apply to all participants.

Statements of Social Insurance

These statements present estimates for several key indicators of the status of the Social Security, Medicare, Railroad Retirement, and Black Lung Programs. The estimates are actuarial present values of cashflow projections as set forth in the relevant trustees' reports and in the relevant agency performance and accountability reports for Railroad Retirement and Black Lung.[1] For example, for

---

[1] Present values recognize that a dollar paid or collected next year is worth less than a dollar today, because a dollar today could be saved and earn a year's-worth of interest. To calculate a present value, future amounts are thus reduced using an assumed interest rate, and those reduced amounts are summmed. The resulting present value is the amount that would have to be put in the bank today as the assumed interest rate to find the future cashflows.

the Federal Old-Age and Survivors Insurance and the Federal Disability Insurance (OASDI) Program as of January 1, 2005, the present value of costs is projected to exceed the present value of cash income by $5,704 billion over the next 75 years. That is the amount that, if invested at the beginning of the period, together with interest earnings, would be just enough to cover excess costs over 75 years. The cashflow projections are analyzed in more detail in later sections. The estimates in the statements below are for persons who are participants or eventually will participate in the programs as contributors (workers) or beneficiaries (retired workers, survivors, and disabled) during a 75-year time period. Refer to the footnotes at the bottom of these statements for the projection valuation date.

United States Government
Statements of Social Insurance
Present Value of Long-Range (75 Years, except Black Lung) Actuarial Projections

(In billions of dollars)

	2005	2004	2003	2002	2001
Federal Old-Age, Survivors and Disability Insurance (Social Security):					
Contributions and Earmarked Taxes from:					
Participants who have attained age 62	464	411	359	348	309
Participants ages 15-61	15,290	14,388	13,576	13,048	12,349
Future participants (under age 15 and births during period)	13,696	12,900	12,213	11,893	11,035
All current and future participants	29,450	27,699	26,147	25,289	23,693
Expenditures for Scheduled Future Benefits for:					
Participants who have attained age 62	5,395	4,933	4,662	4,402	4,255
Participants ages 15-61	23,942	22,418	21,015	20,210	18,944
Future participants (under age 15 and births during period)	5,816	5,578	5,398	5,240	4,700
All current and future participants	35,154	32,928	31,075	29,851	27,899
Present value of future expenditures less future revenue	5,704[1]	5,229[2]	4,927[3]	4,562[4]	4,207[5]
Federal Hospital Insurance (Medicare Part A):					
Contributions and Earmarked Taxes from:					
Participants who have attained eligibility age	162	148	128	125	113
Participants who have not attained eligibility age	5,064	4,820	4,510	4,408	4,136
Future participants	4,209	4,009	3,773	3,753	3,507
All current and future participants	9,435	8,976	8,411	8,286	7,757
Expenditures for Scheduled Future Benefits for:					
Participants who have attained eligibility age	2,179	2,168	1,897	1,747	1,693
Participants who have not attained eligibility age	12,668	12,054	10,028	9,195	8,568
Future participants	3,417	3,246	2,653	2,470	2,225
All current and future participants	18,264	17,468	14,577	13,412	12,487
Present value of future expenditures less future revenue	8,829[1]	8,492[2]	6,166[3]	5,126[4]	4,730[5]
Federal Supplementary Medical Insurance (Medicare Part B):					
Premiums:					
Participants who have attained eligibility age	363	332	283	252	258
Participants who have not attained eligibility age	2,900	2,665	2,148	1,856	1,845
Future participants	924	891	688	600	593
All current and future participants	4,187	3,889	3,119	2,708	2,696
Expenditures for Scheduled Future Benefits for:					
Participants who have attained eligibility age	1,622	1,475	1,306	1,132	1,159
Participants who have not attained eligibility age	11,541	10,577	8,845	7,463	7,415
Future participants	3,408	3,277	2,622	2,238	2,206
All current and future participants	16,571	15,329	12,773	10,833	10,780
Present value of future expenditures less future revenue[6]	12,384[1]	11,440[2]	9,653[3]	8,125[4]	8,084[5]
Federal Supplementary Medical Insurance (Medicare Part D):					
Premiums and State Transfers:					
Participants who have attained eligibility age	185	176			
Participants who have not attained eligibility age	1,790	1,857			
Future participants	572	618			
All current and future participants	2,547	2,651			
Expenditures for Scheduled Future Benefits for:					
Participants who have attained eligibility age	880	773			
Participants who have not attained eligibility age	7,913	7,566			
Future participants	2,440	2,431			
All current and future participants	11,233	10,770			
Present value of future expenditures less future revenue[6]	8,686[1]	8,119[2]			
Railroad Retirement:					
Contributions and Earmarked Taxes from:					
Participants who have attained eligibility	4	4	4	3	3
Participants who have not attained eligibility	37	37	40	40	41
Future participants	41	39	41	41	41
All current and future participants	82	80	85	83	84

Expenditures for Scheduled Future Benefits for:					
Participants who have attained eligibility	84	81	80	74	73
Participants who have not attained eligibility	73	72	73	76	74
Future participants	16	14	14	13	13
All current and future participants	173	167	167	162	161
Present value of future expenditures less future revenues[7]	91[1]	87[2]	83[3]	79[4]	77[5]
Black Lung (Part C) *present value of future expenditures less future revenue*[8]	(5)[9]	(4)[10]	(4)[11]	(5)[12]	(4)[13]

[1] The projection period is 1/1/2005 - 12/31/2079 and the valuation date is 1/1/2005.
[2] The projection period is 1/1/2004 - 12/31/2078 and the valuation date is 1/1/2004.
[3] The projection period is 1/1/2003 - 12/31/2077 and the valuation date is 1/1/2003.
[4] The projection period is 1/1/2002 - 12/31/2076 and the valuation date is 1/1/2002.
[5] The projection period is 1/1/2001 - 12/31/2075 and the valuation date is 1/1/2001.
[6] These amounts represent the present value of the transfers from the General Fund of the Treasury to the Supplementary Medical Insurance Trust Fund. These intragovernmental transfers are included as income in the Centers for Medicare & Medicaid Services' (CMS) Financial Report but are not income from the Governmentwide perspective of this report.
[7] These amounts approximate the present value of the financial interchange and transfers from the General Fund of the Treasury to the Social Security Equivalent Benefit (SSEB) Account (see later discussion of Railroad Retirement Program). They are included as income in the Railroad Retirement Financial Report but are not income from the Governmentwide perspective of this report.
[8] Does not include interest expense accruing on the outstanding debt.
[9] The projection period is 9/30/2005 - 9/30/2040 and the valuation date is 6/30/2005.
[10] The projection period is 9/30/2004 - 9/30/2040 and the valuation date is 6/30/2004.
[11] The projection period is 9/30/2003 - 9/30/2040 and the valuation date is 6/30/2003.
[12] The projection period is 9/30/2002 - 9/30/2040 and the valuation date is 6/30/2002.
[13] The projection period is 9/30/2001 - 9/30/2040 and the valuation date is 6/30/2001.

Note: Details may not add to totals due to rounding.

The following notes are an integral part of this statement.

Notes to the Statements of Social Insurance

Actuarial present values of the projections are computed based on the economic and demographic assumptions representing the trustees' best estimates (the intermediate assumptions) as set forth in the relevant trustees' reports and in the relevant agency performance and accountability reports for Railroad Retirement and Black Lung. The projections are based on the continuation of program provisions contained in current law.

Contributions and earmarked taxes consist of payroll taxes from employers, employees, and self-employed persons; revenue from Federal income taxation of OASDI and railroad retirement benefits; excise tax on coal (Black Lung); and premiums from, and State transfers on behalf of, participants in Medicare. Income for all programs is presented from a consolidated perspective. Interest payments and other intragovernmental transfers have been eliminated. For example, the Centers for Medicare & Medicaid Services' (CMS) 2005 Financial Report presents income from the trust fund's perspective, not a Governmentwide perspective. Therefore, CMS' Financial Report includes $12,384 billion for the present value of future transfers from the General Fund of the Treasury to the Medicare Part B Account and $8,686 billion for the Medicare Part D Account that have been eliminated in this *Financial Report*. Expenditures include scheduled benefit payments and administrative expenses. The term "scheduled" is used to signify that projected benefits are based on the benefit formulas under current law. However, current Social Security and Medicare law does not provide for full benefit payments after the trust funds are exhausted.

Future participants include births during the projection period and individuals below age 15 as of January 1 of the valuation year.

The present values of future expenditures less future revenues is the current amount of funds needed to cover projected shortfalls, excluding the starting trust fund balances, over the projection period. They are calculated by subtracting the actuarial present values of future scheduled contributions and dedicated tax income by and on behalf of current and future participants from the actuarial present value of the future scheduled benefit payments to them or on their behalf. For these calculations, the trust fund balances at the beginning of the valuation period are not included. The beginning-of-year trust fund balances in billions of dollars for the respective programs, including interest earned, are shown in the following table.

Program	2005	2004	2003	2002	2001
Social Security......................	$1,687	$1,531	$1,378	$1,213	$1,049
Medicare					
HI....................................	$268	$256	$235	$209	$177
SMI..................................	$19	$24	$34	$41	$44
Railroad Retirement	$28	$26	$22	$21	$19
Black Lung...........................	($9)	($8)	($8)	($8)	($7)

The projection period for future participants covers the next 75 years for the Social Security and Medicare Programs. The projection period for current participants (i.e., those age 15 and over on January 1 of the valuation year, referred to as the "closed group") would theoretically cover all of their working and retirement years, a period that could be greater than 75 years in a relatively small number of instances.

For Social Security and Medicare, further information can be obtained from the Social Security Administration (SSA) (*The 2005 Annual Report of the Board of Trustees of the Federal Old-Age and Survivors Insurance and Disability Insurance Trust Funds*) and from the Department of Health and Human Services (HHS) (*The 2005 Annual Report of the Boards of the Trustees of the Federal Hospital Insurance and the Federal Supplementary Medical Insurance Trust Funds*).

Social Security and Medicare

Social Security

The Federal Old-Age and Survivors Insurance (OASI) Trust Fund was established on January 1, 1940, as a separate account in the Treasury. The Federal Disability Insurance (DI) Trust Fund, another separate account in the Treasury, was established on August 1, 1956. OASI pays cash retirement benefits to eligible retirees and their eligible dependents and survivors, and the much smaller DI fund pays cash benefits to eligible individuals who are unable to work due to medical conditions. Though the events that trigger benefit payments are quite different, both trust funds have the same earmarked financing structure: primarily payroll taxes and income taxes on benefits. All financial operations of the OASI and DI Programs are handled through these respective funds. The two funds are often referred to as simply the combined OASDI Trust Funds.

The primary receipts of these two funds are taxes paid by workers, their employers, and individuals with self-employment income, based on work covered by the OASDI Program. Since 1990, employers and employees have each paid 6.2 percent of covered earnings. The self-employed pay 12.4 percent of covered earnings. Payroll taxes are computed on wages and net earnings from self-employment up to a specified maximum annual amount ($90,000 in 2005) that increases each year with economy-wide wages.

Since 1984, up to one-half of OASDI benefits have been subject to Federal income taxation. Effective for taxable years beginning after 1993, the maximum percentage of benefits subject to taxation was increased from 50 percent to 85 percent. The revenue from income taxes on 50 percent of benefits is allocated to the OASDI Trust Funds and the rest is allocated to the Hospital Insurance (HI) Trust Fund.

That portion of each trust fund not required to pay benefits and administrative costs is invested, on a daily basis, in interest-bearing obligations of the U.S. Government. The Social Security Act authorizes the issuance by the Treasury of special non-marketable, intragovernmental debt obligations for purchase exclusively by the trust funds. Although the special issues cannot be bought or sold in the open market, they are redeemable at any time at face value and thus bear no risk of fluctuations in principal value due to changes in market yield rates. Interest on the bonds is credited to the trust funds and becomes an asset to the funds and a liability to the general Government fund.

Medicare

The Medicare Program, created in 1965, also has two separate trust funds: the Hospital Insurance (HI, Medicare Part A) and Supplementary Medical Insurance (SMI, Medicare Parts B and D) Trust Funds.[2] HI pays for inpatient acute hospital services and major alternatives to hospitals (skilled nursing services, for example) and SMI pays for hospital outpatient services, physician services, and assorted other services and products through the Part B account and will pay for prescription drugs through the Part D account. Though the events that trigger benefit payments are quite similar, HI and SMI have very different earmarked financing structures. Like OASDI, HI is financed primarily by payroll contributions. Employers and employees each pay 1.45 percent of earnings, while self-employed workers pay 2.9 percent of their net income. Other income to the HI fund includes a small amount of premium income from voluntary enrollees, a portion of the Federal income taxes that beneficiaries pay on Social Security benefits (as explained above), and interest credited on Treasury securities held in the HI Trust Fund.

For SMI, transfers from the General Fund of the Treasury rep-

---

[2] Medicare legislation in 2003 created the new Part D account in the SMI Trust Fund to track the finances of a new prescription drug benefit that will begin in 2006. As in the case of Medicare Part B, approximately three-quarters of revenues to the Part D account will come from general revenues. Consequently, the nature of the relationship between the SMI Trust Fund and the Federal budget described below is largely unaffected by the presence of the Part D account though the magnitude will be greater.

resent the largest source of income covering abot 75 percent of program costs for both Parts B and D. Beneficiaries pay monthly premiums that finance about 25 percent of costs. With Part D drug coverage, Medicaid will no longer be the primary payer for beneficiaries dually eligible for Medicare and Medicaid. For those beneficiaries, States must pay the Part D account a portion of their estimated foregone drug costs for this population (referred to below as State transfers). As with HI, interest due on Treasury securities held in the SMI Trust Fund is credited to the fund, although in the case of SMI, this is quite small.

Social Security, Medicare, and Governmentwide Finances

The current and future financial status of the separate Social Security and Medicare Trust Funds is the focus of the trustees' reports, a focus that may appropriately be referred to as the "trust fund perspective." In contrast, the Federal Government primarily uses the *unified budget* concept as the framework for budgetary analysis and presentation. It represents a comprehensive display of all Federal activities, regardless of fund type or on- and off-budget status, a broader focus than the trust fund perspective that may appropriately be referred to as the "budget perspective" or the "Governmentwide perspective." Social Security and Medicare are among the largest expenditure categories of the U.S. Federal budget. Together, they now account for more than a third of all Federal spending and the percentage is projected to rise dramatically for the reasons discussed below. This section describes in detail the important relationship between the trust fund perspective and the Governmentwide perspective.

Figure 1 is a simplified graphical depiction of the interaction of the Social Security and Medicare Trust Funds with the rest of the

Federal budget.[3] The boxes on the left show sources of funding, those in the middle represent the trust funds and other Government accounts (of which the General Fund is a part) into which that funding flows, and the boxes on the right show simplified expenditure categories. The figure is intended to illustrate how the various sources of program revenue flow through the budget to beneficiaries. The general approach is to group revenues and expenditures that are linked specifically to Social Security and/or Medicare separately from those for other Federal programs. (For ease of understanding, these other Federal programs are referred to here as *other Government* programs.)

Each of the trust funds has its own sources and types of revenue. With the exception of General Fund transfers to SMI, each of these revenue sources is earmarked specifically for the respective trust fund, and cannot be used for other purposes. In contrast, personal and corporate income taxes and other revenue go into the General Fund of the Treasury and are drawn down for any Government program for which Congress has approved spending.[4] The arrows from the boxes on the left represent the flow of these revenues into the trust funds and other Government accounts.

The heavy line between the top two boxes in the middle of

[3] The Federal unified budget encompasses all Federal Government financing and is synonymous with a Governmentwide perspective.

[4] Other programs also have dedicated revenues in the form of taxes and fees (and other forms of receipt) and there are a large number of earmarked trust funds in the Federal budget. Total trust fund receipts account for about 40 percent of total Government receipts with the Social Security and Medicare Trust Funds accounting for about two-thirds of trust fund receipts. For further discussion see *Federal Trust and Other Earmarked Funds*, GAO-01-199SP, January 2001. In the figure and the discussion that follows, we group all other programs, including these other earmarked trust fund programs, under "Other Government Accounts" to simplify the description and maintain the focus on Social Security and Medicare.

Figure 1 represents intragovernmental transfers between the SMI Trust Fund and other Government accounts. The Medicare SMI Trust Fund is shown separately from the two Social Security trust funds (OASI and DI) and the Medicare HI Trust Fund to highlight the unique financing of SMI. SMI is currently the only one of the four programs that receives large transfers from the General Fund of the Treasury, which is a part of the other Government accounts (the Part D account will receive transfers from the States). The transfers make up roughly three-fourths of SMI Program expenses. While the transfers currently support the Part B account, beginning in 2006 additional transfers will be made to the Part D account and are expected to comprise about three-fourths of expenses in that account. The transfers are automatic; their size depends on how much the program spends, not on how much revenue comes into the Treasury. If General Fund revenues become insufficient to cover both the mandated transfer to SMI and expenditures on other general Government programs, Treasury would have to borrow to make up the difference. In the longer run, if transfers to SMI are increasing—as shown below, they are projected to increase significantly in coming years—then Congress must either raise taxes, cut other Government spending, or reduce SMI benefits.

The dotted lines between the middle boxes of Figure 1 also represent intragovernmental transfers but those transfers arise in the form of "borrowing/lending" between the Government accounts. Interest credited to the trust funds arises when the excess of program income over expenses is loaned to the General Fund. The vertical lines labeled *Surplus Borrowed* represent these flows from the trust funds to the other Government accounts. These loans reduce the amount that the General Fund has to borrow from the public to finance a deficit (or likewise increase the amount of debt paid off if there is a surplus). But the General Fund has to credit interest on the loans from the trust fund programs, just as if it borrowed the money from the public. The credits lead to future obligations for the General Fund (which is part of the other Government accounts). These transactions are indicated in Figure 1 by the vertical arrows labeled *Interest Credited.* The credits increase trust fund income exactly as much as they increase credits (future obligations) in the General Fund. So from the standpoint of the Government as a whole, at least in an accounting sense, these interest credits are a wash.

It is important to understand the additional implications of these loans from the trust funds to the other Government accounts. When the trust funds get the receipts that they loan to the General Fund, these receipts provide additional authority to spend on benefits and other program expenses. The General Fund, in turn, has taken on the obligation of paying interest on these loans every year and repaying the principal when trust fund income from other sources falls below expenditures—the loans will be called in and the General Fund will have to reduce other spending, raise taxes, or borrow more from the public to finance the benefits paid by the trust funds.

Figure 1
Social Security, Medicare, and Governmentwide Finances

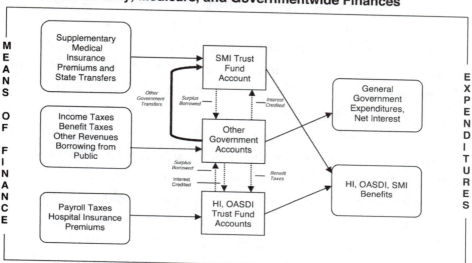

Actual dollar amounts roughly corresponding to the flows presented in Figure 1 are shown in Table 1 for fiscal year 2005. The first three columns show revenues and expenditures for HI, SMI, and OASDI, respectively, and the fourth column is the sum of these three columns. The fifth column has total revenues and expenditures for all other Government programs, which includes the General Fund account, and the last column is the sum of the "combined" and "other Government" columns. In Table 1, revenues from the public (left side of Figure 1) and expenditures to the public (right side of Figure 1) are shown separately from transfers between Government accounts (middle of Figure 1). Note that the transfers ($114.5 billion) and interest credits ($109.5 billion) received by the trust funds appear as negative entries under other Government and are thus offsetting when summed for the total budget column. These two intragovernmental transfers are key to the differences between the trust fund and budget perspectives.

From the Governmentwide perspective, only revenues received from the public (and States in the case of Medicare, Part D) and expenditures made to the public are important for the final balance. Trust fund revenue from the public consists of payroll taxes, benefit taxes, and premiums. For HI, the difference between total expenditures made to the public ($184.1 billion) and revenues ($181.3 billion) was $2.8 billion in 2005, indicating that HI had a relatively small negative effect on the overall budget outcome *in that year.* For the SMI account, revenues from the public (premiums) were relatively small, representing about a quarter of total expenditures made to the public in 2005. The difference, $116.8 billion, resulted in a net draw on the overall budget balance in that year. For OASDI, the difference between total expenditures made to the public ($523.3 billion) and revenues from the public ($604.9 billion) was -$81.6 billion in 2005, indicating that OASDI had a positive effect on the overall budget outcome *in that year.*

The trust fund perspective is captured in the bottom section of each of the three trust fund columns that contain data from the respective trustees' reports. For HI, total revenues exceeded total expenditures by $12.9 billion in 2005, as shown at the bottom of the first column. This surplus would be added to the beginning trust fund (not shown) that leads to budget obligations in future years. For SMI, total revenues of $152.5 billion ($35.9 + $116.6), including $114.0 billion transferred from other Government accounts (the General Fund), fell short of total expenditures by $0.2 billion. Transfers to the SMI Program from other Government accounts (the General Fund), amounting to about 75 percent of program costs, are obligated under current law and therefore appropriately viewed as revenue from the trust fund perspective.

For OASDI, total revenues of $696.7 billion ($604.9 + $91.8), including interest and a small amount of other Government transfers, exceeded total expenditures of $523.3 billion by $174.0 billion.

Table 1
Annual Revenues and Expenditures for Medicare and Social Security Trust Funds and the Total Federal Budget, Fiscal Year 2005

(In billions of dollars)

Revenue and Expenditure Categories	Trust Funds			Com-bined	Other Govern-ment	Total[1]
	HI	SMI	OASDI			
Revenues from the Public:						
Payroll and benefit taxes	177.7	-	604.9	782.6	-	782.6
Premiums	3.6	35.9	-	39.5	-	39.5
Other taxes and fees	-	-	-	-	1,331.2	1,331.2
Total	181.3	35.9	604.9	822.1	1,331.2	2,153.3
Total expenditures to the public[2]	184.1	152.7	523.3	860.2	1,611.6	2,471.8
Net results for budget perspective[3]	2.8	116.8	(81.6)	38.0	280.5	318.5
Revenues from Other Government Accounts:						
Transfers	0.5	114.0	-	114.5	114.5	-
Interest credits	15.1	2.6	91.8	109.5	109.5	-
Total	15.6	116.6	91.8	224.0	224.0	-
Net results for trust fund perspective[3, 4]	(12.9)	0.2	(174.0)	(186.7)	N/A	N/A

[1] This column is the sum of the preceding two columns and shows data for the total Federal budget. The figure $318.5 was the total Federal deficit in fiscal year 2005.
[2] The OASDI figure includes $3.9 billion transferred to the Railroad Retirement Board for benefit payments and is therefore an expenditure to the public.
[3] Net results are computed as expenditures less revenues.
Note: "N/A" indicates not applicable.
[4] Details may not add to totals due to rounding.

Cashflow Projections

Background

Economic and Demographic Assumptions. The Boards of Trustees[5] of the OASDI and Medicare Trust Funds provide in their annual reports to Congress short-range (10-year) and long-range (75-year) actuarial estimates of each trust fund. Because of the inherent uncertainty in estimates for 75 years into the future, the Boards use three alternative sets of economic and demographic assumptions to show a range of possibilities. Assumptions are made about many economic and demographic factors, including gross domestic product (GDP), earnings, the consumer price index (CPI), the unemployment rate, the fertility rate, immigration, mortality, disability incidence and terminations and, for the Medicare projections, health care cost growth. The assumptions used for the most recent set of projections shown in Table 2 are generally referred to as the "intermediate assumptions," and reflect the trustees' best estimate of expected future experience.

---

[5] There are six trustees: the Secretaries of Treasury (managing trustee), Health and Human Services, and Labor; the Commissioner of the Social Security Administration; and two public trustees who are appointed by the President and confirmed by the Senate for a 4-year term. By law, the public trustees are members of two different political parties.

Table 2
Social Security and Medicare Demographic and Economic Assumptions

		Demographic Assumptions				Economic Assumptions			
Year	Total Fertility Rate[1]	Age-Sex Adjusted Death Rate[2]	Life Expectancy at Birth Male[3]	Life Expectancy at Birth Female[3]	Net Immigration[4] (persons)	Productivity Growth[5] (percent change)	Real Wage Differential[6] (percent change)	CPI[7] (percent change)	Average Annual Interest Rate[8] (percent)
2005	2.02	854.2	74.8	79.6	1,075,000	2.0	2.1	2.2	4.2
2006	2.02	849.8	74.9	79.7	1,075,000	2.0	2.2	2.2	5.1
2010	2.01	828.2	75.4	80.0	1,000,000	1.7	1.3	2.8	5.7
2020	1.98	764.7	76.5	80.8	950,000	1.6	1.0	2.8	5.8
2030+	1.95	705.0	77.5	81.7	900,000	1.6	1.1	2.8	5.8

[1] The total fertility rate for any year is the average number of children who would be born to a woman in her lifetime if she were to experience the birth rates by age observed in, or assumed for, the selected year, and if she were to survive the entire childbearing period. The ultimate total fertility rate of 1.95 is assumed to be reached in 2029.
[2] The age-sex-adjusted death rate is a weighted average of age-sex-specific death rates (deaths per 100,000) in a year where the weights are the number of people in the corresponding age-sex group as of April 1, 2000. The death rate is a summary measure and not a basic assumption. Note that after 2030, the death rate continues to fall, to 495.5 by 2080.
[3] The period life expectancy for a group of persons born in a given year is the average that would be attained by such persons if the group were to experience in succeeding years the death rates by age observed in, or assumed for, the given year. It is a summary measure and not a basic assumption; it summarizes the effects of the basic assumptions from which it is derived. Life expectancy continues to increase, to 81.7 for males and 85.2 for females by 2080.
[4] Net immigration is the number of persons who enter during the year (both legally and otherwise) minus the number of persons who leave during the year.
[5] Productivity is the percent change in total economy productivity, defined as the ratio of gross domestic product to hours worked by all workers.
[6] The real-wage differential is the difference between the percentage increases, before rounding, in the average annual wage in covered employment, and the average annual CPI. The ultimate real wage differential eventually trends upwards to an ultimate value of 1.1.
[7] The CPI is the annual average value for the calendar year of the CPI for urban wage earners and clerical workers.
[8] The average annual interest rate is the average of the nominal interest rates, which, in practice, are compounded semiannually for special-issue Treasury obligations sold only to the trust funds in each of the 12 months of the year.

Beneficiary-to-Worker Ratio. Underlying the pattern of expenditure projections for both the OASDI and Medicare Programs is the impending demographic change that will occur as the large baby-boom generation, born in the years 1946 to 1964, retires or reaches eligibility age. The consequence is that the number of beneficiaries will increase much faster than the number of workers who pay taxes that are used to pay benefits. The pattern is illustrated in Chart 1 which shows the ratio of OASDI beneficiaries to workers for the historical period and estimated for the next 75 years. In 2004, there were about 30 beneficiaries for every 100 workers. By 2030, there will be about 46 beneficiaries for every 100 workers. A similar demographic pattern confronts the Medicare Program. For example, for the HI Program, there were about 26 beneficiaries for every 100 workers in 2004; by 2030 there are expected to be about 42 beneficiaries for every 100 workers. This ratio for both programs will continue to increase to about 50 beneficiaries for every 100 workers by the end of the projection period, after the baby-boom generation has moved through the Social Security system due to declining birth rates and increasing longevity.

Chart 1— Beneficiaries per 100 Covered Workers
1970-2079

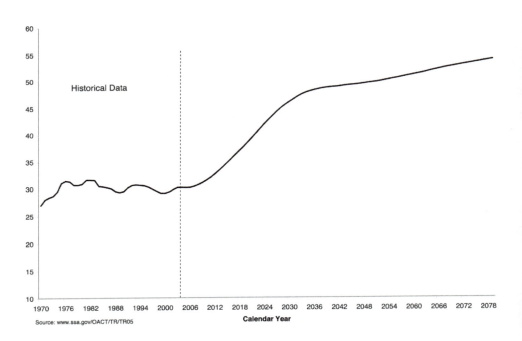

Source: www.ssa.gov/OACT/TR/TR05

Social Security Projections

Nominal Income and Expenditures. Chart 2 shows historical values and actuarial estimates of combined OASDI annual income (excluding interest) and expenditures for 1970-2079 in nominal dollars. The estimates are for the open-group population. That is, the estimates include taxes paid from, and on behalf of, workers who will enter covered employment during the period, as well as those already in covered employment at the beginning of that period. These estimates also include scheduled benefit payments made to, and on behalf of, such workers during that period. Note that expenditure projections in Chart 2 and subsequent charts are based on current-law benefit formulas regardless of whether the income and assets are available to finance them.

**Chart 2—OASDI Income (Excluding Interest) and Expenditures
1970-2079**

(In billions of nominal dollars)

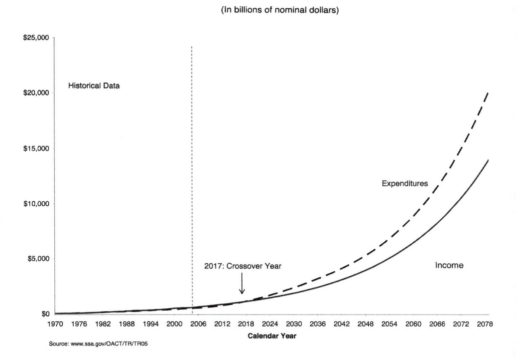

Source: www.ssa.gov/OACT/TR/TR05

Currently, Social Security tax revenues exceed benefit payments and will continue to do so until 2017, when revenues are projected to fall below benefit payments, after which the gap between expenditures and revenues continues to widen.

Income and Expenditures as a Percent of Taxable Payroll. Chart 3 shows annual income (excluding interest but including both payroll and benefit taxes) and expenditures expressed as percentages of taxable payroll, commonly referred to as the income rate and cost rate, respectively.

The OASDI cost rate is projected to decline slightly until about 2008. It then begins to increase rapidly and first exceeds the income rate in 2017, producing cashflow deficits thereafter. As described above, surpluses that occur prior to 2017 are "loaned" to the General Fund and accumulate, with interest, reserve spending authority for the trust fund. The reserve spending authority represents an obligation for the General Fund. Beginning in 2017, Social Security will start using interest credits to meet full benefit obligations. The Government will need to raise taxes, reduce benefits, increase borrowing from the public, and/or cut spending for other programs to meet its obligations to the trust fund. By 2041, the trust fund reserves (and thus reserve spending authority) are projected to be exhausted. Even if a trust fund's assets are exhausted, however, tax income will continue to flow into the fund. Present tax rates would be sufficient to pay 74 percent of scheduled benefits after trust fund exhaustion in 2041 and 68 percent of scheduled benefits in 2079.

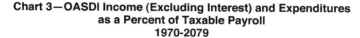

**Chart 3—OASDI Income (Excluding Interest) and Expenditures
as a Percent of Taxable Payroll
1970-2079**

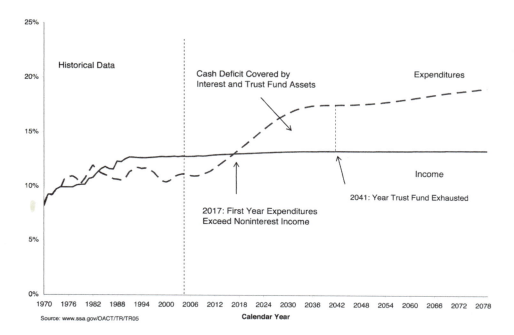

Source: www.ssa.gov/OACT/TR/TR05

Income and Expenditures as a Percent of GDP. Chart 4 shows estimated annual income (excluding interest) and expenditures, expressed as percentages of GDP, the total value of goods and services produced in the United States. This alternative perspective shows the size of the OASDI Program in relation to the capacity of the national economy to sustain it. The gap between expenditures and income widens continuously with expenditures generally growing as a share of GDP and income declining slightly relative to GDP. Social Security's expenditures are projected to grow from 4.3 percent of GDP in 2004 to 6.3 percent by 2034 and to 6.4 percent by 2079. In 2079, expenditures are projected to exceed income by 1.9 percent of GDP.

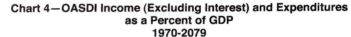

**Chart 4—OASDI Income (Excluding Interest) and Expenditures
as a Percent of GDP
1970-2079**

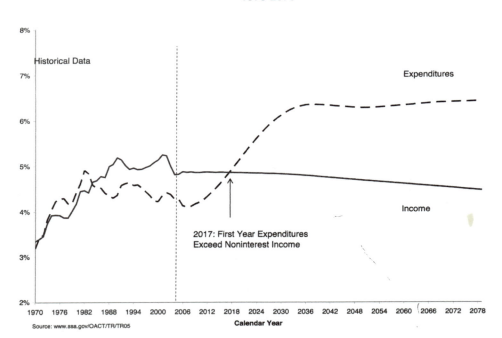

Source: www.ssa.gov/OACT/TR/TR05

Sensitivity Analysis. Actual future income from OASDI payroll taxes and other sources and actual future expenditures for scheduled benefits and administrative expenses will depend upon a large number of factors: the size and composition of the population that is receiving benefits, the level of monthly benefit amounts, the size and characteristics of the work force covered under OASDI, and the level of workers' earnings. These factors will depend, in turn, upon future marriage and divorce rates, birth rates, death rates, migration rates, labor force participation and unemployment rates, disability incidence and termination rates, retirement age patterns, productivity gains, wage increases, cost-of-living increases, and many other economic and demographic factors.

This section presents estimates that illustrate the sensitivity of long-range expenditures and income for the OASDI Program to changes in *selected individual assumptions*. In this analysis, the intermediate assumption is used as the reference point, and one assumption at a time is varied. The variation used for each individual assumption reflects the levels used for that assumption in the low cost (Alternative I) and high cost (Alternative III) projections. For example, when analyzing sensitivity with respect to variation in real wages, income and expenditure projections using the intermediate assumptions are compared to the outcome when projections are done by changing only the real wage assumption to either low cost or high cost alternatives.

The low cost alternative is characterized by assumptions that generally improve the financial status of the program (relative to the intermediate assumption) such as slower improvement in mortality (beneficiaries die younger). In contrast, assumptions under the high cost alternative generally worsen the financial outlook. One exception occurs with the CPI assumption (next page).

Table 3 shows the effects of changing individual assumptions on the present value of estimated OASDI expenditures in excess of income (the *shortfall* of income relative to expenditures in present value terms). The assumptions are shown in parentheses. For example, the intermediate assumption for the annual rate of *reduction in age-sex-adjusted death rates* is 0.72 percent. For the low cost alternative, a slower reduction rate (0.30 percent) is assumed as it means that beneficiaries die at a younger age relative to the intermediate assumption, resulting in lower expenditures. Under the low cost assumption, the shortfall drops from $5,704 billion to $4,376 billion, a 23 percent smaller shortfall. The high cost death rate assumption (1.27 percent) results in an increase in the shortfall, from $5,704 billion to $7,303 billion, a 28 percent increase in the shortfall. Clearly, alternative death rate assumptions have a substantial impact on estimated future cashflows in the OASDI Program.

A higher fertility rate means more workers relative to beneficiaries over the projection period, thereby lowering the shortfall relative to the intermediate assumption. An increase in the rate from 1.95 to 2.2 results in a 10 percent smaller shortfall (i.e., expenditures less income), from $5,704 billion to $5,144 billion.

Higher real wage growth results in faster income growth relative to expenditure growth. Table 3 shows that a real wage differential that is 0.5 greater than the intermediate assumption of 1.1 results in a drop in the shortfall from $5,704 billion to $4,887 billion, a 14 percent decline.

The CPI change assumption operates in a somewhat counterintuitive manner, as seen in Table 3. A lower rate of change results in a higher shortfall. This arises as a consequence of holding the real wage assumption constant while varying the CPI so that wages (the income base) are affected sooner than benefits. If the rate is assumed to be 1.8 percent rather than 2.8 percent, the shortfall rises about 7 percent, from $5,704 billion to $6,094 billion.

The effect of net immigration is similar to fertility in that, over the 75-year projection period, higher immigration results in proportionately more workers (taxpayers) than beneficiaries. The low-cost assumption for net immigration results in an 8 percent drop in the shortfall, from $5,704 billion to $5,270 billion, relative to the intermediate case; and the high-cost assumption results in a 5 percent higher shortfall.

Finally, Table 3 shows the sensitivity of the shortfall to variations in the real interest rate or, in present value terminology, the sensitivity to alternative discount rates. A higher discount rate results in a lower present value. The shortfall of $4,246 billion is 26 percent lower when the real interest rate is assumed to be 3.7 percent rather than 3 percent, and 41 percent higher when the real interest rate is assumed to be 2.2 percent rather than 3 percent.

Table 3
Present Values of Estimated OASDI Expenditures in Excess of Income Under Various Assumptions, 2005-2079

(In billions of dollars)

Assumption	Shortfall		
	Low	Intermediate	High
Average annual reduction in death rates ..	4,376 (0.30)	5,704 (0.72)	7,303 (1.27)
Total fertility rate	5,144 (2.2)	5,704 (1.95)	6,260 (1.7)
Real wage differential	4,887 (1.6)	5,704 (1.1)	6,287 (0.6)
CPI change	5,308 (3.8)	5,704 (2.8)	6,094 (1.8)
Net immigration	5,270 (1,300,000)	5,704 (900,000)	6,010 (672,500)
Real interest rate	4,246 (3.7)	5,704 (3.0)	8,063 (2.2)

Numbers in parentheses are the values of the assumptions used in the respective scenario.

Source: 2005 OASDI Trustees Report and SSA.

Medicare Projections

Recent Medicare Legislation. On December 8, 2003, President Bush signed into law the Medicare Prescription Drug, Improvement, and Modernization Act of 2003. The 2003 law will have a major impact on the operations and finances of Medicare. The law adds a prescription drug benefit to Medicare beginning in 2006 and a new prescription drug account in the SMI Trust Fund. The benefit could be obtained through a private drug-only plan, a private preferred-provider organization or health maintenance organization, or through an employer-sponsored retiree health plan. The preferred-provider organizations will be new to the Medicare Program and will operate on a regional basis. The Federal Government will assume some of the costs of providing prescription drug coverage to people eligible for both Medicare and Medicaid.

The legislation also includes provisions not related to the prescription drug benefit. It includes increases in Medicare provider reimbursements, higher Medicare Part B premiums for people at higher income levels, and an expansion of tax-deductible health savings accounts. The 2003 legislation is expected to have a significant effect on future Medicare finances as seen below and earlier in the Statement of Social Insurance.

Health Care Cost Growth. In addition to the growth in the number of beneficiaries per worker, the Medicare Program has the added pressure of expected growth in the use and cost of health care per person. Continuing development and use of new technology is expected to cause health care expenditures to grow faster than GDP in the long run. For the intermediate assumption, health care expenditures per beneficiary are assumed to grow one percentage point faster than per capita GDP over the long range.

Total Medicare. It is important to recognize the rapidly increasing long-range cost of Medicare and the large role of general revenues and beneficiary premiums in financing the SMI Program. Chart 5 shows expenditures and current-law noninterest revenue sources for HI and SMI combined as a percentage of GDP. The total expenditure line shows Medicare costs rising to almost 14 percent of GDP by 2079. Revenues from taxes and premiums (including State transfers under Part D) are expected to increase from 1.7 percent of GDP in 2004 to 3.5 percent of GDP in 2079. Payroll tax income declines gradually as a percent of GDP as growth in the number of workers paying such taxes slows and wages as a portion of compensation declines, offset by higher premiums combined for Parts B and D of SMI as a percent of GDP. General revenue contributions for SMI, as determined by current law, are projected to rise as a percent of GDP from 0.9 percent to 6.2 percent over the same period. Thus, revenues from taxes and premiums (including State transfers) will fall substantially as a share of total noninterest Medicare income (from 66 percent in 2004 to 36 percent in 2079) while general revenues will rise (from 34 percent to 64 percent). The gap between total noninterest Medicare income (including general revenue contributions) and expenditures begins around 2008 and then steadily continues to widen, reaching 3.9 percent of GDP by 2079.

**Chart 5—Total Medicare (HI and SMI) Expenditures and Noninterest Income
as a Percent of GDP
1970-2079**

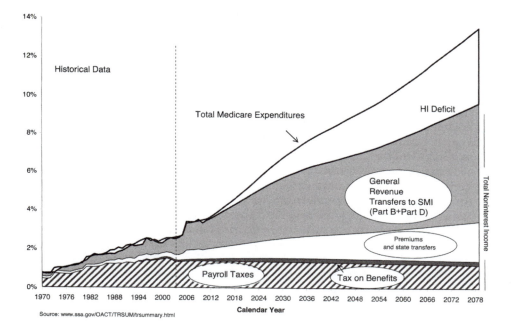

Source: www.ssa.gov/OACT/TRSUM/trsummary.html

Medicare, Part A (Hospital Insurance)—Nominal Income and Expenditures. Chart 6 shows historical and actuarial estimates of HI annual income (excluding interest) and expenditures for 1970-2079 in nominal dollars. The estimates are for the open-group population. The figure reveals a widening gap between income and expenditures after 2004.

Chart 6—Medicare Part A Income (Excluding Interest) and Expenditures 1970-2079

(In billions of nominal dollars)

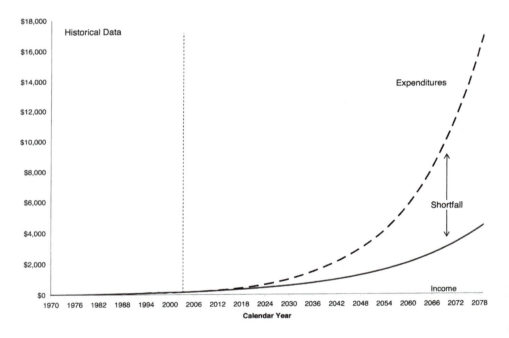

Source: www.ssa.gov/OACT/TRSUM/images/LD_ChartC.html and CMS

Medicare, Part A Income and Expenditures as a Percent of Taxable Payroll. Chart 7 illustrates income (excluding interest) and expenditures as a percentage of taxable payroll over the next 75 years. The chart shows that the expenditure rate exceeds the income rate beginning in 2004, and cash deficits continue thereafter. Trust fund interest earnings and assets provide enough resources to pay full benefit payments until 2020 with general revenues used to finance interest and loan repayments to make up the difference between cash income and expenditures during that period. Pressures on the Federal budget will thus emerge well before 2020. Present tax rates would be sufficient to pay 79 percent of scheduled benefits after trust fund exhaustion in 2020 and 27 percent of scheduled benefits in 2079.

Chart 7—Medicare Part A Income (Excluding Interest) and Expenditures as a Percent of Taxable Payroll 1970-2079

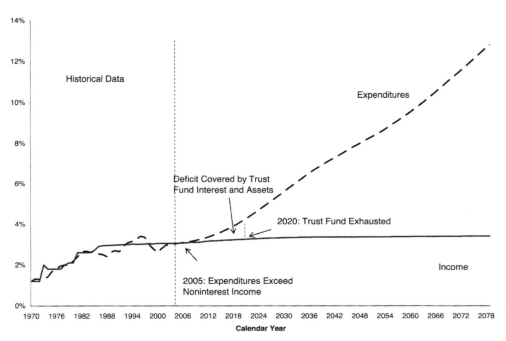

Source:www.ssa.gov/OACT/TRSUM/images/LD_ChartC.html and CMS

Medicare Part A Income and Expenditures as a Percent of GDP. Chart 8 shows estimated annual income (excluding interest) and expenditures, expressed as percentages of GDP, the total value of goods and services produced in the United States. This alternative perspective shows the size of the HI Program in relation to the capacity of the national economy to sustain it. Medicare Part A's expenditures are projected to grow from 1.4 percent of GDP in 2004, to 2.6 percent in 2030, and to 5.4 percent by 2079. The gap between expenditures and income widens continuously with expenditures growing as a share of GDP and income declining slightly relative to GDP. By 2079, expenditures are projected to exceed income by 4.0 percent of GDP.

**Chart 8—Medicare Part A Income (Excluding Interest) and Expenditures as a Percent of GDP
1970-2079**

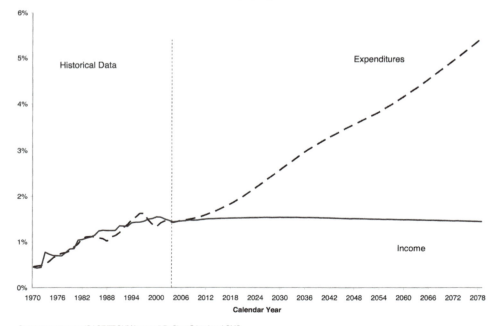

Source:www.ssa.gov/OACT/TRSUM/images/LD_ChartC.html and CMS

Medicare, Parts B and D (Supplementary Medical Insurance).
Chart 9 shows historical and actuarial estimates of Medicare Part
B and Part D premiums (and Part D State transfers) and expenditures for each of the next 75 years, in nominal dollars. The gap
between premiums and State transfer revenues and program
expenditures, a gap that will need to be filled with transfers from
general revenues, grows throughout the projection period.

Chart 9—Medicare Part B and Part D Premium and State Transfer Income and Expenditures 1970-2079

(In billions of nominal dollars)

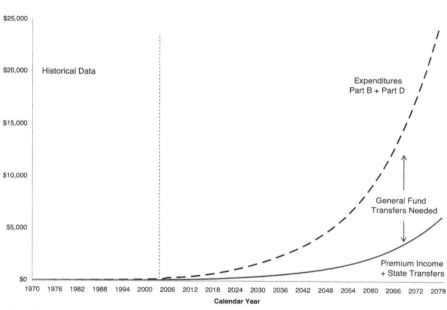

Source: Centers for Medicare & Medicaid Services

Medicare Part B and Part D Premium and State Transfer Income and Expenditures as a Percent of GDP. Chart 10 shows expenditures for the Supplementary Medical Insurance Program over the next 75 years expressed as a percentage of GDP, providing a perspective on the size of the SMI Program in relation to the capacity of the national economy to sustain it. In 2004, SMI expenditures were $141 billion, which was 1.2 percent of GDP. After 2005, this percentage is projected to increase steadily reaching 8.2 percent in 2079. This reflects growth in the volume and intensity of Medicare services provided per beneficiary throughout the projection period, including the prescription drug benefits, together with the effects of the baby boom retirement. Premium and State transfer income grows from under 0.3 percent in 2004 to nearly 2.0 percent of GDP in 2079, so the portion financed by General Fund transfers to SMI is projected to be about 78 percent throughout the projection period.

Chart 10—Medicare Part B and Part D Premium and State Transfer Income and Expenditures as a Percent of GDP
1970-2079

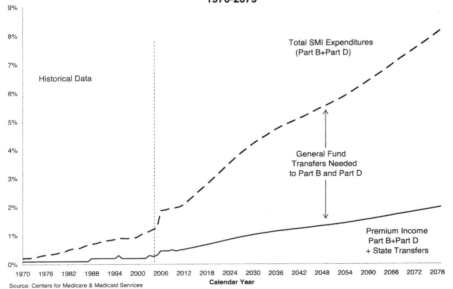

Source: Centers for Medicare & Medicaid Services

Medicare Sensitivity Analysis. This section illustrates the sensitivity of long-range cost and income estimates for the Medicare Program to changes in *selected individual assumptions.* As with the OASDI analysis, the intermediate assumption is used as the reference point, and one assumption at a time is varied. The variation used for each individual assumption reflects the levels used for that assumption in the low cost and high cost projections (see description of sensitivity analysis for OASDI).

Table 4 shows the effects of changing various assumptions on the present value of estimated HI expenditures in excess of income (the *shortfall* of income relative to expenditures in present value terms). The assumptions are shown in parentheses. Clearly, net HI expenditures are extremely sensitive to alternative assumptions about the growth in health care cost. For the low cost alternative, the slower growth in health costs causes the shortfall to drop from $8,829 billion to $3,140 billion, a 64 percent smaller shortfall. The high cost assumption results in a more than doubling of the shortfall, from $8,829 billion to $18,113 billion.

Variations in the next four assumptions in Table 4 result in relatively minor changes in net HI expenditures. The higher or lower fertility assumptions cause a less than 2 percent change in the shortfall relative to the intermediate case. The higher real wage growth rate results in about a 6 percent greater shortfall while a lower growth rate reduces the shortfall by about 8 percent. Wages are a key cost factor in the provision of health care. Higher wages also result in greater payroll tax income. HI expenditures exceed HI income by a wide and increasing margin in the future (Charts 6 to 8). As a result, an assumed higher real wage differential has a larger impact on HI expenditures than HI income, thereby increasing the shortfall of income relative to expenditures. CPI and net immigration changes have very little effect on net HI expenditures. Higher immigration increases the net shortfall modestly as higher payroll tax revenue is more than offset by higher medical care expenditures.

Table 4 also shows that the present value of net HI expenditures is 26 percent lower if the real interest rate is 3.7 percent rather than 3 percent and 37 percent higher if the real interest rate is 2.2 percent rather than 3 percent.

Table 4
Present Values of Estimated Medicare Part A Expenditures in Excess of Income Under Various Assumptions, 2005-2079

(In billions of dollars)

Assumption[1]	Shortfall		
	Low	Intermediate	High
Average annual growth in health costs[2]	3,140 (4.1)	8,829 (5.1)	18,113 (6.1)
Total fertility rate[3]	8,677 (2.2)	8,829 (1.95)	8,978 (1.7)
Real wage differential	8,303 (0.6)	8,829 (1.1)	9,531 (1.6)
CPI change	8,751 (3.8)	8,829 (2.8)	8,863 (1.8)
Net immigration..	8,734 (672,500)	8,829 (900,000)	8,982 (1,300,000)
Real interest rate...	6,544 (3.7)	8,829 (3.0)	12,075 (2.2)

[1] The sensitivity of the projected HI net cashflow to variations in future mortality rates is also of interest. At this time, however, relatively little is known about the relationship between improvements in life expectancy and the associated changes in health status and per beneficiary health expenditures. As a result, it is not possible at present to prepare meaningful estimates of the Part A mortality sensitivity.
[2] Annual growth rate is the aggregate cost of providing covered health care services to beneficiaries. The low cost and high cost alternatives assume that costs increase 1 percent slower or faster, respectively, than the intermediate assumption, relative to growth in taxable payroll.
[3] The total fertility rate for any year is the average number of children who would be born to a woman in her lifetime if she were to experience the birth rates by age observed in, or assumed for, the selected year and if she were to survive the entire childbearing period.

Table 5 shows the effects of various assumptions about the growth in health care costs on the present value of estimated SMI

(Medicare Parts B and D) expenditures in excess of income. As with HI, net SMI expenditures are very sensitive to changes in the health care cost growth assumption. For the low cost alternative, the slower assumed growth in health costs reduces the Governmentwide resources needed for Part B from $12,384 billion to $8,645 billion and in Part D from $8,686 billion to $6,146 billion, about a 30 percent difference in each case. The high-cost assumption increases Governmentwide resources needed to $18,353 billion for Part B and to $12,677 billion for Part D, just under a 50 percent increase in each case.

Table 5
Present Values of Estimated Medicare Parts B and D Future Expenditures Less Premium Income and State Transfers Under Three Health Care Cost Growth Assumptions, 2005-2079

(In billions of dollars)

Medicare Program[1]	Governmentwide Resources Needed		
	Low (4.1)	Intermediate (5.1)	High (6.1)
Part B	8,645	12,384	18,353
Part D	6,146	8,686	12,677

[1] Annual growth rate is the aggregate cost of providing covered health care services to beneficiaries. The low and high scenarios assume that costs increase one percent slower or faster, respectively, than the intermediate assumption.

Source: Centers for Medicare & Medicaid Services.

Sustainability of Social Security and Medicare

75-Year Horizon

According to the 2005 Medicare Trustees Report, the HI Trust Fund is projected to remain solvent until 2020 and, according to the 2005 Social Security Trustees Report, the OASDI Trust Funds are projected to remain solvent until 2041. In each case, some general revenues must be used to satisfy the authorization of full benefit payments until the year of exhaustion. This occurs when the trust fund balances accumulated during prior years are needed to pay benefits, which leads to a transfer from general revenues to the trust funds. Moreover, under current law, General Fund transfers to the SMI Trust Fund will occur into the indefinite future and will continue to grow with the growth in health care expenditures.

The potential magnitude of future financial obligations under these three social insurance programs is therefore important from a unified budget perspective as well as for understanding generally the growing resource demands of the programs on the economy. A common way to present future cashflows is in terms of their *present value*. This approach recognizes that a dollar paid or collected next year is worth less than a dollar today, because a dollar today could be saved and earn a year's-worth of interest (see footnote 1).

Table 6 shows the magnitudes of the primary expenditures and sources of financing for the three trust funds computed on an open-group basis for the next 75 years and expressed in present values. The data are consistent with the Statement of Social Insurance. For HI, revenues from the public are projected to fall short of total expenditures by $8,829 billion in present value terms.[6] From the budget or Governmentwide perspective, that is the additional amount needed in order to pay scheduled benefits over the next 75 years. From the trust fund perspective, the amount needed is $8,561 billion in present value after subtracting the value of the existing trust fund balances (an asset to the trust fund account but an

---

[6] Interest income is not a factor in this table as dollar amounts are in present value terms.

intragovernmental transfer to the overall budget). For SMI, revenues from the public and State transfers are estimated to be $12,384 billion less than total expenditures for the Part B account and $8,686 billion less for the Part D account, amounts that, from a budget perspective, will be needed to keep the program solvent for the next 75 years. From the trust fund perspective, however, the present values of total revenues and total expenditures for the SMI Program are equal due to the annual adjustment of revenue from other Government accounts to meet program costs.[7] For OASDI, projected revenues from the public fall short of total expenditures by $5,704 billion in present value dollars and, from the trust fund perspective, by $4,017 billion.

From the Governmentwide perspective, the present value of the total resources needed for the Social Security and Medicare Programs equals $35,603 billion. These resources needed from the budget are in addition to payroll taxes, benefit taxes, and premium payments. From the trust fund perspective, which counts the trust funds and the general revenue transfers to the SMI Program as dedicated funding sources, in order to meet projected costs for the next 75 years the three programs will require additional resources of $12,558 billion in present value terms, beyond the $21,071 billion in present value of required general revenue transfers to the SMI Program and $1,974 billion to honor the trust fund investments in Treasury securities.

---

[7] The SMI Trust Fund also has a very small amount of existing assets.

Table 6
Present Values of Revenue and Cost Components of 75-Year Open Group Obligations HI, SMI, and OASDI

(In billions of dollars, as of January 1, 2005)

	HI	SMI Part B	SMI Part D	OASDI	Total
Revenues from the Public:					
Taxes	9,435	-	-	29,450	38,885
Premiums, State transfers	-	4,187	2,547	-	6,733
Total	9,435	4,187	2,547	29,450	45,619
Total costs to the public	18,264	16,571	11,233	35,154	81,222
Net results for Government-wide (budget) perspective[1]	8,829	12,384	8,686	5,704	35,603
Revenues from other Government accounts	-	12,384	8,686	-	21,071
Trust fund in 1/1/2005	268	19	-	1,687	1,974
Net results for trust fund perspective[1]	8,561	(19)	-	4,017	12,558

[1] Net results are computed as cost less revenue.

Source: 2005 OASDI and Medicare Trustees' Reports.

Infinite Horizon

The 75-year horizon represented in Table 6 is consistent with the primary focus of the Social Security and Medicare Trustees' Reports. For the OASDI Program, for example, an additional $5.7 trillion in present value will be needed above currently scheduled taxes to pay for scheduled benefits ($4.0 trillion from the trust fund perspective). Yet, a 75-year projection is not a complete representation of all future financial flows through the infinite horizon. For example, when calculating unfunded obligations, a 75-year horizon includes revenue from some future workers but only a fraction of their future benefits. In order to provide a more complete estimate of the long-run unfunded obligations of the programs, estimates can be extended to the infinite horizon. The open-group infinite horizon net obligation is the present value of all expected future program outlays less the present value of all expected future program tax and premium revenues. Such a measure is provided in Table 7 for the three trust funds represented in Table 6.

From the budget or Governmentwide perspective, the values in line 1 plus the values in line 4 of Table 7 represent the value of resources needed to finance each of the programs into the infinite future. The sums are shown in the last line of the table (also equivalent to adding the values in the second and fifth lines). The total resources needed for all the programs sums to more than $81 trillion in present value terms. This need can be satisfied only through increased borrowing, higher taxes, reduced program spending, or some combination.

The second line shows the value of the trust fund at the beginning of 2005. For the HI and OASDI Programs this represents, from the trust fund perspective, the extent to which the programs are funded. From that perspective, when the trust fund is subtracted, an additional $24.0 trillion and $11.1 trillion, respectively, are needed to sustain the programs into the infinite future. As described above, from the trust fund perspective, the SMI Program is fully funded. The substantial gap that exists between premiums and State transfer revenue and program expenditures in the SMI Program ($25.8 trillion + $18.3 trillion) represents future general revenue obligations of the Federal budget.

In comparison to the analogous 75-year number in Table 6, extending the calculations beyond 2079 captures the full lifetime benefits and taxes and premiums of all current and future participants. The shorter horizon understates financial needs by capturing relatively more of the revenues from current and future workers and not capturing all of the benefits that are scheduled to be paid to them.

Table 7
Present Values of Expenditures Less Tax, Premium and State Transfer Revenue through the Infinite Horizon, HI, SMI, OASDI

(in trillions of dollars as of January 1, 2005)

(In trillions of dollars)	HI	SMI Part B	SMI Part D	OASDI	Total
Present value of future expenditures less future taxes and premiums and State transfers for current participants	9.6	9.9	6.8	13.7	40.0
Less current trust fund	0.3	-	-	1.7	2.0
Equals net obligations for past and current participants	9.3	9.9	6.8	12.0	38.1
Plus net obligations for future participants	14.7	15.9	11.5	(0.9)	41.2
Equals net obligations through the infinite future for all participants	24.0	25.8	18.3	11.1	79.3
Present value of future expenditures less the present values of future income over the infinite horizon (line 2 + line 5)	24.3	25.8	18.3	12.8	81.3

Source: 2005 OASDI and Medicare Trustees' Reports.

Railroad Retirement, Black Lung, and Unemployment Insurance

Railroad Retirement

Railroad retirement pays full retirement annuities at age 60 to railroad workers with 30 years of service. The program pays disability annuities based on total or occupational disability. It also pays annuities to spouses, divorced spouses, widow(er)s, remarried widow(er)s, surviving divorced spouses, children, and parents of deceased railroad workers. Medicare covers qualified railroad retirement beneficiaries in the same way as it does Social

Security beneficiaries. The Railroad Retirement and Survivors Improvement Act of 2001 (RRSIA), enacted into law on December 21, 2001, liberalized benefits for 30-year service employees and their spouses, eliminated a cap on monthly benefits for retirement and disability benefits, lowered minimum service requirements from 10 to 5 years, and provided for increased benefits for widow(er)s.

The Railroad Retirement Board (RRB) and SSA share jurisdiction over the payment of retirement and survivor benefits. RRB has jurisdiction if the employee had at least 5 years (if performed after 1995) of railroad service. For survivor benefits, RRB requires that the employee's last regular employment before retirement or death be in the railroad industry. If a railroad employee or his or her survivors do not qualify for railroad retirement benefits, the RRB transfers the employee's railroad retirement credits to SSA.

Payroll taxes paid by railroad employers and their employees provide a primary source of income for the Railroad Retirement and Survivor Benefit Program. By law, railroad retirement taxes are coordinated with Social Security taxes. Employees and employers pay tier I taxes at the same rate as Social Security taxes. Tier II taxes finance railroad retirement benefit payments that are higher than Social Security levels.

Other sources of program income include: financial interchanges with the Social Security and Medicare trust funds, earnings on investments, Federal income taxes on railroad retirement benefits, and appropriations (provided after 1974 as part of a phase out of certain vested dual benefits). The financial interchange is a significant source of income from a trust fund perspective. This transaction between railroad's Social Security

Equivalent Benefit (SSEB) Account, the Federal Old-Age and Survivors Insurance Trust Fund, the Disability Insurance Trust Fund, and the Federal Hospital Insurance Trust Fund is intended to put the three trust funds in the same position they would have been had railroad employment been covered under the Social Security Act. From a Governmentwide (budget) perspective, the financial interchange is an intragovernmental transfer.

Investments are also an important source of income for the Railroad Retirement and Survivors Benefit Program. Provisions in RRSIA modified the manner in which this income is generated. Amounts in the Railroad Retirement Account and the SSEB Account not needed to pay current benefits and administrative expenses are transferred to the National Railroad Retirement Investment Trust (NRRIT). NRRIT's Board[8] of seven trustees is empowered to invest trust assets in nongovernmental assets, such as equities and debt, as well as in Government securities. Prior to RRSIA, all investments were limited to Government securities.

The sole purpose of the NRRIT is to manage and invest railroad retirement assets. Since its inception, NRRIT has received $21.3 billion from RRB (including $19.2 billion in fiscal year 2003, pursuant to RRSIA) and returned $2.7 billion. During fiscal year 2005, the NRRIT made net transfers of $809 million to the RRB to pay retirement benefits. Administrative expenses of the trust are paid out of trust assets.

---

[8] The Board of Trustees is comprised of seven trustees, three selected by railroad labor unions and three by railroad companies. The seventh trustee is an independent trustee selected by the other six trustees. The trustees' terms are for 3 years and are staggered. RRSIA provides that on the initial Board, one each of the Labor and Management members would be selected for 3-year terms, one each for 2-year terms, and one each for a 1-year term. Thereafter, all terms are 3 years. The independent trustees' initial and succeeding terms are 3 years.

Cashflow Projections

Economic and Demographic Assumptions. The economic assumptions include a cost-of-living increase of 3.0 percent, an interest rate of 8 percent, and a wage increase of 4 percent. The demographic assumptions include rates of mortality and total termination rates, remarriage rates for widows, retirement rates, and withdrawal rates. For details on the demographic assumptions and other assumptions, refer to the Railroad Retirement System Annual Report, June 2005 and the 22nd Actuarial Valuation of the Assets and Liabilities under the Railroad Retirement Acts as of December 31, 2001, with Technical Supplement.

The average railroad employment is assumed to be 222,000 in 2005. The employment assumption, based on a model developed by the Association of American Railroads, assumes that (1) passenger service employment will remain at the level of 43,000 and (2) the employment base, excluding passenger service employment, will decline at a constant 3 percent annual rate for 25 years, at a falling rate over the next 25 years, and remain level thereafter.

Nominal Income and Expenditures. Chart 11 shows, in nominal dollars, estimated railroad retirement income (excluding interest and financial interchange income) and expenditures for the period 2005-2079 based on the intermediate set of assumptions used in the Railroad Retirement Board's actuarial evaluation of the program. The estimates are for the open-group population, which includes all persons projected to participate in the Railroad Retirement Program as railroad workers or beneficiaries during the period. Thus, the estimates include payments from, and on behalf of, those who are projected to be employed by the railroads during the period as well as those already employed at the beginning of the period. They also include expenditures made to, and on behalf of, such workers during that period.

Chart 11—Estimated Railroad Retirement Income (Excluding Interest and Financial Interchange Income) and Expenditures 2005-2079

(In billions of nominal dollars)

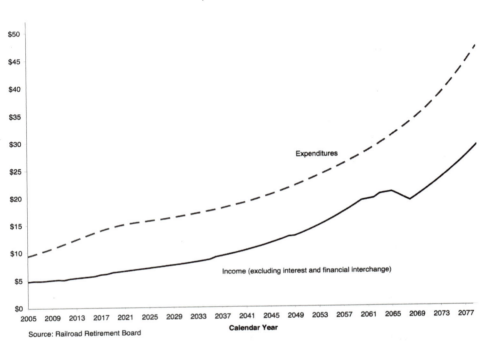

Source: Railroad Retirement Board

As Chart 11 shows, expenditures are expected to exceed tax income for the entire projection period. The imbalances continue to widen until about 2020, after which their growth slows for the next 45 years (until 2050). After a slight narrowing from 2050 to 2060, the imbalances begin to grow again after 2060, due in part to reductions in tax rates from 2061 to 2068.

Income and Expenditures as a Percent of Taxable Payroll. Chart 12 shows estimated expenditures and income as a percent of tier II taxable payroll. The imbalances grow until about 2020 but then begin to decrease steadily as expenditures fall. Tax rates begin to decline after 2060, stabilizing after 2068. Compared to last year, projected tax rates are lower. Beginning in calendar year 2004, the tier II tax rate is determined from a tax rate table based on the average account benefit ratio. The lower projected tax rates generally result from favorable employment and investment return experience. Actual calendar year 2004 employment exceeded the range projected for 2004 in last year's report, resulting in a higher starting employment level in this year's report. In addition, actual calendar year 2004 investment return of approximately 11.5 percent exceeded expected investment return of 8 percent.

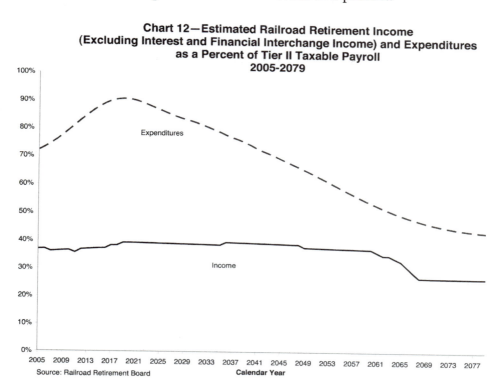

**Chart 12—Estimated Railroad Retirement Income
(Excluding Interest and Financial Interchange Income) and Expenditures
as a Percent of Tier II Taxable Payroll
2005-2079**

Source: Railroad Retirement Board

Calendar Year

Sensitivity Analysis. Actual future income from railroad payroll taxes and other sources and actual future expenditures for scheduled benefits and administrative expenses will depend upon a large number of factors as mentioned above. Two crucial assumptions are employment growth and the interest rate. Table 8 shows the sensitivity of the shortfall in the Railroad Retirement Program to variations in these two assumptions. The low-cost employment scenario has a 4.1 percent smaller shortfall of income to expenditures, and the high-cost scenario has a 3.9 percent higher shortfall. A higher discount rate reduces future values relative to a lower rate. As seen in the table, the shortfall is 30.4 percent lower if the interest rate is 12 percent rather than 8 percent and 77.4 percent higher when the interest rate is 4 percent rather than 8 percent.

Table 8
Present Values of Railroad Retirement Expenditures in Excess of Income Under Various Employment and Interest Rate Assumptions

(In millions of dollars)

Assumption	Low	Middle	High
Employment[1]	87,108 (1.5%)	90,849 (3.0%)	94,408 (4.5%)
Interest rate	63,216 (12%)	90,849 (8%)	161,122 (4%)

[1] The low and middle employment scenarios have passenger service employment remaining at 43,000 and the remaining employment base declining at 1.5 percent and 3 percent, respectively, for the next 25 years. The high cost scenario has passenger service employment declining by 500 per year until a level of 35,000 is reached with the remaining employment base declining by 4.5 percent per year for 25 years, at a reducing rate over the next 25 years, and remaining level thereafter.

Source: Railroad Retirement Board.

Sustainability of Railroad Retirement

Table 9 shows the magnitudes of the primary expenditures and sources of financing for the Railroad Retirement Program computed on an open-group basis for the next 75 years and expressed in present values as of January 1, 2005. The data are consistent with the Statement of Social Insurances.

From a Governmentwide (budget) perspective, revenues are expected to fall short of expenditures by $91 billion, which represents the present value of resources needed from the budget to sustain the Railroad Retirement Program. From a trust fund perspective, when the trust fund balance and the financial interchange are included, the combined balance of the NRRIT, the Railroad Retirement Account, and the SSEB Account show a slight surplus.

Table 9
Present Values of 75-Year Projections of Revenues and Expenditures for the Railroad Retirement Program[1,2]

(In billions of present-value dollars as of January 1, 2005)

Estimated Future Income (Excluding Interest)[3] Received from or on Behalf of:

Current participants who have attained retirement age	4.1
Current participants not yet having attained retirement age	36.8
Those expected to become participants	41.1
All participants	81.9

Estimated Future Expenditures:[4]

Current participants who have attained retirement age	84.1
Current participants not yet having attained retirement age	72.9
Those expected to become participants	15.8
All participants	172.8

Net obligations from budget perspective (expenditures less income)	90.8
Railroad Retirement Program assets (mostly investments stated at market)[5]	28.2
Financial Interchange from Social Security Trust	63.1
Net Obligations from Trust Fund Perspective	(0.5)

[1] Represents combined values for the Railroad Retirement Account, SSEB Account, and NRRIT, based on middle employment assumption.
[2] The data used reflect the provisions of RRSIA of 2001.
[3] Future income (excluding interest) includes tier I taxes, tier II taxes, and income taxes on benefits.
[4] Future expenditures include benefits and administrative expenditures.
[5] The value of the fund reflects the 8 percent interest rate assumption. The RRB uses the relatively high rate due to investments in private securities.

Note: Detail may not add to totals due to rounding. Employee and beneficiary status are determined as of 1/1/2004 whereas present values are as of 1/1/2005.

Black Lung

The Black Lung Disability Benefit Program provides compensation for medical and survivor benefits for eligible coal miners who are disabled due to pneumoconiosis (black lung disease) arising out of their coal mine employment. The U.S. Department of Labor (DOL) operates the Black Lung Disability Benefit Program. The Black Lung Disability Trust Fund (BLDTF) provides benefit payments to eligible coal miners disabled by pneumoconiosis when no responsible mine operator can be assigned the liability. The beneficiary population has been declining as the incidence of black lung disease has fallen, and the group of miners affected by the disease (and their widows) has been dying at a more rapid rate than new awards have been made.

Excise taxes on coal mine operators, based on the sale of coal, is the primary source of financing black lung disability payments and related administrative costs. Though excise tax revenues currently exceed costs (and are expected to in the future), that was not always the case. The Black Lung Benefits Revenue Act provides for repayable advances to the BLDTF from the General Fund of the Treasury, in the event that BLDTF resources are not adequate to meet program obligations. During earlier years of the program, general revenues were needed to pay for cash shortfalls in the program. BLDTF financial statements continue to report a balance payable and interest paid to the General Fund.

On September 30, 2005, total liabilities of the BLDTF exceeded assets by $9.2 billion. This deficit fund balance represented the accumulated shortfall of excise taxes necessary to meet benefit payment and interest expenses. This shortfall was financed by repayable advances (with interest) to the BLDTF. Outstanding advances on September 30, 2005, were $9.2 billion, bearing interest rates ranging from 4.500 to 13.875 percent. Excise tax revenues of $610.4 million, benefit payment expense of $327.9 million, and interest expense of $674.9 million were recognized for the year ended September 30, 2005.

Chart 13 shows projected black lung expenditures (excluding interest payments) and excise tax collections for the period 2006-2040. The significant assumptions used in the projections are coal production estimates, the tax rate structure, the number of beneficiaries, life expectancy, and medical costs. Analysts project that a scheduled reduction in taxes on coal sales will decrease cash inflows by 52 percent between the years 2013 to 2015. After 2015, cash surpluses continue to widen due to a declining beneficiary population and increasing revenues. Including projected interest payments, however, the BLDTF's overall liabilities will continue to exceed its assets, and that shortfall will get larger in each successive year.

Chart 13—Estimated Black Lung Total Income and Expenditures (Excluding Interest) 2006-2040

(In millions of nominal dollars)

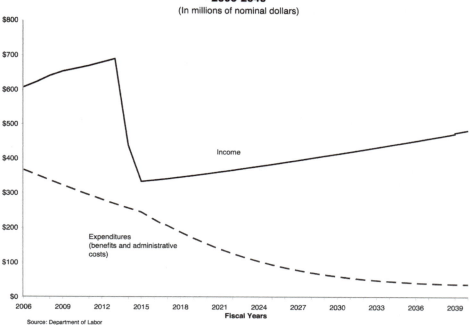

Source: Department of Labor

Table 10 shows present values of 35-year projections of expenditures and revenues for the Black Lung Program computed as of October 1, 2005, using a discount rate of 6.42 percent, the average of the interest rates underlying the projections (the interest rate is higher than the current Government borrowing rate, reflecting the fact that the program borrowed from the General Fund during periods of relatively high interest rates). From a Governmentwide (budget) perspective, the present value of expenditures is expected to be less than the present value of income by $4.0 billion (a surplus). From a trust fund perspective, a large balance ($9.2 billion) is owed to the General Fund. From that perspective, when that accumulated balance is combined with the cashflow surplus, the program shows a negative balance of $5.2 billion in present value dollars.

Table 10
Present Values of 35-Year Projections of Revenues and Expenditures for the Black Lung Program

(In billions of present value dollars, as of October 1, 2005)

Estimated future tax income	7.0
Estimated future expenditures	3.0
Net obligations from budget perspective (expenditures less income)	(4.0)
Accumulated balance due General Fund	9.2
Net obligations from trust fund perspective	5.2

Source: Department of Labor. The projections were based on data from the 2005 Mid-Session Review.

Unemployment Insurance

The Unemployment Insurance Program was created in 1935 to provide temporary partial wage replacement to unemployed workers who lose their jobs. The program is administered through a unique system of Federal and State partnerships established in Federal law but administered through conforming State laws by State agencies. DOL interprets and enforces Federal law requirements and provides broad policy guidance and program direction, while program details such as benefit eligibility, duration, and amount of benefits are established through individual State unemployment insurance statutes and administered through State unemployment insurance agencies.

The program is financed through the collection of Federal and State unemployment taxes that are credited to the Unemployment Trust Fund (UTF) and reported as Federal tax revenue. The fund was established to account for the receipt, investment, and disbursement of unemployment taxes. Federal unemployment taxes are used to pay for Federal and State administration of the Unemployment Insurance Program, veterans' employment services, State employment services, and the Federal share of extended unemployment insurance benefits. Federal unemployment taxes also are used to maintain a loan account within the UTF, from which insolvent State accounts may borrow funds to pay unemployment insurance benefits.

Chart 14 shows the projected cash contributions and expenditures over the next 10 years under expected economic conditions (described below). The significant assumptions used in the projections include total unemployment rates, civilian labor force levels, percent of unemployed receiving benefits, total wages, distribution of benefit payments by State, State tax rate structures, State taxable wage bases, and interest rates on UTF investments. These projections, excluding interest earnings, indicate net cash inflows for the next 4 years. There is a crossover back to net outflows in fiscal years 2010 through 2012, after which net inflows resume for the remainder of the projection period.

**Chart 14—Estimated Unemployment Fund Cashflow
Using Expected Economic Conditions
2006-2015**

(In billions of nominal dollars)

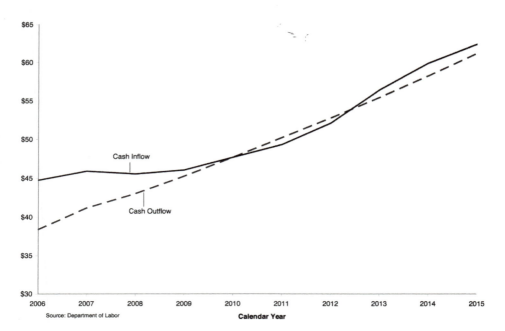

Source: Department of Labor

Calendar Year

Table 11 shows present values of 10-year projections of revenues and expenditures for the Unemployment Insurance Program using a discount rate of 6.04 percent (up from 5.03 percent last year due to higher expected yields on the trust fund assets), the average of the interest rates underlying the 10-year projections. Three sets of numbers are presented in order to show the effects of varying economic conditions as reflected in different assumptions about the unemployment rate. For expected economic conditions, the estimates are based on an unemployment rate of 5.12 percent during fiscal year 2006, decreasing to 5.00 percent in fiscal year 2009 and thereafter. Under the mild recessionary scenario, the unemployment rate peaks at 7.43 percent in fiscal year 2008 and declines gradually until reaching 5.0 percent in 2014. Finally, under the deep recession scenario, the unemployment rate is assumed to peak at 10.15 percent in 2009 and gradually fall to 5.18 percent by the end of the projection period.

Each scenario uses an open group that includes current and future participants of the Unemployment Insurance Program. Table 11 shows that, as economic conditions worsen, while tax income is projected to increase as higher layoffs result in higher employer taxes, benefit outlays increase much faster. From the Governmentwide (budget) perspective, under expected conditions, the present value of income exceeds the present value of expenditures by $14 billion. From the same perspective, under a deep recession scenario, the present value of expenditures exceeds the present value of income by $29 billion. From a trust fund perspective, the program has more than $54 billion in assets. When combined with the present value of net cash income under expected economic conditions, the program has a surplus of $69 billion.

Table 11
Present Values of 10-Year Projections of Revenues and Expenditures for Unemployment Insurance Under Three Alternative Scenarios for Economic Conditions

(In billions of present value dollars, as of October 1, 2005)

| | | Economic Conditions | |
	Expected	Mild Recession	Deep Recession
Future cash income	367.9	412.0	463.5
Future expenditures	353.7	405.6	492.8
Net obligations from budget perspective (expenditures less income)	(14.2)	(6.4)	29.3
Trust fund assets	54.4	54.4	54.4
Net obligations from trust fund perspective[1]	(68.6)	(60.8)	(25.1)

[1]Net obligations from the trust fund perspective=net obligations from the budget perspective-trust fund assets. The negative values in this line are indicative of surpluses.

Source: Data for the present value calculations are from the Department of Labor.

Unemployment Trust Fund Solvency

Each State's accumulated UTF net assets or reserve balance should provide a defined level of benefit payments over a defined period. To be minimally solvent, a State's reserve balance should provide for 1 year's projected benefit payment needs based on the highest levels of benefit payments experienced by the State over the last 20 years. A ratio of 1.0 or greater prior to a recession indicates a State is minimally solvent. States below this level are vulnerable to exhausting their funds in a recession. States exhausting their reserve balance must borrow funds from the Federal Unemployment Account (FUA) to make benefit payments. The Missouri and New York State accounts had loans payable to FUA at the end of fiscal year 2005. In addition, Texas, Illinois, and North Carolina had outstanding debts to other sources. During periods of high-sustained unemployment, balances in the FUA may be depleted. In these circumstances, FUA is authorized to borrow from the Treasury General Fund.

Chart 15 presents the State by State results of this analysis as of September 30, 2005. As the table illustrates, 27 State funds were below the minimal solvency ratio on September 30, 2005.

Chart 15—Unemployment Trust Fund Solvency as of September 30, 2005

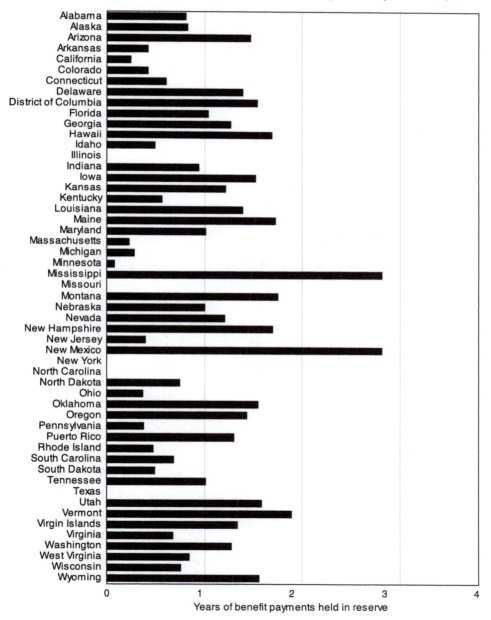

Years of benefit payments held in reserve

Stewardship Assets

The Government holds stewardship assets for the benefit of the Nation. Because the Government has been entrusted with, and made accountable for, these resources and responsibilities, they are recognized in this *Financial Report.*

When acquired, stewardship assets are generally treated as expenses in the financial statements. This section provides more detailed stewardship information on these resources to highlight their long-term benefit and to demonstrate accountability. This information facilitates the understanding of the operations and financial condition of the Government.

Stewardship Land

Stewardship land refers to federally-owned land that is set aside for the use and enjoyment of present and future generations and land on which military bases are located. Except for military bases, this land is not used or held for use in general Government operations. Stewardship land is land that the Government does not expect to use to meet its obligations, unlike the assets listed in the balance sheets. Stewardship land is measured in nonfinancial units such as acres of land and lakes, miles of parkways, and miles of wild and scenic rivers. Examples of stewardship land include national parks, national forests, wilderness areas, and land used to enhance ecosystems to encourage animal and plant species and to conserve nature. This category excludes lands administered by the Bureau of Indian Affairs and held in trust.

Most stewardship land managed by the Government was once

part of the 1.8 billion acres of public domain land acquired between 1781 and 1867. Stewardship land accounts for 28 percent of the current U.S. landmass. Stewardship land acquired totaled $419.5 million and $312.5 million for the years ended September 30, 2005, and 2004, respectively. Table 12 depicts the stewardship land owned by the Government and administered by the Department of the Interior (DOI), the Department of Defense (DOD), and the Department of Agriculture (USDA). Detailed information concerning stewardship land can be obtained in the financial statements of DOI, DOD, and USDA.

Table 12
United States Government Stewardship Land as of September 30

Agency	Predominate Use	Millions of Acres		Percentage	
		2005	2004	2005	2004
Bureau of Land Management.....	Public land	261.7	261.8	40.4	40.5
U.S. Forest Service	National forest system	193.2	192.9	29.8	29.8
U.S. Fish and Wildlife Service....	National wildlife refuge system	90.4	90.3	13.9	14.0
National Park Service.................	National park system	79.0	79.0	12.2	12.2
Department of Defense..............	Mission land	16.7	16.7	2.6	2.6
Bureau of Reclamation..............	Water, power, and recreation	5.8	5.7	0.9	0.9
	All other	1.6	-	0.2	-
Total acres...		648.4	646.4	100.0	100.0

Note: Not included in this table is the Department of Commerce which has designated 19,000 square miles of coastal waters as national marine sanctuaries and is also developing plans for the Coral Reef Ecosystem Reserve which covers 132,000 thousand square miles. Also not included is the Environmental Protection Agency which currently has title to 62 remedial cleanup sites.

Heritage Assets

Heritage assets are Government-owned assets that have one or more of the following characteristics:

- Historical or natural significance.
- Cultural, educational, or artistic importance.
- Significant architectural characteristics.

The cost of heritage assets often is not determinable or relevant to their significance. Like stewardship land, the Government does not expect to use these assets to meet its obligations. The most relevant information about heritage assets is nonfinancial. The public entrusts the Government with these assets and holds it accountable for their preservation. Examples of heritage assets include Mount Rushmore National Memorial, Yosemite National Park, and museum objects on display at the Smithsonian Institution. Other examples of heritage assets include the Declaration of Independence, the U.S. Constitution, and the Bill of Rights preserved by the National Archives. Also included are national monuments/structures such as the Vietnam Veterans Memorial, the Jefferson Memorial, and the Washington Monument, as well as the Library of Congress. Many other sites such as battlefields, historic structures, and national historic landmarks are placed in this category, as well.

Some heritage assets are used both to remind us of our heritage and for day-to-day operations. These assets are referred to as multi-use heritage assets. One typical example is the White House. The cost of acquisition, betterment or reconstruction of all multi-use heritage assets is capitalized as general property, plant, and equipment and is depreciated.

The following discussion of the Government's heritage assets is not all-inclusive. Rather, it highlights significant heritage assets reported by Federal agencies.

The Government classifies heritage assets into three broad categories:

- Collection-type
- Natural
- Cultural

Collection-type heritage assets include objects gathered and maintained for museum and library collections. Natural heritage assets include national wilderness areas, wild and scenic rivers, natural landmarks, forests and grasslands. Cultural heritage assets include historic places and structures, memorials and monuments, national cemeteries and archeological sites.

Collection-Type Heritage Assets

The Smithsonian Institution holds some of the most prominent Federal museum collections. The Smithsonian acquires, protects, and preserves approximately 143.7 million individual objects for public exhibition, education, and research.

Similarly, the Library of Congress holds the world's largest library collection, comprising more than 131.8 million items. The Library of Congress receives two copies of every book, pamphlet, map, print, photograph, and piece of music registered for copyright in the United States.

The National Archives holds about 3.2 million cubic feet of records. These records ensure ready access to essential information documenting the rights of citizens, the actions of Federal officials, and the effects of those actions on the national experience. These records include text and legislative records; cartographic and architectural records; motion picture, sound, and video records; and still pictures and graphics. The National Archives also maintains historically important documents such as the U.S. Constitution and the Louisiana Purchase Treaty.

Collection-type heritage assets acquired totaled $12.2 million and $19.0 million for the years ended September 30, 2005, and 2004, respectively.

Natural Heritage Assets

Congress has designated several wilderness areas to preserve their natural conditions. DOI manages approximately 72.0 million acres of these wilderness areas comprised of almost 68 percent of the Nation's more than 106.0 million wilderness acres. The Cebolla Wilderness in New Mexico is one such area.

The national wild and scenic rivers system includes protected free-flowing rivers. The Government protects these areas because of their fish and wildlife, or for their scenic, recreational, geologic, historic, or cultural value. DOI manages 51 percent of these 10,930 river miles, including the Bluestone National Scenic River in West Virginia.

The Government also sets aside natural landmarks that exemplify a region's natural characteristics. The U.S. Fish and Wildlife Service manages 9 national historic landmarks, the Bureau of Land Management manages 21 natural historic landmarks, and the National Park Service manages 179 national natural landmarks, such as the Grand Coulee Gorge in Washington State.

The U.S. Forest Service manages 155 national forests and 20 national grasslands on more than 193.2 million acres of public land. These areas encompass significant heritage resources. Examples include the White Mountain National Forest in New Hampshire and the Thunder Basin National Grassland in Wyoming.

Natural heritage assets acquired totaled $54.9 million and $199.5 million for the years ended September 30, 2005, and 2004, respectively.

Any acreage cited above for natural heritage assets, such as wilderness areas, are also included in the acreage cited in the Stewardship Land section.

Cultural Heritage Assets

The National Register of Historic Places lists historic sites and structures. This is America's official list of cultural resources worthy of preservation. Official properties include districts, sites, buildings, structures, and objects significant to American history. It also includes significant architectural, archaeological engineering, and cultural properties. Forest Service land encompasses 3,397 such properties.

The Nation's monuments and memorials include the Washington Monument, the Vietnam Veterans Memorial, the World War II Memorial (new), and the Jefferson Memorial in Washington, D.C. The National Park Service manages these. In addition, the American Battle Monuments Commission administers, operates, and maintains 24 permanent American military cemeteries on foreign soil and 29 stand-alone memorials, monuments, and markers around the world. This includes the Belleau Wood Marine Monument in France.

Archeological and historical sites contain the remains of human activity. DOI manages numerous archaeological sites. The National Park Service manages approximately 63,007 archeological and historical sites; the U.S. Fish and Wildlife Service and the Bureau of Reclamation manage approximately 14,685 archaeological and historical properties. The Bureau of Land Management no longer reports on the number of archeological and historic sites reflecting the withdrawal of 271,474 acres for fiscal year 2005.

The ancient earthen mounds at the Hopewell Culture National Historic Site in Ohio are a notable example.

National cemeteries include the Arlington National Cemetery in Virginia and the Fort Logan National Cemetery in Colorado. The Department of the Army (Army) manages the Arlington National Cemetery. The Department of Veterans Affairs (VA) manages Fort Logan National Cemetery and other cemeteries.

Cultural heritage assets acquired totaled $172.6 million and $117.1 million for the years ended September 30, 2005, and 2004, respectively.

Stewardship Investments

Stewardship investments focus on Government programs aimed at providing long-term benefits by improving the Nation's productivity and enhancing economic growth. These investments can be provided through direct Federal spending or grants to State and local governments for certain education and training programs, research and development, and federally financed but not federally-owned property, such as bridges and roads. When incurred, these investments are included as expenses in determining the net cost of operations.

Non-Federal Physical Property

The Government makes grants and provides funds for the purchase, construction, and/or major renovation of State and local government physical properties. Cost for non-Federal physical property programs are included as expenses in the Statements of Net Cost and are reported as investments in Table 13. They are measured on the same accrual basis of accounting used in the *Financial Report* statements. The amounts reported in fiscal year 2005 for investments in prior years (fiscal years 2004-2001) have been restated because agencies are continuously reviewing, correcting, and updating this data.

Table 13
Stewardship Investments
for the Years Ended September 30

(In billions of dollars)	Fiscal Year 2005	Restated Fiscal Year 2004	Restated Fiscal Year 2003	Restated Fiscal Year 2002	Restated Fiscal Year 2001
Investments in non-Federal physical property	47.6	47.0	50.4	51.6	41.6
Investments in human capital	89.5	78.0	72.2	62.6	51.0
Research and development:					
Investments in basic research	26.3	23.9	24.6	22.7	18.8
Investments in applied research	21.1	20.8	21.5	21.6	17.7
Investments in development	62.3	57.2	48.9	45.3	39.8
Total investments	246.8	226.9	217.6	203.8	168.9

Human Capital

The Government runs several programs that invest in human capital. Those investments go toward increasing and maintaining a healthy economy by educating and training the general public. Costs do not include training expenses for Federal workers.

Research and Development

Federal investments in research and development comprise those expenses for basic research, applied research, and development that are intended to increase or maintain national economic productive capacity or yield other future benefits.

- Investments in basic research are for systematic studies to gain knowledge or understanding of the fundamental aspects of phenomena and of observable facts without specific applications toward processes or products in mind.

- Investments in applied research are for systematic studies to gain knowledge or understanding necessary for determining the means by which a recognized and specific need may be met.

- Investments in development are the systematic use of the knowledge and understanding gained from research for the production of useful materials, devices, systems, or methods, including the design and development of prototypes and processes.

United States Government Notes to the Financial Statements for the Years Ended September 30, 2005, and September 30, 2004

Note 1. Summary of Significant Accounting Policies

A. Reporting Entity

This *Financial Report* includes the financial status and activities of the executive branch, the legislative branch (the U.S. Senate and the U.S. House of the Representatives report on a cash basis), and the judicial branch (which also reports on a cash basis) of the Government. The judicial branch reports on a limited basis because it is not required by law to submit financial statement information to Treasury. The Appendix section of this report contains a list of significant Government entities included in the *Financial Report*, as well as examples of entities excluded. The excluded entities are not part of the *Financial Report* because they are Government sponsored enterprises, such as Fannie Mae, Freddie Mac, etc.; or their activities are not included in the Federal budget's totals, such as the Thrift Savings Fund, and the Board of Governors of the Federal Reserve System, etc.

Material intragovernmental transactions are eliminated in consolidation, except as described in Note 17—Unreconciled Transactions Affecting the Change in Net Position. The financial reporting period ends September 30 and is the same as used for the annual budget.

B. Basis of Accounting and Revenue Recognition

These financial statements were prepared using U.S. generally accepted accounting principles (GAAP), primarily based on Statements of Federal Financial Accounting Standards (SFFAS). Under these principles:

- Expenses are generally recognized when incurred except that the costs of social insurance programs including Social Security, Medicare, Railroad Retirement, Black Lung, and Unemployment are recognized only for amounts currently due and payable.
- Nonexchange (unearned) revenues, including taxes, duties, fines, and penalties, are recognized when collected and adjusted to the change in net measurable and legally collectable amounts receivable. Related refunds and other offsets, including those that are measurable and legally payable, are netted against nonexchange revenue.
- Exchange (earned) revenues are recognized when the Government provides goods and services to the public for a price. Exchange revenues include user charges such as admission to Federal parks and premiums for certain Federal insurance.

The basis of accounting used for budgetary purposes, which is primarily on a cash and obligation basis and follows budgetary concepts and policies, differs from the basis of accounting used for the financial statements which follow U.S. GAAP. See the

Reconciliations of Net Operating Cost and Unified Budget Deficit in the Financial Statements section.

C. Direct Loans and Loan Guarantees

Direct loans obligated and loan guarantees committed after fiscal year 1991 are reported based on the present value of the net cashflows estimated over the life of the loan or guarantee. The difference between the outstanding principal of the direct loans and the present value of their net cash inflows is recognized as a subsidy cost allowance; the present value of estimated net cash outflows of the loan guarantees is recognized as a liability for loan guarantees.

The subsidy expense for direct or guaranteed loans disbursed during a year is the present value of estimated net cash outflows for those loans or guarantees. A subsidy expense also is recognized for modifications made during the year to loans and guarantees outstanding and for reestimates made as of the end of the year to the subsidy allowances or loan guarantee liability for loans and guarantees outstanding.

Direct loans obligated and loan guarantees committed before fiscal year 1992 are valued under two different methodologies within the Government: the allowance-for-loss method and the present-value method. Under the allowance-for-loss method, the outstanding principal of direct loans is reduced by an allowance for uncollectible amounts; the liability for loan guarantees is the amount the agency estimates would more likely than not require future cash outflow to pay default claims.

Under the present-value method, the outstanding principal of direct loans is reduced by an allowance equal to the difference between the outstanding principal and the present value of the expected net cashflows. The liability for loan guarantees is the present value of expected net cash outflows due to the loan guarantees.

D. Accounts and Taxes Receivable

Accounts receivable represents claims to cash or other assets from entities outside the Government that arise from the sale of goods or services, duties, fines, certain license fees, recoveries, or other provisions of the law.

The category taxes receivable consists primarily of uncollected tax assessments, penalties, and interest when taxpayers have agreed the amounts are owed, or a court has determined the assessments are owed. The balance sheets do not include unpaid assessments when neither taxpayers nor a court have agreed that the amounts are owed (compliance assessments) or the Government does not expect further collections due to factors such as the taxpayer's death, bankruptcy, or insolvency (writeoffs). Taxes receivable are reported net of an allowance for the estimated portion deemed to be uncollectible.

E. Inventories and Related Property

Inventories within the Government are valued using historical cost, net realizable value, and latest acquisition cost (see Note 5—Inventories and Related Property, Net). Historical cost methods include first-in-first-out, weighted average, and moving average. Estimated repair costs reduce the value of inventory held for repair. Excess, obsolete, and unserviceable inventories are valued at estimated net realizable value. When latest acquisition cost is used to value inventory held for sale, it is adjusted for holding gains and losses in order to approximate historical cost.

The related property portion of the inventory and related property line includes operating materials and supplies, stockpile materials, commodities, seized and monetary instruments, and forfeited property. Operating materials and supplies are valued at historical cost, latest acquisition cost, and standard price using the purchase and consumption method of accounting. Operating materials and supplies that are valued at latest acquisition cost and standard pricing are not adjusted for holding gains and losses.

F. Property, Plant, and Equipment

Property, plant, and equipment used in Government operations are carried at cost. Depreciation and amortization expense applies to property, plant, and equipment reported on the balance sheets except for land, unlimited duration land rights and construction in progress. Depreciation and amortization are recognized using the straight-line method over the estimated useful lives of the assets. The cost of acquisition, betterment, or reconstruction of all multi-use heritage assets is capitalized as general property, plant, and equipment and is depreciated.

G. Federal Employee and Veteran Benefits Payable

Federal employee and veteran benefits payable are recorded during the time employee services are rendered. The related liabilities for defined benefit pension plans and post-retirement health benefits and veterans' compensation and burial benefits are recorded at estimated present value of future benefits, less any estimated present value of future normal cost contributions. The estimated present value for veteran's benefits is disclosed but is not included in the Federal employee and veteran benefits payable line. However, the estimated present value for veteran health benefits is not estimated, these benefits are expensed when services are provided.

Normal cost is the portion of the actuarial present value of projected benefits allocated as an expense for employee services rendered in the current year. Actuarial gains and losses (and prior service cost, if any) are recognized immediately in the year they occur, without amortization.

H. Environmental and Disposal Liabilities

Environmental and disposal liabilities are recorded at the estimated current cost of removing, containing and/or disposing of hazardous waste and environmental contamination, assuming the use of current technology. Hazardous waste is a solid, liquid, or gaseous waste that, because of its quantity or concentration, presents a potential hazard to human health or the environment. Remediation consists of removal, decontamination, decommissioning, site restoration, site monitoring, closure and post-closure cost, treatment, and/or safe containment. Where technology does not exist to clean up hazardous waste, only the estimable portion of the liability, typically safe containment, is recorded.

I. Deferred Maintenance

Deferred maintenance is maintenance that was not performed when it should have been or scheduled maintenance that was delayed or postponed. Maintenance is the act of keeping fixed assets in acceptable condition, including preventative maintenance, normal repairs, and other activities needed to preserve the assets, so they continue to provide acceptable services and achieve their expected life. Maintenance excludes activities aimed at expanding the capacity of assets or otherwise upgrading them to serve needs different from those originally intended. Deferred maintenance expenses are not accrued in the Statements of Net Cost or recognized as liabilities on the balance sheets. However, deferred maintenance information is disclosed in the Supplemental Information section of this report.

J. Contingent Liabilities

Liabilities for contingencies are recognized on the balance sheets when both:

- A past transaction or event has occurred.
- A future outflow or other sacrifice of resources is probable and measurable.

The estimated contingent liability may be a specific amount or a range of amounts. If some amount within the range is a better estimate than any other amount within the range, then that amount is recognized. If no amount within the range is a better estimate than any other amount, then the minimum amount in the range is recognized.

Contingent liabilities that do not meet the above criteria for recognition, but for which there is at least a reasonable possibility that a loss may have been incurred, are disclosed in Note 19—Contingencies.

K. Commitments

In the normal course of business, the Government has a number of unfulfilled commitments that may require the use of its financial resources. Note 20—Commitments describes the components of the Government's actual commitments that need to be disclosed because of their nature and/or their amount. They include long-term leases, undelivered orders, and other commitments.

Discussion of treaties and other international agreements entered into by the United States Government are included in the Commitments section.

L. Social Insurance

A liability for social insurance programs (Social Security, Medicare, Railroad Retirement, Black Lung, and Unemployment) is recognized for any unpaid amounts due as of the reporting date. No liability is recognized for future benefit payments not yet due. For further information, see the Stewardship Information section on Stewardship Responsibilities, and Note 21—Dedicated Collections.

M. Related Party Transactions

Federal Reserve banks (FRBs) and private banks, which are not part of the reporting entity, serve as the Government's depositary and fiscal agent. They process Federal payments and deposits to Treasury's account and service Treasury securities. FRBs owned $732.7 billion and $698.0 billion of Treasury securities held by the public as of September 30, 2005, and 2004, respectively. FRB earnings that exceed statutory amounts of surplus established for FRBs are paid to the Government and are recognized as nonexchange revenue. Those earnings totaled $19.3 billion and $19.7 billion for the years ended September 30, 2005, and 2004, respectively. The primary source of these earnings is from interest earned on Treasury securities held by the FRBs. Also, as described in Note 15—Other Liabilities, the FRB holds certificates and special drawing rights certificates.

FRBs issue Federal Reserve notes, the circulating currency of the United States. Specific assets owned by FRBs, typically Treasury securities, collateralize these notes. Federal Reserve notes are backed by the full faith and credit of the Government.

The Government does not guarantee payment of the liabilities of Government-sponsored enterprises such as the Federal National Mortgage Association or the Federal Home Loan Mortgage Corporation, which are privately owned. These enterprises also are excluded from the reporting entity.

Note 2. Cash and Other Monetary Assets

Cash and Other Monetary Assets as of September 30

(In billions of dollars)	2005	2004
Operating cash	28.3	31.0
Other cash-not restricted	10.1	9.3
Other cash-restricted	4.5	4.0
Total cash	42.9	44.3
International monetary assets	32.0	41.5
Gold	10.9	10.9
Domestic monetary assets	-	0.3
Total cash and other monetary assets	85.8	97.0

Cash

Total cash consists of:

- Operating cash of the Government representing balances from tax collections; customs duties; other revenues; Federal debt receipts; and other various receipts, net of checks outstanding, which are held in the FRBs and in Treasury tax and loan accounts.

- Other cash representing the balances of cash equivalents and other funds held in agencies' books, such as demand deposits, amounts held in trust, deposits in transit, imprest funds, undeposited collections, and amounts representing the balances of petty cash. Restricted cash represents cash that is restricted due to the imposition on cash deposits by law, regulation, or agreement.

Operating cash and the other cash of the Government are either insured (for balances up to $100,000) by the Federal Deposit

Insurance Corporation (FDIC), or collateralized by securities pledged by financial institutions.

International Monetary Assets

International monetary assets include the U.S. reserve position in the International Monetary Fund (IMF), U.S. holdings of Special Drawing Rights (SDRs), and official reserves of foreign currency and gold.

The U.S. reserve position in the IMF reflects the reserve asset portion of the financial subscription that the United States has paid in as part of its participation in the IMF. The IMF promotes international monetary cooperation and a stable payments system to facilitate growth in the world economy. Its primary activities are surveillance of member economies, financial assistance as appropriate, and technical assistance.

Only a portion of the U.S. financial subscriptions to the IMF is made in the form of reserve assets, the remainder is provided in the form of a letter of credit from the United States to the IMF.

The balance available under the letter of credit totaled $40.4 billion and $35.0 billion for the years ended September 30, 2005, and 2004, respectively. The U.S. reserve position in the IMF has a U.S. dollar equivalent of $13.2 billion and $19.4 billion for the years ended September 30, 2005, and 2004, respectively.

SDRs are international monetary reserves issued by the IMF. These interest-bearing assets can be obtained by IMF allocations, transactions with IMF member countries, interest earnings on SDR holdings, or U.S. reserve position in the IMF. SDR holdings are an asset of Treasury's Exchange Stabilization Fund (ESF), which held SDRs totaling $8.2 billion and $12.8 billion equivalent for the years ended September 30, 2005, and 2004, respectively.

The IMF allocates SDRs to its members in proportion to each member's quota in the IMF. The SDR Act of 1968 authorized the Secretary of the Treasury to issue SDR Certificates (SDRCs) to the Federal Reserve in exchange for dollars. The amount of SDRCs outstanding cannot exceed the dollar value of SDR holdings. The Secretary of the Treasury determines when Treasury will issue or redeem SDRCs. SDRCs outstanding totaled $2.2 billion for the years ended September 30, 2005, and 2004, and are included in Note 15—Other Liabilities.

As of September 30, 2005, and 2004, other liabilities included $7.1 billion and $7.2 billion, respectively, of interest-bearing liability to the IMF for SDR allocations. The SDR allocation item represents the cumulative total of SDRs distributed by the IMF to the United States in allocations that occurred in 1970, 1971, 1972, 1979, 1980, and 1981.

Gold

Gold is valued at the statutory price of $42.2222 per fine troy ounce. The number of fine troy ounces was 258,713,310 as of September 30, 2005, and 2004. The market value of gold on the London Fixing as of the reporting date was $473 and $416 per fine troy ounce for the years ended September 30, 2005, and 2004, respectively. Gold totaling $10.9 billion for the years ending September 30, 2005, and 2004, was pledged as collateral for gold certificates issued and authorized to the FRBs by the Secretary of the Treasury. Treasury may redeem the gold certificates at any time. See Note 15—Other Liabilities.

Domestic Monetary Assets

Domestic monetary assets consist of liquid assets, other than cash, that are based on the U.S. dollar, including coins, silver bullion, and other coinage metals.

Note 3. Accounts and Taxes Receivable, Net

Accounts receivable includes related interest receivable of $4.8 billion and $6.2 billion for the years ended September 30, 2005, and 2004, respectively, and represents claims to cash or other assets from entities outside the Government. An allowance for estimated losses due to uncollectible amounts is established when it is more likely than not the receivables will not be totally collected. The allowance method varies among the agencies in the Government and is usually based on past collection experience. Methods include statistical sampling of receivables, specific identification and intensive analysis of each case, aging methodologies, and percentage of total receivables based on historical collection. Accounts receivable are net of an allowance for uncollectible accounts. The allowance amounts are $13.2 billion and $16.7 billion for the years ended September 30, 2005 and 2004, respectively.

Taxes receivable are the gross tax receivables net of allowance for doubtful accounts. Gross taxes receivable consists primarily of assessments, penalties, and related interest that were not paid or abated and which the taxpayers have agreed the amounts are owed or a court has determined the assessments are owed. The allowance for doubtful accounts is based on projections of collectibility from a statistical sample of taxes receivable.

Accounts and Taxes Receivable as of September 30

(In billions of dollars)	2005	2004
Department of Agriculture	9.4	2.5
Department of Defense	7.6	7.5
Social Security Administration	7.0	6.2
Department of Energy	4.0	4.0
Department of the Interior	2.7	1.3
Department of Health and Human Services	2.1	2.1
Pension Benefit Guaranty Corporation	1.7	2.5
Tennessee Valley Authority	1.1	1.0
Department of Labor	1.0	1.1
Office of Personnel Management	0.9	0.9
All other departments	6.2	6.0
Accounts receivable, net	43.7	35.1
Gross taxes receivable	90.7	91.4
Allowance for doubtful accounts	(68.3)	(70.1)
Taxes receivable, net	22.4	21.3
Total accounts and taxes receivable, net	66.1	56.4

Note 4. Loans Receivable and Loan Guarantee Liabilities, Net

The Government uses two methods, direct loans and loan guarantee programs, to accomplish the same goals. These goals are to promote the Nation's welfare by making direct Federal loans and guaranteeing non-Federal loans to segments of the population not served adequately by non-Federal institutions. For those unable to afford credit at the market rate, Federal credit programs provide subsidies in the form of direct loans offered at an interest rate lower than the market rate. For those to whom non-Federal financial institutions are reluctant to grant credit because of the high risk involved, Federal credit programs guarantee the payment of these non-Federal loans and absorb the cost of defaults.

The amount of the long-term cost of post-1991 direct loans

and loan guarantees outstanding equals the subsidy cost allowance for direct loans and the liability for loan guarantees as of the fiscal yearend. The amount of the longterm cost of pre-1992 direct loans and loan guarantees equals the allowance for uncollectible amounts (or present value allowance) for direct loans and the liability for loan guarantees. The long-term cost is based on all direct loans and guaranteed loans disbursed in this fiscal year and previous years that are outstanding as of the end of this fiscal year. It includes the subsidy cost of these loans and guarantees estimated as of the time of loan disbursement and subsequent adjustments such as modifications, reestimates, amortizations, and writeoffs.

Direct Loans and Loan Guarantees as of September 30

(In billions of dollars)	Face Value of Loans Outstanding		Long-term Cost of Loans and Guarantees Outstanding		Net Loans Receivable		Amount Guaranteed by the Government		Subsidy Expense for the Fiscal Year Ended September 30	
	2005	2004	2005	2004	2005	2004	2005	2004	2005	2004
Direct Loan Programs:										
Federal Direct Student Loans	97.7	92.1	2.0	(1.6)	95.7	93.7			5.2	(0.6)
Electric loans-USDA	30.2	27.5	2.2	(2.2)	28.0	29.7			(0.1)	(0.1)
Rural Housing Service	26.8	26.5	6.0	6.8	20.8	19.7			(0.5)	0.2
Federal Family Education Loan	20.2	20.0	8.5	9.3	11.7	10.7			-	-
Water and Environmental Loans-USDA	8.3	6.0	0.8	0.7	7.5	5.3			-	-
Export Loans-USDA	11.7	15.8	4.7	7.7	7.0	8.1			(0.3)	(0.1)
Housing for the Elderly and Disabled	6.5	9.7	(0.1)	2.6	6.6	7.1			-	-
Farm Loans-USDA	6.9	7.4	0.6	0.5	6.3	6.9			0.1	(0.1)
Export-Import Bank Loans	8.4	13.2	2.9	5.5	5.5	7.7			-	-
U.S. Agency for International Development	7.7	8.7	2.6	2.5	5.1	6.2			-	-
Housing and Urban Development	4.0	13.2	(0.1)	9.3	4.1	3.9			0.4	-
Telecommunications Loans-USDA	4.1	4.4	0.1	0.1	4.0	4.3			-	-
All Other Direct Loan Programs	25.3	21.4	5.8	3.8	19.5	17.6			0.2	0.1
Total	257.8	265.9	36.0	45.0	221.8	220.9			5.0	(0.6)
Guaranteed Loan Programs:										
Federal Family Education Loans	289.2	245.3	30.4	23.3			288.1	240.6	9.8	9.0
Federal Housing Administration Loans, HUD	454.3	509.7	4.6	5.2			416.4	471.4	1.2	(2.9)
Veterans Housing Benefit Program	202.1	207.4	3.5	4.7			62.1	64.7	(1.5)	0.2
Export-Import Bank Guarantees	50.9	47.5	2.3	3.1			50.9	47.5	0.2	0.3
Small Business Loans	73.3	67.5	2.1	2.5			61.1	56.4	(0.3)	0.1
Israeli Loan Guarantee Program, AID	13.0	12.3	1.1	0.8			13.0	12.3	0.2	-
Overseas Private Investment Corporation Credit Program	3.6	3.7	0.6	0.7			3.6	3.7	-	-
Rural Housing Service	14.8	13.6	0.6	0.4			13.3	12.2	0.1	0.1
Air Transportation Stabilization Board	0.9	1.3	0.6	0.7			0.8	1.1	-	-
Federal Ship Financing Fund	3.1	3.4	0.4	0.4			3.1	3.4	-	-
Business and Industry Loans	4.2	4.2	0.4	0.3			3.1	3.1	0.1	-
Export Credit Guarantee Programs	4.2	5.0	0.3	0.2			4.1	4.8	(0.3)	0.1
All Other Guaranteed Loan Programs	20.2	16.2	0.8	0.8			18.6	15.2	(0.1)	0.7
Total	1,133.8	1,137.1	47.7	43.1			938.2	936.4	9.4	7.6

Net loans receivable includes related interest and foreclosed property, and is included in the assets section of the balance sheets.

The total subsidy expense is the cost of direct loans and loan guarantees recognized during the fiscal year. It consists of the subsidy expense incurred for direct and guaranteed loans disbursed during the fiscal year, for modifications made during the fiscal year of loans and guarantees outstanding, and for reestimates as of the end of the fiscal year of the cost of loans and guarantees outstanding. This expense is included in the Statements of Net Cost.

Major Loan Programs

The Department of Education has two major education loan programs. The first major education loan program, the Federal Direct Student Loan Program, established in fiscal year 1994, offers four types of education loans: Stafford, Unsubsidized Stafford, PLUS for parents, and consolidation loans. Evidence of financial need is required for a student to receive a subsidized Stafford loan. The other three types of loans are available to borrowers at all income levels. These loans usually mature 9 to 13 years after the student is no longer enrolled. They are unsecured. The second major education loan program, the Federal Family Education Loan Program established in fiscal year 1965, has guaranteed loan programs. Like the Federal Direct Student Loan Program, it offers four types of loans: Stafford, Unsubsidized Stafford, PLUS for parents, and consolidation loans.

The USDA offers direct and guaranteed loans through credit programs in the Farm and Foreign Agricultural Services (FFAS) Mission Area through the Farm Service Agency (FSA) and the Commodity Credit Corporation (CCC), and in the Rural Development Mission Area (RD).

The FFAS delivers commodity, credit, conservation, disaster and emergency assistance programs that help strengthen and stabilize the agricultural economy.

The FSA offers direct and guaranteed loans to farmers who are unable to obtain private commercial credit and through this supervised credit to graduate its borrowers to commercial credit.

The CCC offers both guarantee credit and direct credit programs for buyers of U.S. exports, suppliers, and sovereign countries in need of food assistance.

The RD provides affordable housing and essential community facilities to rural communities through its housing loan and grant programs. These programs include:

- Very low- and low-to-moderate-income home ownership loans and guarantees.
- Very low-income housing repair loans.
- Multifamily housing loans and guarantees.
- Domestic farm labor housing loans.
- Housing site loans.
- Credit sales of acquired property.

The Rural Utilities Program administers a variety of loan programs for electric energy, telecommunications, and water and environmental projects in rural America.

The Department of Housing and Urban Development, Federal Housing Administration (FHA) provides mortgage insurance to encourage lenders to make credit available to expand home ownership. FHA predominately serves borrowers that the conventional market does not serve adequately. This includes first-time homebuyers, minorities, low-income families, and residents of under-served areas.

The VA's Veterans Housing Benefit Program provides partial guarantee of residential mortgage loans issued to eligible veterans, reservists, and service members by private lenders. This guarantee allows veterans, reservists, and service members to purchase a home without a substantial down payment.

The Export-Import Bank aids in financing and promoting

U.S. exports. To accomplish its objectives, the bank's authority and resources are used to:

- Assume commercial and political risk that exporters or private institutions are unwilling or are unable to undertake.
- Overcome maturity and other limitations in private sector financing.
- Assist U.S. exports to meet foreign officially sponsored export credit competition.
- Provide leadership and guidance in export financing to the U.S. exporting and banking communities and to foreign borrowers.

The average repayment terms for these loans are approximately 7 years.

The U.S. Agency for International Development (USAID) provides economic assistance to selected countries in support of U.S. efforts to promote stability and security interests in strategic regions of the world.

Other loan programs include the Small Business Administration general business loan guarantees and disaster loans; and the Farm Service Agency's farm ownership, emergency, and disaster loans.

Government-sponsored enterprises have the authority to request borrowings totaling $10 billion, subject to the approval of the Secretary of the Treasury.

Note 5. Inventories and Related Property, Net

Inventories and Related Property as of September 30

(In billions of dollars)	Defense	All Others	Total	Defense	All Others	Total
		2005			2004	
Inventory purchased for resale	80.0	0.6	80.6	76.0	0.7	76.7
Inventory held in reserve for future sale	-	-	-	-	0.1	0.1
Inventory and operating material and supplies held for repair	45.3	0.4	45.7	48.1	0.3	48.4
Inventory—excess, obsolete, and unserviceable	6.8	-	6.8	5.4	0.1	5.5
Operating materials and supplies held for use	126.3	5.2	131.5	127.8	4.8	132.6
Operating materials and supplies held in reserve for future use	-	0.2	0.2	-	0.2	0.2
Operating materials and supplies—excess, obsolete, and unserviceable	3.7	(0.3)	3.4	3.1	-	3.1
Stockpile materials	0.1	42.2	42.3	0.1	41.2	41.3
Stockpile materials held for sale	1.2	0.3	1.5	1.4	-	1.4
Other related property	0.9	1.2	2.1	1.1	1.8	2.9
Total allowance for inventories and related property	(41.7)	(0.4)	(42.1)	(49.8)	(0.9)	(50.7)
Total inventories and related property, net	222.6	49.4	272.0	213.2	48.3	261.5

Inventory is tangible personal property that is (1) held for sale, principally to Federal agencies, (2) in the process of production for sale, or (3) to be consumed in the production of goods for sale or in the provision of services for a fee.

Inventory purchased for resale is the cost or value of tangible personal property purchased by an agency for resale. DOD, which accounts for nearly all of the inventory purchased for resale in the Government, generally uses the Latest Acquisition Cost (LAC) method, which is revalued for holding gains and losses. DOD is transitioning their inventory to the moving average cost (MAC) method to be compliant with SFFAS No. 3 and approximately 35% of their inventory is now reported using MAC.

Inventory held in reserve for future sale is inventory not readily available, or inventory that will be needed in the future.

Inventory and operating materials and supplies held for repair are damaged inventory that require repair to make them suitable for sale (inventory) or is more economic to repair than to dispose of (operating materials and supplies). Inventory—excess, obsolete, and unserviceable:

- Excess inventory is that which exceeds the demand expected in the normal course of operations and which does not meet management's criteria to be held in reserve for future sale.
- Obsolete inventory is that which no longer is needed due to changes in technology, laws, customs, or operations.
- Unserviceable inventory is inventory damaged beyond economic repair.

Excess, obsolete, and unserviceable inventory is reported at net realizable value.

Operating materials and supplies held for use are tangible personal property to be consumed in normal operations.

Operating materials and supplies held in reserve for future use are materials retained because they are not readily available in the market or because they will not be used in the normal course of operations, but there is more than a remote chance that they will eventually be needed. DOD, which accounts for most of the reported operating materials and supplies held for use, uses LAC and Standard Price under the purchase and consumption methods of accounting and does not adjust for holding gains and losses, which does not approximate historical cost.

Operating materials and supplies—excess, obsolete, and unserviceable:

- Excess operating materials and supplies are materials that exceed the demand expected in the normal course of operations, and do not meet management's criteria to be held in reserve for future use.
- Obsolete operating materials and supplies are materials no longer needed due to changes in technology, laws, customs, or operations.
- Unserviceable operating materials and supplies are materials damaged beyond economic repair.

DOD, which accounts for most of the reported excess, obsolete, and unserviceable operating materials and supplies, revalues it to a net realizable value of zero through the allowance account.

Stockpile materials include strategic and critical materials held in reserve for use in national defense, conservation, or national emergencies due to statutory requirements; for example, nuclear materials and oil, and stockpile materials that are authorized to be sold. The majority of the amount reported by the DOD is stockpile materials held for sale, and the amount reported in all others is stockpile materials held in reserve, with the majority of it being reported by the Department of Energy (DOE).

Other related property:

- Commodities include items of commerce or trade that have an exchange value used to stabilize or support market prices.

- Seized monetary instruments are comprised of only monetary instruments that are awaiting judgment to determine ownership. The related liability is included in other liabilities. Other property seized by the Government, such as real property and tangible personal property, is not included as a Government asset. It is accounted for in agency property-management records until the property is forfeited, returned, or otherwise liquidated.
- Forfeited property is comprised of monetary instruments, intangible property, real property, and tangible personal property acquired through forfeiture proceedings; property acquired by the Government to satisfy a tax liability; and unclaimed and abandoned merchandise.
- Other property not classified above.

Note 6. Property, Plant, and Equipment, Net

The category of property, plant, and equipment consists of tangible assets including land, buildings, structures, automated data processing software, and other assets used to provide goods and services. Depreciation and amortization is recognized using the straight-line method over the estimated useful lives of the assets.

Property, Plant, and Equipment as of September 30, 2005

(In billions of dollars)	Cost Defense	Cost All Others	Accumulated Depreciation/ Amortization Defense	Accumulated Depreciation/ Amortization All Others	Net Defense	Net All Others
Buildings, structures, and facilities	163.9	172.7	95.4	87.3	68.5	85.4
Furniture, fixtures, and equipment	1,266.4	121.7	908.8	71.1	357.6	50.6
Construction in progress	20.3	44.0	N/A	N/A	20.3	44.0
Land	10.5	10.7	N/A	N/A	10.5	10.7
Automated data processing software	7.9	7.4	4.4	2.7	3.5	4.7
Assets under capital lease	0.6	1.6	0.4	0.5	0.2	1.1
Leasehold improvements	0.3	4.0	0.1	2.3	0.2	1.7
Other property, plant, and equipment	0.2	49.3	-	30.1	0.2	19.2
Subtotal	1,470.1	411.4	1,009.1	194.0	461.0	217.4
Total property, plant, and equipment, net		1,881.5		1,203.1		678.4

Property, Plant, and Equipment as of September 30, 2004

(In billions of dollars)	Cost Defense	Cost All Others	Accumulated Depreciation/ Amortization Defense	Accumulated Depreciation/ Amortization All Others	Net Defense	Net All Others
Buildings, structures, and facilities	159.4	165.1	91.5	80.1	67.9	85.0
Furniture, fixtures, and equipment	1,192.4	112.7	852.1	66.8	340.3	45.9
Construction in progress	19.6	40.0	N/A	N/A	19.6	40.0
Land	10.1	16.7	N/A	N/A	10.1	16.7
Automated data processing software	6.1	5.8	3.6	2.0	2.5	3.8
Assets under capital lease	0.6	1.7	0.4	0.5	0.2	1.2
Leasehold improvements	0.1	3.7	0.1	2.0	-	1.7
Other property, plant, and equipment	0.1	46.5	-	28.8	0.1	17.7
Subtotal	1,388.4	392.2	947.7	180.2	440.7	212.0
Total property, plant, and equipment, net		1,780.6		1,127.9		652.7

For physical quantity information related to the multiuse heritage assets, refer to agency supplemental stewardship reporting for heritage assets.

The National Aeronautics and Space Administration's (NASA) property, plant, and equipment has been reclassified for fiscal year 2004 in fiscal year 2005. They reclassified approximately $40.5 billion from furniture, fixtures, and equipment to other property, plant, and equipment ($38.0 billion) and to building, structures, and facilities ($2.5 billion) for its theme assets. The theme assets consist of property, plant, and equipment specifically designed for use in a NASA program and includes special tooling, special test equipment, the Space Shuttle, and other configurations of spacecraft: engines, unlaunched satellites, rockets, and other scientific components unique to the space program.

Note 7. Securities and Investments

Securities and Investments as of September 30

(In billions of dollars)	2005	2004
Securities and investments:		
Pension Benefit Guaranty Corporation	30.8	13.8
NRRIT[1]	26.1	24.6
Exchange Stabilization Fund	9.4	10.9
All other	9.0	7.8
Total securities and investments	75.3	57.1

[1] For more information, see Railroad Retirement in the Stewardship Information section (page 116).

These securities and investments do not include non-marketable Treasury securities, which have been eliminated in consolidation. They are presented at cost, net of unamortized premiums and discounts. The Pension Benefit Guaranty Corporation (PBGC) invests primarily in fixed maturity and equity securities. As discussed in the Stewardship Information section of this report, the NRRIT manages and invests railroad retirement assets that are to be used to pay retirement benefits to the Nation's railroad workers under the Railroad Retirement Program, a social insurance program. Treasury's Exchange Stabilization Fund invests primarily in foreign currency, bonds, and bills.

Note 8. Other Assets

Other Assets as of September 30

(In billions of dollars)	2005	2004
Advances and prepayments	32.8	27.0
Other	23.9	24.7
Total other assets	56.7	51.7

Other assets include advances and prepayments which represent funds disbursed in contemplation of the future performance of services, receipt of goods, the incurrence of expenditures, or the receipt of other assets. These include advances to contractors and grantees, travel advances, and prepayments for items such as rents, taxes, insurance, royalties, commissions, and supplies.

Other items included in other assets are regulatory assets, purchased power generating capacity, deferred nuclear generating units, nonmarketable equity investments in international financial institutions, the balance of assets held by the experience-rated carriers participating in the Health Benefits and Life Insurance Program carriers (pending disposition on behalf of OPM), and receivables from bank and thrift resolutions.

Note 9. Accounts Payable

Accounts Payable as of September 30

(In billions of dollars)	2005	2004
Department of Defense	28.6	28.4
Pension Benefit Guaranty Corporation	9.3	1.2
Department of Agriculture	4.3	3.4
Department of Homeland Security	3.3	2.8
Agency for International Development	3.2	2.0
U.S. Postal Service	2.3	2.5
General Services Administration	2.1	2.3
National Aeronautics and Space Administration	2.1	2.0
Department of Justice	1.9	2.1
Department of Energy	1.4	1.3
Department of State	1.3	1.2
Department of Labor	1.1	1.0
Department of the Interior	1.0	0.6
Department of Housing & Urban Development	0.8	0.8
Tennessee Valley Authority	0.8	0.9
All other departments	4.4	7.6
Total accounts payable	67.9	60.1

The accounts payable table includes accounts payable for goods and property ordered and received, services rendered by other than Federal employees, and accounts payable for cancelled appropriations.

Note 10. Federal Debt Securities Held by the Public and Accrued Interest

Definitions of Debt

Debt Held by the Public—Federal debt held outside the Government by individuals, corporations, State or local governments, Federal Reserve banks, and foreign governments and central banks.
Intragovernmental Debt Holdings—Federal debt held by Government trust funds, revolving funds, and special funds.

Federal Debt Securities Held by the Public and Accrued Interest

(In billions of dollars)	Balance September 30, 2004	Net Change During Fiscal Year 2005	Balance September 30, 2005	Average Interest Rate 2005	Average Interest Rate 2004
Treasury Securities (Public):					
Marketable securities:					
Treasury bills	961.5	(51.2)	910.3	3.4%	1.6%
Treasury notes..............................	2,109.6	218.6	2,328.2	3.7%	3.5%
Treasury bonds..............................	551.9	(31.4)	520.5	7.9%	8.0%
Treasury inflation-protected securities (TIPS).........................	223.0	84.0	307.0	2.4%	2.8%
Total marketable Treasury securities	3,846.0	220.0	4,066.0		
Nonmarketable securities	461.5	73.7	535.2	4.9%	5.1%
Net unamortized premium/ (discounts)...............................	(34.8)	(0.7)	(35.5)		
Total Treasury securities, net (public)	4,272.7	293.0	4,565.7		
Agency Securities:					
Tennessee Valley Authority..........	23.3	(0.4)	22.9		
All other agencies	0.7	(0.4)	0.3		
Total agency securities, net of unamortized premiums and discounts	24.0	(0.8)	23.2		
Accrued interest payable	32.7	2.6	35.3		
Total Federal debt securities held by the public and accrued interest	4,329.4	294.8	4,624.2		

Types of marketable securities:
Bills – Short-term obligations issued with a term of 1 year or less.
Notes – Medium-term obligations issued with a term of at least 1 year, but not more than 10 years.
Bonds – Long-term obligations of more than 10 years.
TIPS – Term of more than 5 years.

This table details Government borrowing to finance operations and shows marketable and nonmarketable securities at face value less net unamortized discounts including accrued interest.

Securities that represent Federal debt held by the public are issued primarily by the Treasury and include:

- Interest-bearing marketable securities (bills, notes, bonds, and inflation-protected).

- Interest-bearing nonmarketable securities (foreign series, State and local government series, domestic series, and savings bonds).
- Non interest-bearing marketable and nonmarketable securities (matured and other).

Section 3111 of Title 31, United States Code (U.S.C.) authorizes the Secretary of the Treasury to use money received from the sale of an obligation and other money in the General Fund of the Treasury to buy, redeem, or refund, at or before maturity, outstanding bonds, notes, certificates of indebtedness, Treasury bills, or savings certificates of the Government. There were no buyback operations in fiscal years 2005 and 2004.

As of September 30, 2005, and 2004, respectively, $7,871.0 billion and $7,333.4 billion of debt were subject to a statutory limit (31 U.S.C. § 3101). That limit was $8,184.0 billion as of September 30, 2005, and $7,384.0 billion as of September 30, 2004. The debt subject to the limit includes Treasury securities held by the public and Government guaranteed debt of Federal agencies (shown in the previous table) and intragovernmental debt holdings (shown in the next table).

Intragovernmental debt holdings represent the portion of the gross Federal debt held as investments by Government entities. This includes major trust funds. For more information on trust funds, see Note 21—Dedicated Collections. These intragovernmental debt holdings are eliminated in the consolidation of these financial statements.

**Intragovernmental Debt Holdings: Federal Debt Securities
Held as Investments by Government Accounts as of September 30**

(In billions of dollars)	Balance 2004	Net Change During Fiscal Year 2005	Balance 2005
Social Security Administration, Federal Old-Age and Survivors Insurance	1,452.6	163.5	1,616.1
Office of Personnel Management, Civil Service Retirement and Disability	631.9	28.9	660.8
Department of Health and Human Services, Federal Hospital Insurance	264.4	12.9	277.3
Social Security Administration, Federal Disability Insurance	182.8	10.5	193.3
Department of Defense, Military Retirement Fund	177.3	-	177.3
Department of Labor, Unemployment	45.2	9.6	54.8
Department of Defense, Medicare-Eligible Retiree Health Care Fund	35.9	17.0	52.9
Federal Deposit Insurance Corporation Funds	47.0	1.2	48.2
Housing and Urban Development, Federal Housing	23.3	(0.7)	22.6
Office of Personnel Management, Employees' Life Insurance	28.1	1.4	29.5
Department of Energy, Nuclear Water Disposal	30.5	3.0	33.5
Department of Health and Human Services, Federal Supplementary Medical Insurance	17.4	(0.2)	17.2
Department of Treasury, Exchange Stabilization Fund	10.3	4.9	15.2
Department of State, Foreign Services Retirement and Disability Fund	12.9	0.5	13.4
Department of Veterans Affairs, National Service Life Insurance Fund[1]	10.9	(0.3)	10.6
Pension Benefit Guaranty Corporation Fund	13.2	(0.2)	13.0
Office of Personnel Management, Employees Health Benefits	10.7	1.8	12.5
Department of Transportation, Airport and Airway Trust Fund	9.9	0.1	10.0
Department of Transportation, Highway Trust Fund	10.2	(1.9)	8.3
All other programs and funds	57.2	7.8	65.0
Subtotal	3,071.7	259.8	3,331.5
Unamortized net (discounts)/premiums	(0.6)	15.3	14.7
Total intragovernmental debt holdings, net	3,071.1	275.1	3,346.2

[1] This line now only reflects activity for the National Service Life Insurance Fund. Other Department of Veterans Affairs funds that were included on this line in the fiscal year 2004 Report are now included in the all other programs funds line of this table.

Note 11. Federal Employee and Veteran Benefits Payable

The Government offers its employees life and health insurance, as well as retirement and other benefits. These benefits, which include actuarial and amounts due and payable to beneficiaries and health care carriers, apply to civilian and military employees.

The Federal Government administers more than 40 pension plans. OPM administers the largest civilian plan. DOD, meanwhile, administers the largest military plan. Other significant pension plans with more than $10 billion in accrued benefits payable include those of the Coast Guard and the Foreign Service. The changes in the accrued post-retirement pension and health benefit liability and components of related expense for the years ended September 30, 2005, and 2004, respectively, are presented below.

Federal Employee and Veteran Benefits Payable as of September 30

	Civilian		Military		Total	
(In billions of dollars)	**2005**	**2004**	**2005**	**2004**	**2005**	**2004**
Pension and accrued benefits	1,273.8	1,230.2	895.4	837.7	2,169.2	2,067.9
Post-retirement health and accrued benefits	290.7	266.1	833.9	725.3	1,124.6	991.4
Veterans compensation and burial benefits	N/A	N/A	1,122.6	924.8	1,122.6	924.8
Liability for other benefits	48.5	54.4	26.9	23.6	75.4	78.0
Total Federal employee and veteran benefits payable...........................	1,613.0	1,550.7	2,878.8	2,511.4	4,491.8	4,062.1

Change in Pension and Accrued Benefits

(In billions of dollars)	Civilian	Military	Total
Actuarial accrued pension liability as of September 30, 2004	1,230.2	837.7	2,067.9
Pension Expense:			
Normal costs..	26.5	15.1	41.6
Plan amendment changes..	-	25.8	25.8
Assumption changes	0.2	4.9	5.1
Interest on liability...	75.5	51.4	126.9
Prior (and past) service cost......................................	(0.2)	-	(0.2)
Actuarial (gains)/losses..	(1.5)	(0.8)	(2.3)
Total pension expense...	100.5	96.4	196.9
Less benefits paid...	56.9	38.7	95.6
Actuarial accrued pension liability as of September 30, 2005	1,273.8	895.4	2,169.2

Significant Long-Term Economic Assumptions Used in Determining Pension Liability and the Related Expense

	Civilian		Military	
(In percentages)	2005	2004	2005	2004
Rate of interest	6.25%	6.25%	6.25%	6.25%
Rate of inflation	3.25%	3.25%	3.00%	3.00%
Projected salary increases	4.00%	4.00%	3.75%	3.75%

Change in Post-Retirement Health and Accrued Benefits

(In billions of dollars)	Civilian	Military	Total
Actuarial accrued post-retirement health benefits liability, as of September 30, 2004	266.1	725.3	991.4
Post-Retirement Health Benefits Expense:			
Normal costs	15.0	18.3	33.3
Interest on liability	16.9	45.5	62.4
Assumption change liability	-	53.6	53.6
Other actuarial (gains)/losses	3.4	5.4	8.8
Total post-retirement health benefits expense	35.3	122.8	158.1
Less claims paid	10.7	14.2	24.9
Actuarial accrued post-retirement health benefits liability, as of September 30, 2005	290.7	833.9	1,124.6

Significant Long-Term Economic Assumptions Used in Determining Post-Retirement Health Benefits and the Related Expense

	Civilian		Military	
(In percentages)	2005	2004	2005	2004
Rate of interest	6.25%	6.25%	6.25%	6.25%
Rate of health care cost inflation	7.00%	7.00%	6.25%	6.25%

Separate boards of actuaries for OPM and DOD determine the actuarial assumptions used in calculating the pension liability and the post-retirement health benefit liability for the civilian and military personnel. Both boards use generally accepted actuarial methodologies. The board for OPM uses a fixed rate of inflation and projected salary increases over all years for both the pension and post-retirement health benefit liabilities. These rates are shown in the tables above. The board for DOD uses a range of rates for the inflation and the projected salary increases, with an ultimate rate for the long term. The board for DOD also uses different health care cost inflation rates for inpatient, outpatient, and prescription drugs. The long-term ultimate rate is shown in the previous tables.

The long-term ultimate rate for fiscal year 2005 of 6.25 percent is shown in the previous tables. For disclosure and comparison purposes, DOD's estimate of a single equivalent fixed rate of health care cost inflation for fiscal year 2005 is 7.8 percent, which is an approximation of the single equivalent rate that would produce that same actuarial liability as the actual rates used.

Civilian Employees

Pensions

OPM administers the largest civilian pension plan, which covers approximately 90 percent of all Federal civilian employees. This plan includes two components of defined benefits. These are the Civil Service Retirement System (CSRS) and the Federal Employees' Retirement System (FERS). The basic benefit components of the CSRS and the FERS are financed and operated through the Civil Service Retirement and Disability Fund (CSRDF).

CSRDF monies are generated primarily from employees' contributions, agency contributions, payments from the General Fund, and interest on investments in Treasury securities. See Note 21—Dedicated Collections.

The Federal Retirement Thrift Investment Board, an independent Government agency, administers the Thrift Savings Plan

(TSP) Fund. The TSP Fund includes the C-Fund, S-Fund, F-Fund, I-Fund, and G-Fund, and the newly established L-Funds. These financial statements exclude this fund because the CSRS and FERS employees own its assets.

Treasury securities held in the G-Fund are included and classified as Treasury securities held by the public. FERS employees may contribute up to 15 percent of base pay to the plan, which the Government matches up to 5 percent. CSRS employees may contribute up to 10 percent of base pay with no Government match.

The G-Fund held $63.5 billion and $56.4 billion in nonmarketable Treasury securities on September 30, 2005, and 2004, respectively. The Federal Government's related liability is included in total Federal debt securities held by the public and accrued interest in the balance sheets.

The L-Funds, established August 1, 2005, diversifies participant accounts among the G, F, C, S, and I Funds, using professionally determined investment mixes (allocations) that are tailored to different time horizons.

Health Benefits

The post-retirement civilian health benefit liability is an estimate of the Government's future cost of providing post-retirement health benefits to current employees and retirees. Although active and retired employees pay an insurance premium under the Federal Employees Health Benefits Program, these premiums cover only a portion of the costs. The OPM actuary applies economic assumptions to historical cost information to estimate the liability, which is then reduced by certain operating costs and premiums received during the year.

Other Benefits

One of the largest other employee benefits is the Federal Employee Group Life Insurance Program. Employee and annuitant contributions and interest on investments fund a portion of this liability. The actuarial life insurance liability is the expected present value of future benefits to pay to, or in behalf of, existing Life Insurance Program participants. The OPM actuary uses interest rate, inflation, and salary increase assumptions that are consistent with the pension liability.

Military Employees (Including Veterans)

Pensions

The DOD Military Retirement Fund (MRF) finances military retirement and survivor benefit programs. The National Defense Authorization Act increased survivor benefits in fiscal year 2005 resulting in a $25.8 billion increase in pension liability.

Projected revenues into the MRF come from three sources: interest earnings on MRF assets, monthly DOD contributions, and annual contributions from the Treasury Department. Beginning with fiscal year 2005, the contributions made by Treasury were increased by an amount equal to the annual expense for the new concurrent receipt provision of the Fiscal Year 2004 National Defense Authorization Act.

The military retirement system consists of a funded, non-contributory, defined benefit plan. It applies to the Departments of the Army, Navy, Air Force, and Marine Corps. This system includes nondisability retirement pay, disability retirement pay, and retirement pay for reserve service and survivor annuity programs.

Military personnel (Army, Navy, Marine Corps, and Air Force) who remain on active duty for 20 years or longer are eligible for retirement. There are three different retirement systems that are currently being used by the military: Final Pay, High-3 Year Average, and the Military Retirement Reform Act of 1986 (REDUX). The date each individual enters the military determines which retirement system they would fall under and if they have the option to pick their retirement system.

Final Pay Retirement System: Final Pay applies to individuals who entered the Service before September 8, 1980. Each year of service is worth 2.5 percent towards the retirement multiplier. The longer an individual stays on active duty, the higher the multiplier and the higher the retirement income, up to the maximum of 75 percent. This multiplier is applied against the final basic pay of the individual's career. A cost of living adjustment (COLA) is given annually based on the increase in the CPI.

High-3 Year Average Retirement System: High-3 Year Average applies to members who first entered the Service after September 8, 1980, but before August 1, 1986. It also applies to individuals who entered on or after August 1, 1986, who do not elect the REDUX retirement system with the $30,000 career status bonus (CSB) at their 15th year of service. The High-3 Year Average calculation is similar to the Final Pay except the High-3 Year Average uses the multiplier against basic pay for the highest 36 months of the individual's career. A COLA is given annually based on the increase in the CPI.

CSB/REDUX Retirement System: The REDUX applies to those who entered the Service on or after August 1, 1986, and who elected to receive the $30,000 CSB at their 15th year of service. Under the CSB/REDUX retirement system, each of the first 20 years of service is worth 2 percent towards the retirement multiplier and each year after 20 years of service is worth 3.5 percent. The retirement multiplier under this retirement system is applied against the average basic pay for the highest 36 months of the individual's basic pay. A COLA is given annually based on the increase in the CPI minus 1 percent. Members retiring under CSB/REDUX receive a one-time catchup at age 62 that restores the retired pay to what it would have been at that point had the member retired under High-3 Year Average. Thereafter, CSB/REDUX members receive reduced (i.e., based on the increase in the CPI minus 1 percent) COLAs for life.

On October 30, 2000, the Floyd D. Spence National Defense Authorization Act for Fiscal Year 2001 (Public Law No. 106-398) was signed into law. This law extended participation in the TSP to members of the uniformed services. Members may contribute from their pay, and their contributions and earnings attributable to their TSP belongs to them even if they do not serve the 20 or more years ordinarily required to receive retirement pay.

Health Benefits

Military benefits entitle retirees and their dependents to health care in military medical facilities if a facility can provide the needed care. Until they reach age 65, military retirees and their dependents also are entitled to be reimbursed for the cost of health care from civilian providers. A premium is charged to enroll in DOD's civilian care program. In addition, there are deductible and copayment requirements for civilian care. Medicare, and since fiscal year 2002, Tricare as secondary payer, covers military retirees after they reach 65 years of age.

Military retiree health care figures include the cost of education and training, staffing, buildings and equipment, as well as the operation and maintenance of medical facilities. They also include claims paid to civilian providers and the cost of administering the program.

Chapter 56 of Title 10, U.S.C. created the DOD Medicare-Eligible Retiree Health Care Fund effective October 1, 2002. The purpose of this fund is to account for the health benefits of Medicare-eligible members and former members of the DOD Uniformed Services who are entitled to retirement or retainer pay, and their eligible dependents who are Medicare eligible.

In addition to the health care benefits for civilian and military retirees and their dependents, the VA also provides medical care to veterans on an "as available" basis, subject to the limits of the annual appropriations. In accordance with 38 CFR 17.36 (c), VA's Secretary makes an annual enrollment decision that defines the veterans, by priority, who will be treated for that fiscal year subject to change based on funds appropriated, estimated collections, usage, the severity index of enrolled veterans, and changes in cost. VA recognizes the medical care expenses in the period the medical care services are provided. For the time period 2001-2005, the average medical cost per year was $24.1 billion.

Veterans Compensation and Burial Benefits

The Government compensates disabled veterans and their survivors. Veterans compensation is payable as a disability benefit or a survivor's benefit. Entitlement to compensation depends on the veteran's disabilities having been incurred in, or aggravated during, active military service; death while on duty; or death resulting from service-connected disabilities, if not in active duty.

Burial benefits include a burial and plot or interment allowance payable for a veteran who, at the time of death, is qualified to receive compensation or a pension, or whose death occurred in a VA facility.

The liability for veteran's compensation and burial benefits payable increased by $197.8 billion in fiscal year 2005 and decreased by $30 billion in fiscal year 2004. The primary factors contributing to these fluctuations were changes in interest rates and other actuarial assumptions; various assumptions in the actuarial model, such as the number of veterans and dependents receiving payments; and life expectancy.

Veterans Compensation and Burial Benefits as of September 30

(In billions of dollars)	2005	2004
Veterans	925.4	775.3
Survivors	193.4	146.2
Burial benefits	3.8	3.3
Total compensation and burial benefits payable	1,122.6	924.8

Significant Economic Assumptions Used in Determining Veterans Compensation and Burial Benefits as of September 30

(In percentages)	2005	2004
Rate of interest	3.93%	2.00%
Rate of inflation	3.60%	2.70%

Other Benefits

Veterans insurance includes the following programs:

- United States Government Life Insurance, established in 1919 to handle new issues and the conversion of World War I Risk Term Insurance.
- National Service Life Insurance, established in 1940 to meet the needs of World War II service personnel.

- Veterans Special Life Insurance, established in 1951 for Korean veterans who did not have service-connected disabilities.
- Service-Disabled Veterans Insurance, established in 1951 for veterans with service-connected disabilities.
- Veterans Reopened Insurance, which established a 1-year reopening in 1965 of National Service Life Insurance for certain disabled World War II and Korean veterans.

The VA also provides certain veterans and/or their dependents with pension benefits, based on annual eligibility reviews, if the veteran died or was disabled for nonservice-related causes. The actuarial present value of the future liability for pension benefits is a nonexchange transaction and is not required to be recorded on the balance sheet. The projected amounts of future payments for pension benefits as of September 30, 2005, and 2004 were $96.8 and $102.2 billion, respectively.

Note 12. Environmental and Disposal Liabilities

Environmental and Disposal Liabilities as of September 30

(In billions of dollars)	2005	2004
Department of Energy:		
Environmental management facilities	121.4	112.8
Active and surplus facilities	26.0	30.4
Long-term stewardship	17.5	17.5
High-level waste and spent nuclear fuel	15.1	14.9
All other Energy environmental liabilities	9.8	6.1
Total Department of Energy	189.8	181.7
Department of Defense:		
Environmental restoration	36.0	37.0
Disposal of Weapon Systems Program	23.2	22.3
Base realignment and closure	4.1	4.0
Other	1.7	1.0
Total Department of Defense	65.0	64.3
All other agencies	5.0	3.2
Total environmental and disposal liabilities	259.8	249.2

During World War II and the Cold War, DOE developed a massive industrial complex to research, produce, and test nuclear weapons. The nuclear weapons complex included nuclear reactors, chemical-processing buildings, metal machining plants, laboratories, and maintenance facilities.

At all the sites where these activities took place, some environmental contamination occurred. This contamination was caused by the production, storage, and use of radioactive materials and hazardous chemicals, which resulted in contamination of soil, surface water, and groundwater. The environmental legacy of nuclear weapons production also includes thousands of contaminated areas and buildings, and large volumes of waste and special nuclear materials requiring treatment, stabilization, and disposal.

Of those environmental liabilities, this report presents only cleanup costs from Federal operations known to result in hazardous and radioactive waste that the Government is required to clean up by Federal, State, or local statutes and/or regulations. Some of these statutes are the Comprehensive Environmental Response, Compensation, and Liability Act (CERCLA); the Resource Conservation and Recovery Act; and the Nuclear Waste Policy Act of 1982, which provides for permanent disposal of the Nation's high-level radioactive waste and spent nuclear fuel; and Public Law No. 105-204, which requires a plan for the conversion of depleted uranium hexaflouride.

DOE is responsible for managing the legacy of contamination from the nuclear weapons complex. The environmental management baseline estimate includes projections of the technical scope, schedule, and costs for environmental restoration; managing nuclear materials waste treatment, storage and disposal activities; and postcleanup monitoring and stewardship at each installation. The baseline estimate includes costs for related activities such as landlord responsibilities, program management, and legally prescribed grants for participation and oversight by Native American tribes, regulatory agencies, and other stakeholders. Active and surplus facilities represent anticipated remediation costs for those facilities that are conducting ongoing operations but ultimately will require stabilization, deactivation, and decommissioning.

Estimated cleanup costs at sites for which there are no current feasible remediation approach are excluded from the baseline estimates, although applicable stewardship and monitoring costs for these sites are included. Significant projects not included are:

- Nuclear explosion test areas (e.g., Nevada test site).
- Large surface water bodies (e.g., Clinch and Columbia Rivers).
- Most ground water (even with treatment, future use will be restricted).

Estimating DOE's environmental cleanup liability requires making assumptions about future activities and is inherently uncertain. The future course of DOE's environmental management program will depend on a number of fundamental technical and policy choices to be made in the future. The sites and facilities could be restored to a pristine condition suitable for any desirable use, or could be restored to a point where they pose no near-term health risks. Achieving pristine conditions would have a higher cost but may, or may not, warrant the costs and potential ecosystem disruption, or be legally required. The environmental liability estimates are dependent on annual funding levels and achievement of work as scheduled. DOE is also required to recognize closure and post closure costs for its general property, plant, and equipment and environmental corrective action costs for current operations.

The cleanup cost associated with general property, plant, and equipment that is allocated to operating periods beyond the balance sheet date is identified as the unrecognized portion. The DOE unrecognized portion of the cleanup cost associated with general property, plant, and equipment is $440 million and $357 million for fiscal years 2005 and 2004, respectively. The unrecognized portion of the cleanup cost is recognized over a predetermined period of time.

DOD is required to clean up contamination resulting from

waste disposal practices, leaks, spills, and other activities that have created a public health or environmental risk. DOD must restore active installations, installations affected by base realignment and closure, and other areas formerly used as defense sites. DOD also bears responsibility for disposal of chemical weapons and environmental costs associated with the disposal of weapons systems (primarily nuclear powered aircraft carriers and submarines). DOD is responsible, as well, for training range and other nonrange unexploded ordnance cleanup.

DOD is required by law to adhere to CERCLA and the Superfund Amendment and Reauthorization Act to clean up contamination resulting from past waste disposal practices, leaks, spills, and other activities which have created a risk to public health or the environment. The Army is DOD's executive agent for cleaning up contamination at sites formerly used by DOD. CERCLA requires DOD to cleanup contamination in coordination with regulatory agencies, other responsible parties, and current property owners.

DOD is currently using two independently validated estimating models, in addition to engineering estimates, to report its environmental liabilities. The models are the Remedial Action Cost Engineering Requirements and the Department of Navy Cost-to-Complete module. These two methods of valuation are used in this note's table. Additionally, cost estimates are based on the following: (1) historic comparable project, (2) a specific bid or independent Government cost estimate for the project, (3) site level data, and (4) annual cost-to-complete estimate.

DOD has not identified any unrecognized portion of the estimated total cleanup cost associated with general property, plant, and equipment. DOD's financial management regulation requires the unrecognized cleanup cost associated with property, plant, and equipment to be disclosed. DOD is working to ensure the regulation is properly implemented.

Note 13. Benefits Due and Payable

These amounts are the benefits owed to program recipients or medical service providers as of the fiscal yearend that have not been paid. For a description of the programs, see the Stewardship Responsibilities section under Stewardship Information.

Benefits Due and Payable as of September 30

(In billions of dollars)	2005	2004
Federal Old-Age and Survivors Insurance	39.3	37.1
Grants to States for Medicaid	20.1	19.3
Federal Disability Insurance	19.2	12.8
Federal Hospital Insurance (Medicare Part A)	16.8	15.0
Federal Supplementary Medical Insurance (Medicare Part B)	16.6	14.8
Supplemental Security Income	2.8	1.8
Unemployment Insurance	0.9	1.1
Other benefits due and payable	1.3	1.0
Total benefits due and payable	117.0	102.9

Note 14. Insurance Program Liabilities

Insurance Program Liabilities as of September 30

(In billions of dollars)	2005	2004
Insurance Program Liabilities:		
Pension Benefit Guaranty Corporation	69.8	60.8
National Flood Insurance Program –DHS	23.4	1.4
Total insurance program liabilities	93.2	62.2

Insurance programs are Federal programs that provide protection to individuals or entities against specified risks except for those Federal employees or veterans, which are discussed in Note

11. These funds are commonly held in revolving funds with the Federal Government, and losses sustained by participants are paid from these funds. Many of these programs receive appropriations to pay excess claims and/or have authority to borrow from the Treasury. Insurance programs do not include social insurance, loan guarantee programs, and programs designed to benefit only current, former, and dependents of Federal employees PBGC.

PBGC insures pension benefits of participants in covered defined benefit pension plans. As a wholly owned corporation of the U.S. Government, PBGC's financial activity and balances are included in the consolidated financial statements of the U.S. Government. However, under current law, PBGC's liabilities may be paid only from PBGC's assets and not from the General Fund of the Treasury or assets of the Government generally. As of September 30, 2005, PBGC had total liabilities of $80.7 billion, and its total liabilities exceeded its total assets by $23.1 billion. In addition, as discussed in Note 19—Contingencies, PBGC reported reasonably possible contingent losses of about $108 billion.

The Federal Emergency Management Agency of the Emergency Preparedness and Response Directorate, Department of Homeland Security, administers the National Flood Insurance Program (NFIP). The NFIP is administered through sale or continuation-in-force of insurance in communities that enact and enforce appropriate flood plain management measures. This liability represents an estimate of NFIP losses that are unpaid at the balance sheet date and is based on the loss and loss adjustment expense factors inherent in the NFIP insurance underwriting operations experience and expectations.

Note 15. Other Liabilities

Other Liabilities as of September 30

(In billions of dollars)	2005	2004
Other accrued liabilities	23.2	5.9
Nuclear Waste Fund	19.6	18.1
Accrued wages and benefits	16.0	38.2
Actuarial liabilities	11.6	10.4
Deposited funds and undeposited collections	11.2	8.5
Gold certificates	10.9	10.9
Accrued grant liability	10.4	10.2
Exchange Stabilization Fund	9.3	9.4
Other debt	8.8	9.1
Accrued annual leave	8.6	8.0
Deferred revenue	8.5	6.9
District of Columbia pension liabilities	8.5	8.4
Energy Employees Occupational Illness Compensation Act	7.4	2.8
Custodial liabilities	7.3	6.5
Contingent liabilities	6.6	2.2
Miscellaneous liabilities	45.3	42.6
Total other liabilities	213.2	198.1

The following are descriptions of some of the other categories (i.e., those over $8 billion) classified as other liabilities:

- Other accrued liabilities include amounts accrued by the Department of Agriculture for the Tobacco Transition Program, Direct and Counter-Cyclical Program, Conservation Reserve Program, and other accrued liabilities.
- Nuclear Waste Fund (NWF) refers to revenues that are accrued by the Department of Energy based on fees assessed against owners and generators of high-level radioactive waste and spent nuclear fuel and interest accrued on investments in Treasury securities. These

revenues are recognized as a financing source as costs are incurred for NWF activities.

- Accrued wages and benefits consist of the estimated liability for civilian and military salaries and wages earned but unpaid.
- Actuarial liabilities includes the estimated liability for the future benefit payments of contracted employees at the DOE. These are not for employee related benefit payments and therefore are not reflected in the Federal Employee and Veteran Benefits Payable footnote.
- Deposit funds and undeposited collections are deposits held and maintained by the Government on behalf of a third party and include unclassified deposited funds that are amounts offsetting undeposited collections, as well as funds deposited in clearing accounts and suspense accounts that await disposition or reclassification.
- Gold certificates include monetized portions of gold and certificates deposited in FRBs.
- Accrued grant liability represents the accruals related to grant program funds provided primarily to State and local governments, as well as universities and nonprofit organizations.
- Exchange stabilization fund includes SDR certificates issued to the FRBs and allocations from the IMF.
- Other debt includes Government obligations, whether secured or unsecured, not included in public debt.
- Accrued annual leave represents the dollar value of annual leave accrued to employees for annual leave hours earned but not used, and that is expected to be paid from

future years' appropriations. Annual leave is an expense which accrues as it is earned by employees.

- Deferred revenue refers to revenue received but not yet earned, such as payments received in advance from outside sources for future delivery of products or services.

- District of Columbia (D.C.) pension liability represents the amount payable to the Judicial Retirement Fund and the D.C. Federal Pension Fund by Treasury for the annual amortized payments that are required to be made from the General Fund of the U.S. Government to fund certain D.C. retirement plans.

- Miscellaneous liabilities include amounts accrued for other liabilities from DOD, VA, Treasury, DOI, PBGC, the United States Postal Service, and the Tennessee Valley Authority (TVA).

Note 16. Collections and Refunds of Federal Revenue

Collections of Federal Revenue for the Year Ended September 30, 2005

(In billions of dollars)	Federal Revenue Collections	Tax Year to Which Collections Relate			
		2005	2004	2003	Prior Years
Individual income and tax withholdings............................	1,864.7	1,212.1	620.9	13.9	18.0
Corporation income taxes..........	306.9	209.4	83.1	1.2	13.2
Unemployment taxes	40.1	22.2	9.9	7.9	0.1
Excise taxes...............................	72.4	52.8	19.0	0.1	0.6
Estate and gift taxes	25.6	0.1	16.6	1.3	7.6
Railroad retirement taxes...........	4.5	3.5	1.1	-	-
Federal Reserve earnings..........	19.3	14.2	5.1	-	-
Fines, penalties, interest, and other revenue	4.3	4.0	0.4	-	-
Custom duties	23.2	23.2	-	-	-
Subtotal	2,361.0	1,541.5	756.1	24.4	39.5
Less: Amounts collected for non-Federal entities	0.9				
Total	2,360.1				

Treasury is the Government's principal revenue-collecting agency. Collections of individual income tax and tax withholdings consist of FICA/SECA and other taxes including payroll taxes collected from other agencies.

Federal Tax Refunds Disbursed for the Year Ended September 30, 2005

(In billions of dollars)	Refunds Disbursed	Tax Year to Which Refunds Relate			
		2005	2004	2003	Prior Years
Individual income tax and tax withholdings.............................	230.0	0.6	211.1	12.8	5.5
Corporation income taxes............	35.1	1.0	7.2	5.5	21.5
Unemployment taxes	0.1	-	0.1	-	-
Excise taxes...................................	1.0	0.3	0.3	-	0.3
Estate and gift taxes	0.9	-	0.3	0.4	0.3
Custom duties	1.2	0.7	0.1	-	0.3
Total...	268.3	2.6	219.1	18.7	27.9

Reconciliation of Collections to Revenue

(In billions of dollars)	2005	2004
Total revenue per the Statements of Operations and Changes in Net Position..	2,185.5	1,912.7
Tax refunds	268.3	279.5
Earned Income Tax Credit and Child Tax Credit Imputed Revenue	(55.3)	(47.1)
Nontax related fines and penalties reported by agencies......................	(19.2)	(21.6)
Nontax related earned revenue	(19.2)	(13.8)
Collections of Federal revenue	2,360.1	2,109.7

Total revenue in the Statements of Operations and Changes in Net Position are presented on a modified cash basis, is net of tax refunds, and includes Earned Income Tax Credit (EITC) payments and other nontax related revenue. EITC and Child Tax Credit amounts are included in gross cost in the Statements of Net Cost as a component of Treasury.

On the other hand, collections of Federal revenue reported in the table in this Note are reported on a gross cash basis. The table above reconciles total revenue to collections.

Collections of Federal Revenue for the Year Ended September 30, 2004

(In billions of dollars)	Federal Revenue Collections	Tax Year to Which Collections Relate			
		2004	2003	2002	Prior Years
Individual income and tax withholdings.............................	1,695.3	1,128.1	541.0	13.2	13.0
Corporation income taxes..........	230.4	150.6	67.3	1.1	11.4
Unemployment taxes	36.9	20.7	9.0	7.2	-
Excise taxes...............................	73.4[1]	54.3[1]	18.6	0.5	-
Estate and gift taxes	25.6	0.1	16.9	1.1	7.5
Railroad retirement taxes...........	4.5	3.4	1.1	-	-
Federal Reserve earnings..........	19.7	13.1	6.6	-	-
Fines, penalties, interest, and other revenue	3.7	3.6	0.1	-	-
Custom duties	21.0	21.0	-	-	-
Subtotal	2,110.5[1]	1,394.9[1]	660.6	23.1	31.9
Less: amounts collected for non-Federal entities	(0.8)[1]				
Total	2,109.7[1]				

[1] Restated.

Federal Tax Refunds Disbursed for the Year Ended September 30, 2004

(In billions of dollars)	Refunds Disbursed	Tax Year to Which Refunds Relate			
		2004	2003	2002	Prior Years
Individual income tax and tax withholdings.................................	230.1	0.6	210.0	12.6	6.9
Corporation income taxes..............	46.6	1.5	8.9	6.7	29.5
Unemployment taxes	0.1	-	0.1	-	-
Excise taxes...................................	0.9	0.3	0.3	0.1	0.2
Estate and gift taxes	0.8	-	0.2	0.3	0.3
Custom duties	1.0	1.0	-	-	-
Total..	279.5	3.4	219.5	19.7	36.9

Note 17. Unreconciled Transactions Affecting the Change in Net Position

The reconciliation of the change in net position requires that the difference between ending and beginning net position equals the excess of revenues over net cost, plus or minus prior period adjustments.

The unreconciled transactions needed to bring the change in net position into balance amounted to a net value of $4.3 billion and ($3.4) billion for the years ended September 30, 2005, and 2004, respectively.

The three primary factors affecting this out-of-balance situation are:

- Improper recording of intragovernmental transactions by agencies.
- Transactions affecting balance sheet assets and liabilities not identified properly by agencies as prior period adjustments.
- Timing differences and errors in reporting transactions.

The Federal financial community considers the identification and accurate reporting of these unreconciled transactions a priority.

Note 18. Change in Accounting Principle and Prior Period Adjustments

Change in Accounting Principle and Prior Period Adjustments to Fiscal Years 2005 and 2004

	Increases to Net Position	
(In billions of dollars)	2005	2004
Change in Accounting Principle:		
Department of Defense	3.6	-
Prior Period Adjustments:		
Department of Defense	7.3	-
Other agencies	0.2	-
Total change in accounting principle and prior period adjustments	11.1	-

For fiscal year 2005, DOD recorded $10.9 billion (net) in prior period adjustments to cumulative results of operations. $3.6 billion (net) of these adjustments were due to a change in accounting principle and $7.3 (net) was due to prior period adjustments. DODs adjustments were the result of the Air Force completing the conversion of its inventory valuation method from Latest Acquisition Cost to Moving Average Cost. This resulted in adjustments to eliminate allowance for gains and losses, establish an allowance for repair, and revalue the inventory. The total inventory revaluation was $11.3 billion. The revaluation was offset by the $0.4 billion reversal of erroneous gains and losses from prior years. Other agencies recorded $0.2 (net) as prior period adjustments.

Note 19. Contingencies

Financial Treatment of Loss Contingencies

Loss contingencies that are assessed to be at least reasonably possible are disclosed in this note. Loss contingencies involve situations where there is an uncertainty of a possible loss. The reporting of loss contingencies depends on the likelihood that a future event or events will confirm the loss or impairment of an asset or the incurrence of a liability. Terms used to assess the range for the likelihood of loss are probable, reasonably possible, and remote. Loss contingencies that are assessed as probable and measurable are accrued in the financial statements. Loss contingencies that are assessed as remote are not reported in the financial statements, nor disclosed in the notes. All other material loss contingencies are disclosed in this note. For an overview of the standards that provide criteria for how Federal agencies are to account for loss contingencies, based on the likelihood of the loss and measurability,[1] see the following table.

Likelihood of future outflow or other sacrifice of resources.	Loss amount can be reasonably measured.	Loss range can be reasonably measured.	Loss amount or range cannot be reasonably measured.
Probable. Future confirming event(s) are more likely to occur than not.[2]	Accrue the liability. Reported on Balance Sheet & Statements of Net Cost.	Accrue liability of best estimate or minimum amount in loss range if there is no best estimate, and disclose nature of contingency and range of estimated liability.	Disclose nature of contingency and include a statement that an estimate cannot be made.
Reasonably possible. Possibility of future confirming event(s) occurring is more than remote and less than likely.	Disclose nature of contingency and estimated loss amount.	Disclose nature of contingency and estimated loss range.	Disclose nature of contingency and include a statement that an estimate cannot be made.
Remote. Possibility of future event(s) occurring is slight.	No disclosure.	No disclosure.	No disclosure.

[1] In addition, a third condition must be met to be a loss contingency: a past event or an exchange transaction must occur.

[2] For loss contingencies related to litigation, probable is defined as the future confirming event or events are more likely than not to occur, with the exception of pending or threatened litigation and unasserted claims. For the pending or threatened litigation and unasserted claims, the future confirming event or events are likely to occur.

The Government is subject to loss contingencies which include insurance and litigation cases. These loss contingencies arise in the normal course of operations and their ultimate disposition is unknown. Based on information currently available, however, it is management's opinion that the expected outcome of these matters, individually or in the aggregate, will not have a material adverse effect on the financial statements, except for the insurance and litigation described in the following sections:

Insurance Contingencies

At the time that an insurance policy is issued, a contingency arises. The contingency is the risk of loss assumed by the insurer, that is, the risk of loss from events that may occur during the term of the policy. For example, the estimated aggregate unfunded vested benefits exposure to PBGC for companies' single-employer and multi-employer defined pension plans is $108.4 billion and $96 billion for 2005 and 2004, respectively.

Legal Contingencies

The Federal Government is party to various administrative claims and legal actions brought against it, some of which may ultimately result in settlements or decisions against the Federal Government.

Management and legal counsel have determined that it is "probable" that some of these actions will result in a loss to the Federal Government and the loss amounts are reasonably measurable. The estimated liabilities for these cases are $5 billion and $4.4 billion for 2005 and 2004, respectively, and are recorded in the balance sheet line items "Insurance Liabilities," or "Other Liabilities." A few of the major cases are summarized below:

- HHS has unasserted claims that resulted from processing errors where incorrect Medicare eligibility determinations were made. Estimated amounts payable to States to reimburse them for payments they paid on behalf of beneficiaries at an amount of $1.6 billion and $1.9 billion for 2005 and 2004, respectively.
- DOI's estimated potential liability for breach of contract case filed by lessees under Federal oil and gas leases on the offshore California Outer Continental Shelf that are not yet developed to production in the amount of $550 million.
- VA has recorded liabilities for pending legal claims related to medical malpractice and other tort claim exposure in the amounts of $522 million and $501 million for 2005 and 2004, respectively.

There are also administrative claims and legal actions pending where adverse decisions are considered by management and legal counsel as "probable" with an estimated range of losses. The best estimate or the minimum range is recorded in the balance sheet. The estimated potential losses for such claims and actions range from $814 million to $1.7 billion for September 2005, and from $843 million to $1.5 billion for September 2004. For example, DOI has numerous lawsuits and claims filed against the agency related to the Federal Tort Claims Act, personnel and employment-related matters, and various land and resource claims in the range of $587 million to $1.2 billion and $726 million to $1.3 billion for 2005 and 2004, respectively.

There are also administrative claims and legal actions pending where adverse decisions are considered by management and legal counsel as "reasonably possible" with an estimate of possible liability or a range of possible liability. The estimated potential losses for such claims and actions range from $1.2 billion to $7.9 billion for September 2005, and from $2.3 billion to $3.7 billion for September 2004. Two of the major cases are summarized below:

- HHS reported as of September 30, 2005, $2.8 billion could be owed in payment adjustments to hospitals that serve a significantly disproportionate share of low-income patients.
- DHS has pending legal claims in the range of $319 million to $2.5 billion for refunds of user fees, harbor maintenance tax claims, and tariff claims as of September 30, 2005.

Numerous litigation cases are pending where the outcome is uncertain or there is at least a reasonable possibility that a loss has been incurred and where estimates cannot be made. There are other litigation cases where the plaintiffs have not made claims for specific dollar amounts, but the claimed amounts may be significant. The ultimate resolution of these legal actions for which the potential loss could not be determined may materially affect the U.S. Government's financial position or operating results. Examples of specific cases are summarized below:

- Native Americans allege that the Departments of Interior and Treasury have breached trust obligations with respect to the management of the plaintiffs' individual Indian monies. The plaintiffs have not made claims for specific dollar amounts in the Federal district court proceedings, but in public statements have asserted that the class is owed tens of billions of dollars.

• North American Free Trade Agreement (NAFTA) allows Canadian and Mexican investors to bring arbitration proceedings against the United States for breaches of certain NAFTA provisions. These cases raise allegations of expropriation as well as other claims of treatment inconsistent with international law or specific treaty commitments that provide investment protections. The United States has successfully defended itself against two claims submitted to arbitration under Chapter 11 of the NAFTA. The United States is currently defending itself against eight claims submitted to arbitration and nine claims not yet submitted under Chapter 11 of NAFTA. These claims total approximately $3.4 billion. The United States has also received notice of another claim not submitted in the amount of either $5.8 billion or $13.6 billion, depending on how one interprets the notice.

Environmental and Disposal Contingencies

The Government is subject to loss contingencies for a variety of environmental cleanup costs for the storage and disposal of hazardous material and the operations and closures of facilities at which environmental contamination may be present and remediation costs.

Management and legal counsel have determined that it is "probable" that some of these actions will result in a loss to the Federal Government and the loss amounts are reasonably measurable. The estimated liabilities for these cases are $5.2 billion and $2.1 billion for 2005 and 2004, respectively, and are recorded in the balance sheet line items "Environmental Liabilities," or "Other Liabilities." For example, DOE is subject to Spent Nuclear Fuel litigation for damages suffered by all utilities as a result of the delay in beginning disposal of spent nuclear fuel. Significant claims for partial breach of contract have been filed with estimated liability amounts of $5 billion and $1.9 billion for 2005 and 2004, respectively.

There are also administrative claims and legal actions pending where adverse decisions are considered by management and legal counsel as "reasonably possible" with an estimate of possible liability or a range of possible liability. The estimated potential losses for such claims are $927 million and $1.7 billion for 2005 and 2004, respectively. The Department of Commerce has estimated liabilities for a variety of cleanup costs, many of which are associated with the Second World War at various sites within the United States in the amounts of $832 million and $1.6 billion for 2005 and 2004, respectively.

Other Contingencies

DOT has large contingency amounts for "Advance Construction" projects and Full Funding Grant Agreements authorizing States to establish budgets and incur costs with their own funds in advance of annual appropriation from Congress totaling $42.9 billion and $38.9 billion for 2005 and 2004, respectively.

Note 20. Commitments

The Government has entered into contractual commitments that require future use of financial resources. It has significant amounts of long-term lease obligations and undelivered orders as shown in the following table. Undelivered orders represent the value of goods and services ordered that have not yet been received.

The Government has other contractual commitments that may require future use of financial resources. For example, the Government has callable subscriptions in the Multilateral Development Banks (MDB), which are autonomous international financial entities that finance economic and social development projects in developing countries. Callable capital resembles promissory notes to honor MDB debts if the MDB cannot otherwise meet its obligations through its other available resources. MDBs are able to use callable capital as backing to obtain very favorable financing terms when borrowing from world capital markets. Treasury officials do not anticipate any calls on MDB subscriptions. To date, there has never been a call on this capital for any of the major MDBs.

Commitments as of September 30

(In billions of dollars)	Capital Leases	Operating Leases	Capital Leases	Operating Leases
	2005		2004	
General Services Administration	0.3	22.9	0.3	22.1
U.S. Postal Service	-	9.6	0.6	9.6
Department of Homeland Security	0.1	1.4	0.1	0.5
Department of Health and Human Services	-	1.4	-	1.0
Securities and Exchange Commission	-	0.9	-	0.6
Other long-term leases	1.1	3.8	0.9	2.8
Total long-term leases	1.5	40.0	1.9	36.6

	Undelivered Orders	
	2005	2004
Department of Defense	174.5	185.7
Department of Housing and Urban Development	68.4	71.6
Department of Transportation	68.1	68.1
Department of Health and Human Services	67.9	67.4
Department of Education	46.4	46.4
Department of the Treasury	44.4	39.1
Department of Homeland Security	23.3	16.7
Department of Agriculture	16.0	14.0
Agency for International Development	13.0	11.4
Department of Energy	10.3	10.1
Environmental Protection Agency	9.7	9.7
Department of Justice	9.1	9.9
Department of State	7.3	7.1
National Science Foundation	7.1	6.9
Department of Interior	6.4	5.6
Other undeliverable orders	25.4	26.6
Total undelivered orders	597.3	596.3

	Other Commitments	
	2005	2004
Callable capital subscriptions for multi-lateral development banks	62.0	61.7
Department of Agriculture	23.0	52.0
Department of Energy	12.7	14.5
Department of Commerce	7.5	7.7
Tennessee Valley Authority	7.4	8.0
Department of Transportation	3.6	4.7
Department of the Treasury	-	8.5
Total other commitments	116.2	157.1

Other Commitments and Risks

The U.S. Government is a party to major treaties and other international agreements. These treaties and other international agreements address various issues including, but not limited to, trade, commerce, security, and arms that may involve financial obligations or give rise to possible exposure to losses. A comprehensive analysis to determine any such financial obligations or possible exposure to loss and their related effect on the consolidated financial statements of the U.S. Government has not yet been performed.

In addition, the United States Government has entered into other agreements that could potentially require claims on Government resources in the future. Examples include war risk and terrorism risk insurance.

Note 21. Dedicated Collections

Dedicated Collections as of September 30, 2005*

(In millions of dollars)	Federal Old-Age & Survivors Insurance Trust Fund	Civil Service Retirement & Disability Fund	Federal Hospital Insurance Trust Fund (Medicare Part A)	Federal Disability Insurance Trust Fund	Military Retirement Fund	Medicare-Eligible Retiree Health Care Fund (MERHCF)
Assets:						
Fund balance	(384.0)	23.0	366.0	(73.0)	22.9	5.0
Investments	1,616,159.0	660,750.0	280,996.0	193,263.0	197,807.1	60,691.7
Other Federal assets	20,936.0	9,684.0	17,978.0	2,539.0	-	32.9
Non-Federal assets	1,965.0	276.0	3,126.0	2,480.0	26.7	11.3
Total assets	1,638,676.0	670,733.0	302,466.0	198,209.0	197,856.7	60,740.9
Liabilities:						
Liabilities due and payable to beneficiaries	39,213.0	4,323.0	16,806.0	22,375.0	-	-
Other liabilities	3,940.0	1,215,432.0	18,906.0	697.0	895,434.0	538,401.0
Total liabilities	43,153.0	1,219,755.0	35,712.0	23,072.0	895,434.0	538,401.0
Total net position	1,595,523.0	(549,022.0)	266,754.0	175,137.0	(697,577.3)	(477,660.1)
Total liabilities and net position	1,638,676.0	670,733.0	302,466.0	198,209.0	197,856.7	60,740.9
Change in Net Position:						
Beginning net position	1,433,278.0	(537,448.0)	253,259.0	170,598.0	(649,695.1)	(466,096.2)
Nonexchange revenue	585,819.0	-	184,457.0	95,591.0	-	-
Other financing sources	16.0	25,652.0	9,431.0	47.0	-	-
Other changes in fund balance	9,416.0	-	-	(1,221.0)	-	-
Exchange revenue	-	57,864.0	2,314.0	-	48,812.2	28,412.4
Program expenses	433,006.0	95,090.0	180,380.0	89,878.0	96,694.4	39,976.3
Other expenses	-	-	2,327.0	-	-	-
Ending net position	1,595,523.0	(549,022.0)	266,754.0	175,137.0	(697,577.3)	(477,660.1)

* By law, certain expenses (costs), revenues, and other financing sources related to the administration of the above funds are not charged to the funds and are therefore financed and/or credited to other sources.

Dedicated Collections as of September 30, 2005*

(In millions of dollars)	Unemploy- ment Trust Fund	Federal Supplemen- tary Medical Insurance Trust Fund (Medicare Part B)	Railroad Retirement Trust Fund	Land and Water Conserva- tion Fund	Foreign Service Retirement and Disability Fund
Assets:					
Fund balance	(273.0)	1,303.0	43.3	-	0.1
Investments	54,805.9	17,448.0	2,156.3	14,303.5	13,359.4
Other Federal assets	979.0	29,345.0	3,644.3	-	196.8
Non-Federal assets	1,418.1	3,424.0	26,438.8	-	1.9
Total assets	56,930.0	51,520.0	32,282.7	14,303.5	13,558.2
Liabilities:					
Liabilities due and payable to beneficiaries	931.7	16,593.0	787.4	-	45.9
Other liabilities	1,501.8	25,661.0	3,784.2	-	13,439.8
Total liabilities	2,433.5	42,254.0	4,571.6	-	13,485.7
Total net position	54,496.5	9,266.0	27,711.1	14,303.5	72.5
Total liabilities and net position	56,930.0	51,520.0	32,282.7	14,303.5	13,558.2
Change in Net Position:					
Beginning net position	45,395.9	10,043.0	25,319.5	13,859.2	(345.8)
Nonexchange revenue	44,404.4	1,336.0	5,010.7	-	-
Other financing sources	0.1	115,784.0	3,176.0	444.3	-
Other changes in fund balance	(3,815.0)	(2,577.0)	-	-	-
Exchange revenue	-	35,945.0	4,868.5	-	1,206.8
Program expenses	31,488.9	149,463.0	10,664.2	-	-
Other expenses	-	1,802.0	(0.6)	-	788.5
Ending net position	54,496.5	9,266.0	27,711.1	14,303.5	72.5

* By law, certain expenses (costs), revenues, and other financing sources related to the administration of the above funds are not charged to the funds and are therefore financed and/or credited to other sources.

Dedicated Collections as of September 30, 2005*

(In millions of dollars)	National Service Life Insurance Fund	Airport and Airway Trust Fund	Highway Trust Fund	Hazardous Substance Superfund	Black Lung Disability Trust Fund
Assets:					
Fund balance	9.0	692.3	2,549.0	7.2	41.9
Investments	10,758.0	10,047.4	8,270.6	2,293.0	-
Other Federal assets	505.0	85.6	-	4.2	-
Non-Federal assets	-	-	-	-	9.1
Total assets	11,272.0	10,825.3	10,819.6	2,304.4	51.0
Liabilities:					
Liabilities due and payable to beneficiaries	142.0	-	-	-	24.4
Other liabilities	10,846.0	3,507.7	11,708.0	-	9,186.6
Total liabilities	10,988.0	3,507.7	11,708.0	-	9,211.0
Total net position	284.0	7,317.6	(888.4)	2,304.4	(9,160.0)
Total liabilities and net position	11,272.0	10,825.3	10,819.6	2,304.4	51.0
Change in Net Position:					
Beginning net position	283.0	6,959.1	5,562.3	2,394.5	(8,711.4)
Nonexchange revenue	-	10,699.9	37,892.6	69.0	611.1
Other financing sources	1.0	-	34.8	1,247.5	-
Other changes in fund balance	-	-	-	-	(56.7)
Exchange revenue	1,081.0	-	-	52.5	-
Program expenses	1,081.0	10,341.4	44,378.1	1,459.1	1,003.0
Other expenses	-	-	-	-	-
Ending net position	284.0	7,317.6	(888.4)	2,304.4	(9,160.0)

* By law, certain expenses (costs), revenues, and other financing sources related to the administration of the above funds are not charged to the funds and are therefore financed and/or credited to other sources.

Dedicated Collections as of September 30, 2004*

(In millions of dollars)	Federal Old-Age & Survivors Insurance Trust Fund	Civil Service Retirement & Disability Fund	Federal Hospital Insurance Trust Fund (Medicare Part A)	Federal Disability Insurance Trust Fund	Military Retirement Fund	Medicare-Eligible Retiree Health Care Fund (MERHCF)
Assets:						
Fund balance	46.0	13.0	600.0	(14.0)	20.7	5.0
Investments	1,452,599.0	631,859.0	268,080.0	182,799.0	187,962.5	38,585.2
Other Federal assets	19,822.0	9,525.0	16,185.0	2,493.0	-	-
Non-Federal assets	1,850.0	258.0	750.0	2,105.0	25.2	8.0
Total assets	1,474,317.0	641,655.0	285,615.0	187,383.0	188,008.4	38,598.2
Liabilities:						
Liabilities due and payable to beneficiaries	37,055.0	4,114.0	15,043.0	16,048.0	-	-
Other liabilities	3,984.0	1,174,989.0	17,313.0	737.0	837,703.5	504,694.4
Total liabilities	41,039.0	1,179,103.0	32,356.0	16,785.0	837,703.5	504,694.4
Total net position	1,433,278.0	(537,448.0)	253,259.0	170,598.0	(649,695.1)	(466,096.2)
Total liabilities and net position	1,474,317.0	641,655.0	285,615.0	187,383.0	188,008.4	38,598.2
Change in Net Position:						
Beginning net position	1,294,528.0	(529,025.0)	241,670.0	158,005.0	(556,416.7)	(458,080.9)
Nonexchange revenue	557,167.0	-	168,775.0	90,110.0	-	-
Other financing sources	12.0	25,957.0	9,187.0	73.0	-	(2,843.3)
Other changes in fund balance	(5,656.0)	-	(45.0)	(2,317.0)	-	-
Exchange revenue	-	56,159.0	1,807.0	-	42,384.5	25,342.4
Program expenses	412,773.0	90,539.0	167,215.0	75,273.0	135,662.9	30,514.4
Other expenses	-	-	920.0	-	-	-
Ending net position	1,433,278.0	(537,448.0)	253,259.0	170,598.0	(649,695.1)	(466,096.2)

* By law, certain expenses (costs), revenues, and other financing sources related to the administration of the above funds are not charged to the funds and are therefore financed and/or credited to other sources.

Dedicated Collections as of September 30, 2004*

(In millions of dollars)	Unemploy- ment Trust Fund	Federal Supplemen- tary Medical Insurance Trust Fund (Medicare Part B)	Railroad Retirement Trust Fund	Land and Water Conserva- tion Fund	Foreign Service Retirement and Disability Fund
Assets:					
Fund balance	157.6	1,943.0	21.6	13,859.2	-
Investments	45,239.4	17,712.0	1,302.2	-	12,827.6
Other Federal assets	911.3	30,441.0	3,714.8	-	196.0
Non-Federal assets	1,638.6	1,251.0	24,681.7	-	2.5
Total assets	47,946.9	51,347.0	29,720.3	13,859.2	13,026.1
Liabilities:					
Liabilities due and payable to beneficiaries	1,128.5	14,832.0	770.7	-	44.1
Other liabilities	1,422.5	26,472.0	3,630.1	-	13,327.8
Total liabilities	2,551.0	41,304.0	4,400.8	-	13,371.9
Total net position	45,395.9	10,043.0	25,319.5	13,859.2	(345.8)
Total liabilities and net position	47,946.9	51,347.0	29,720.3	13,859.2	13,026.1
Change in Net Position:					
Beginning net position	47,577.2	14,100.0	23,374.5	13,443.8	(653.8)
Nonexchange revenue	41,744.4	1,602.0	4,892.7	-	-
Other financing sources	-	95,493.0	3,330.1	415.4	-
Other changes in fund balance	(3,028.1)	2,265.0	-	-	-
Exchange revenue	-	30,344.0	7,562.6	-	1,185.6
Program expenses	40,897.6	132,458.0	13,841.1	-	-
Other expenses	-	1,303.0	(0.7)	-	877.6
Ending net position	45,395.9	10,043.0	25,319.5	13,859.2	(345.8)

* By law, certain expenses (costs), revenues, and other financing sources related to the administration of the above funds are not charged to the funds and are therefore financed and/or credited to other sources.

Dedicated Collections as of September 30, 2004*

(In millions of dollars)	National Service Life Insurance Fund	Airport and Airway Trust Fund	Highway Trust Fund	Hazardous Substance Superfund	Black Lung Disability Trust Fund
Assets:					
Fund balance	10.0	642.0	3,349.7	188.2	43.8
Investments	11,121.0	9,891.6	10,211.9	2,217.3	-
Other Federal assets	545.0	129.5	-	-	-
Non-Federal assets	-	-	-	-	10.7
Total assets	11,676.0	10,663.1	13,561.6	2,405.5	54.5
Liabilities:					
Liabilities due and payable to beneficiaries	142.0	-	-	-	25.3
Other liabilities	11,251.0	3,704.0	7,999.3	11.0	8,740.6
Total liabilities	11,393.0	3,704.0	7,999.3	11.0	8,765.9
Total net position	283.0	6,959.1	5,562.3	2,394.5	(8,711.4)
Total liabilities and net position	11,676.0	10,663.1	13,561.6	2,405.5	54.5
Change in Net Position:					
Beginning net position	309.0	8,123.5	11,799.7	2,517.0	(8,227.0)
Nonexchange revenue	-	9,674.5	34,710.8	77.8	566.3
Other financing sources	1.0	-	(398.0)	1,257.5	-
Other changes in fund balance	-	-	-	-	(55.7)
Exchange revenue	1,184.0	-	-	27.4	-
Program expenses	1,211.0	10,838.9	40,550.2	1,485.2	995.0
Other expenses	-	-	-	-	-
Ending net position	283.0	6,959.1	5,562.3	2,394.5	(8,711.4)

* By law, certain expenses (costs), revenues, and other financing sources related to the administration of the above funds are not charged to the funds and are therefore financed and/or credited to other sources.

The previous tables above depict selected trust funds that have been chosen based on their financial activity. Additionally, the Federal Government has many other dedicated collections and trust funds.

In the Federal budget, the term "trust fund" means only that the law requires a particular fund be accounted for separately, used only for a specified purpose, and designated as a trust fund.

A change in law may change the future receipts and the terms under which the fund's resources are spent. In the private sector, trust fund refers to funds of one party held and managed by a second party (the trustee) in a fiduciary capacity.

The line item "investments," listed under assets in the previous tables, refers to investments in Federal debt securities, net of unamortized discounts and premiums. Total assets represent the unexpended balance from all sources of receipts and amounts due the trust funds, regardless of source, including related Governmental transactions. These are transactions between two different entities within the Government (for example, monies received by one entity of the Government from another entity of the Government).

Most of the trust fund assets are invested in intragovernmental debt holdings. These securities require redemption if a fund's disbursements exceed its receipts. Redeeming these securities will increase the Government's financing needs and require more borrowing from the public (or less repayment of debt), or will result in higher taxes than otherwise would have been needed, or less spending on other programs than otherwise would have occurred, or some combination thereof.

Depicted on the next page is a description of all the funds included in the table Dedicated Collections as of September 30, which also includes the names of the Government agencies that administer each particular fund. For detailed information regarding trust funds, please refer to the financial statements of the corresponding administering agencies. For information on the actuarial and other liabilities associated with the funds in this report, see Note 11—Federal Employee and Veteran Benefits Payable and Note 13—Benefits Due and Payable.

Federal Old-Age and Survivors Insurance Trust Fund

The Federal Old-Age and Survivors Insurance Trust Fund, administered by SSA, provides a basic annuity to workers to protect them from loss of income at retirement and provides a guaranteed income to survivors in the event of the death of a family's primary wage earner.

Payroll and self-employment taxes primarily fund the Federal Old-Age and Survivors Insurance Trust Fund. Interest earnings on Treasury securities, Federal agencies' payments for the Social Security benefits earned by military and Federal civilian employees, and Treasury payments for a portion of income taxes collected on Social Security benefits provide the fund with additional income. The law establishing the Federal Old-Age and Survivors Insurance Trust Fund and authorizing the depositing of amounts to the credit of the trust fund is set forth in 42 U.S.C. § 401.

Civil Service Retirement and Disability Fund

The CSRDF covers two Federal civilian retirement systems: CSRS—for employees hired before 1984, and FERS—for employees hired after 1983. OPM administers the CSRS and the FERS systems. The laws establishing the CSRDF and authorizing the depositing of amounts to the credit of the trust fund are set forth in 5 U.S.C. § 8334-8348. Funding sources include:

- Federal civilian employees' contributions.
- Agencies' contributions on behalf of employees.
- Appropriations.
- Interest earned on investments in Treasury securities.

Federal Hospital Insurance Trust Fund (Medicare Part A)

The Federal Hospital Insurance Trust Fund finances the Hospital Insurance Program (Medicare Part A). This program funds the cost of inpatient hospital and related care for individuals age 65 or older who meet certain insured status requirements, and eligible disabled people. HHS administers the program.

The Federal Hospital Insurance Trust Fund is financed primarily by payroll taxes, including those paid by Federal agencies. It also receives income from interest earnings on Treasury securities and a portion of income taxes collected on Social Security benefits. The law establishing the Federal Hospital Insurance Trust Fund and authorizing the depositing of amounts to the credit of the trust fund is set forth in 42 U.S.C. § 1395i.

Federal Disability Insurance Trust Fund

The Federal Disability Insurance Trust Fund provides assistance and protection against the loss of earnings due to a wage earner's disability in the form of money payments. SSA administers the Federal Disability Insurance Trust Fund.

Like the Federal Old-Age and Survivors Insurance Trust Fund, payroll taxes primarily fund the Federal Disability Insurance Trust Fund. The fund also receives income from interest earnings on Treasury securities, Federal agencies' payments for the Social Security benefits earned by military and Federal civilian employees, and a portion of income taxes collected on Social Security benefits. The law establishing the Federal Disability Insurance Trust Fund and authorizing the depositing of amounts to the credit of the trust fund is set forth in 42 U.S.C. § 401.

Military Retirement Fund

The Military Retirement Fund provides retirement benefits for Army, Navy, Marine Corps, and Air Force personnel and their survivors. The fund is financed by DOD contributions, appropriations, and interest earned on investments in Federal debt securities. DOD administers the Military Retirement Fund. The laws establishing the Military Retirement Fund and authorizing the depositing of amounts to the credit of the trust fund are set forth in 10 U.S.C. § 1461-1467.

Medicare-Eligible Retiree Health Care Fund

The Medicare-Eligible Retiree Health Care Fund, administered by DOD and established by 10 U.S.C. § 1111, finances and pays the liabilities under the DOD retiree health care programs for Medicare-eligible beneficiaries. Such beneficiaries include qualifying members, former members, and dependents of the Uniformed Services. The assets of the fund are comprised of any amounts appropriated to the fund, payments to the fund authorized by 10 U.S.C. § 1116, and interest on investments authorized by 10 U.S.C. § 1117.

Unemployment Trust Fund

The UTF provides temporary assistance to workers who lose their jobs. The program is administered through a unique system of Federal and State partnerships, established in Federal law, but executed through conforming State laws by State officials. DOL administers the Federal operations of the program.

Taxes on employers provide the primary funding source for the UTF. However, interest earned on investments in Treasury securities also provides income to the fund. Appropriations have supplemented the fund's income during periods of high and extended unemployment. The law establishing the UTF and authorizing the depositing of amounts to the credit of the trust fund is set forth in 42 U.S.C. § 1104.

Federal Supplementary Medical Insurance Trust Fund (Medicare Part B)

The Federal Supplementary Medical Insurance Trust Fund finances the Supplementary Medical Insurance Program (Medicare Part B) that provides supplementary medical insurance for enrolled eligible participants to cover physician and out-patient services not covered by Medicare Part A. HHS administers the program.

Medicare Part B financing is not based on payroll taxes; it is based on monthly premiums and income from the General Fund of the Treasury. The law establishing the Federal Supplementary Medical Insurance Trust Fund and authorizing the depositing of amounts to the credit of the trust fund is set forth in 42 U.S.C. § 1395t.

Railroad Retirement Trust Fund

The Railroad Retirement Trust Fund provides annuities and survivor benefits to eligible railroad employees and their survivors.

The fund also pays disability annuities based on total or occupational disability. Payroll taxes paid by railroad employers and their employees provide the primary source of income for the Railroad Retirement Survivor Benefit program. The law establishing the Railroad Retirement Trust Fund and authorizing the depositing of amounts to the credit of the trust fund is set forth in 45 U.S.C. § 231n and 45 U.S.C. § 231n-1.

The Railroad Retirement and Survivors' Improvement Act, enacted on December 21, 2001, created the National Railroad Retirement Investment Trust to administer the new fund, which is allowed to invest in Federal debt securities as well as other investments outside of the U.S. Government (see Railroad Retirement in the Stewardship Information section).

Land and Water Conservation Fund

The Land and Water Conservation Fund (LWCF) is administered by DOI and was enacted in 1964, Public Law 88-578, to create and maintain a nationwide legacy of high quality recreation areas and facilities. The LWCF Act established a funding source for both Federal acquisition of authorized national park, conservation, and recreation areas as well as grants to State and local governments to help them acquire, develop, and improve outdoor recreation areas. Annually, $903 million for the LWCF are transferred from the Minerals Management Service to the National Park Service, the majority of which are from royalties from Outer Continental Shelf oil deposits. Each year, amounts from the LWCF are warranted to some of the bureaus within the DOI and the rest to the Department of Agriculture's Forest Service. The law establishing the Land and Water Conservation Fund and authorizing the depositing of amounts to the credit of the trust fund is set forth in 16 U.S.C. § 4601-11.

Foreign Service Retirement and Disability Fund

The Foreign Service Retirement and Disability Fund (FSRD) is administered by the Department of State and provides pensions to retired and disabled members of the Foreign Service. The FSRD's revenues consist of contributions from active participants and their U.S. Government agency employers, appropriations, and interest on investments in Treasury securities. Monthly annuity payments are made to eligible retired employees or their survivors. Separated employees without title to an annuity may take a refund of their contributions. P.L. 96-465 limits the amount of administrative expense that can be charged to the fund to $5,000 per year. Cash is invested in U.S. Treasury securities until it is needed. The laws establishing the Foreign Service Retirement and Disability Fund and authorizing the deposit of amounts to the credit of the trust fund are set forth in 22 U.S.C. § 4042 and 22 U.S.C. § 4045.

National Service Life Insurance Fund

The National Service Life Insurance Program (NSLI) covers policyholders who served during World War II. The program opened October 8, 1940, when it became clear that large-scale military inductions were imminent. Over 22 million policies were issued under the NSLI Program. The majority of policies administered directly by the Department of Veteran's Affairs are NSLI policies. This program remained opened until April 25, 1951, when two new programs were established for Korean War service members and veterans. The financing sources for the NSLI come from the public and veterans. The law establishing the NSLI Program and authorizing the depositing of amounts to the credit of the trust fund is set forth in 38 U.S.C. § 1920.

Airport and Airway Trust Fund

The Airport and Airway Trust Fund provides for airport improvement and airport facilities maintenance. It also funds airport equipment, research, and a portion of the Federal Aviation Administration's administrative operational support. DOT administers the Airport and Airway Trust Fund. The law establishing the Airport and Airway Trust Fund and authorizing the depositing of amounts to the credit of the trust fund is set forth in 26 U.S.C. § 9502. Funding sources include:

- Taxes received from transportation of persons and property in the air, as well as fuel used in non-commercial aircraft.
- International departure taxes.
- Interest earned on investments in Treasury securities.

Highway Trust Fund

The Highway Trust Fund was established to promote domestic interstate transportation and to move people and goods. The fund provides Federal grants to States for highway construction, certain transit programs, and related transportation purposes. DOT administers programs financed by the Highway Trust Fund.

The law establishing the Highway Trust Fund and authorizing the depositing of amounts to the credit of the trust fund is set forth in 26 U.S.C. § 9503. Funding sources include earmarked taxes on gasoline and other fuels, certain tires, the initial sale of heavy trucks, and highway use by commercial motor vehicles. Deposits not needed immediately for payments are invested by the Treasury's Bureau of Public Debt in noninterest bearing public debt securities. As funds are needed for payments, the Highway Trust Fund Corpus investments are liquidated and funds are transferred to the Federal Highway Administration for payment of obligations.

Hazardous Substance Superfund

The Hazardous Substance Superfund was authorized to address public health and environmental threats from spills of hazardous materials and from sites contaminated with hazardous substances. The Environmental Protection Agency administers the fund. The law establishing the Hazardous Substance Superfund and authorizing the depositing of amounts to the credit of the trust fund is set forth in 26 U.S.C. § 9507. Funding sources include:

- Fines, penalties, and cost recoveries from responsible parties.
- Appropriations.
- Interest earned on investments in Treasury securities.

Black Lung Disability Trust Fund

The BLDTF provides benefits to coal miners who are totally disabled due to pneumoconiosis (black lung disease). It also covers surviving dependents of miners who died due to pneumoconiosis.

Excise taxes on coal mine operators, based on the sale of coal, partially fund black lung disability payments as well as related administrative and interest costs. Intragovernmental advances to the BLDTF, which must be repaid with interest, fund the shortfall. DOL administers the BLDTF. The law establishing the BLDTF and authorizing the depositing of amounts to the credit of the trust fund is set forth in 26 U.S.C. § 9501.

Note 22. Indian Trust Funds

The Indian Trust Funds differ from other dedicated collections reported in Note 21—Dedicated Collections. DOI has responsibility for the assets held in trust on behalf of American Indian tribes and individuals.

DOI, through the Office of the Special Trustee's (OST's) Office of Trust Funds Management, holds trust funds in accounts for Indian tribes. It maintains approximately 1,400 accounts for Tribal and Other Special Trust Funds (including the Alaska Native Escrow Fund). The OST was established by the American Indian Trust Fund Management Reform Act of 1994 (Public Law 103-412) and was created to improve the accountability and management of Indian funds held in trust by the Federal Government.

The balances that have accumulated in the Tribal and Other Special Trust Funds have resulted from judgment awards, settlements of claims, land use agreements, royalties on natural resource depletion, and other proceeds derived directly from trust resources and investment income.

The trust fund balances included in the Trust Funds Held for Indian Tribes and Other Special Trust Funds contain two categories: trust funds held for Indian tribes (considered non-Federal funds) and trust funds held by DOI for future transfer to a tribe upon satisfaction of certain conditions or where the corpus of the fund is non-expendable (considered Federal funds).

The tables below depict the U.S. Government as trustee for Indian Trust Funds Held for Indian Tribes and Other Special Trust Funds. The Other Special Trust Funds included in the table below ($277.3 billion and $266.4 billion for fiscal years 2005 and 2004, respectively, identified in DOI's financial statements) and trust funds considered Federal funds are included in DOI's financial statements.

U.S. Government as Trustee for Indian Trust Funds Held for Indian Tribes and Other Special Trust Funds
Statement of Assets and Trust Fund Balances as of September 30

(In millions of dollars)	2005	2004
Assets		
Current Assets:		
Cash and cash equivalents	501.6	490.4
Due from other Federal agencies[1]	-	7.8
Investments	2,380.2	2,477.0
Total assets	2,881.8	2,975.3[2]
Trust fund balances, held for Indian Tribes and by DOI	2,881.8	2,975.3

[1]This represents an amount that the Bureau of Indian Affairs (BIA) erroneously transferred from the trust funds' account at the U.S. Treasury into the BIA's account at the U.S. Treasury. This amount was transferred on September 30, 2004, and was returned to the proper U.S. Treasury account in October of 2004. The erroneous transfer, which was identified through OST's reconciliation and internal control process, did not impact the interest earnings to the trust funds.
[2]Details may not add to totals due to rounding.

U.S. Government as Trustee for Indian Trust Funds Held for Indian Tribes and Other Special Trust Funds
Statement of Changes in Trust Fund Balances as of September 30

(In millions of dollars)	2005	2004
Receipts	517.7	413.7
Disbursements	(611.2)	(318.5)
Increase (decrease) in trust fund balances, net	(93.5)	95.2
Trust fund balances, beginning of year	2,975.3	2,880.1
Trust fund balances, end of year	2,881.8	2,975.3

OST also maintains about 266,000 open Individual Indian Monies (IIM) accounts. The IIM fund is primarily a deposit fund for individuals who have a beneficial interest in the trust funds. The IIM account-holders realize receipts primarily from royalties on natural resource depletion, land use agreements, and enterprises that have a direct relationship to trust fund resources and investment income. Funds related to the IIM Trust Fund are included in the following tables.

U.S. Government as Trustee for Indian Trust Funds Held for Individual Indian Monies Trust Funds
Statement of Assets and Trust Fund Balances as of September 30

(In millions of dollars)	2005	2004
Assets:		
Cash and cash equivalents	28.3	21.4
Investments	388.6	371.7
Accrued interest receivable	3.0	3.6
Total assets	419.9	396.7
Trust fund balances, held for individual Indians	419.9	396.7

U.S. Government as Trustee for Indian Trust Funds Held for Individual Indian Monies Trust Funds
Statement of Changes in Trust Fund Balances as of September 30

(In millions of dollars)	2005	2004
Receipts	301.6	204.6
Disbursements	(278.4)	(221.0)
Increase (decrease) in trust fund balances, net	23.2	(16.4)
Trust fund balances, beginning of year	396.7	413.1
Trust fund balances, end of year	419.9	396.7

The amounts presented in the four tables of this note were prepared using a cash basis of accounting, which is a comprehensive basis of accounting other than GAAP. Receivables and payables are not recorded, and investment premiums and discounts are not amortized in the Trust Funds Held for Indian Tribes and Other Special Trust Funds. Receipts are recorded when received and disbursements when paid, and investments are stated at historical cost. The only basis of accounting difference between the Trust Funds Held for Indian Tribes and Other Special Trust Funds and the IIM Trust Fund is that the latter records the receivables and payables related to accrued interest and dividends when earned, including amortization of investment discounts and premiums, and investments are stated at amortized cost.

United States Government Supplemental Information (Unaudited) for the Years Ended September 30, 2005, and September 30, 2004

Deferred Maintenance

Deferred maintenance is the estimated cost to bring Government-owned property to an acceptable condition, resulting from not performing maintenance on a timely basis. Deferred maintenance excludes the cost of expanding the capacity of assets or upgrading them to serve needs different from those originally intended. The consequences of not performing regular maintenance could include increased safety hazards, poor service to the public, higher costs in the future, and inefficient operations. Estimated deferred maintenance costs are not accrued in the Statements of Net Cost or recognized as a liability on the balance sheets.

The amounts disclosed for deferred maintenance on the following table have been measured using the following three methods:

- Condition assessment surveys are periodic inspections of the Government-owned property to determine the current condition and estimated cost to bring the property to an acceptable condition.
- Life-cycle cost forecast is an acquisition or procurement technique that considers operation, maintenance, and other costs in addition to the acquisition cost of assets.
- Management analysis method is founded on inflation-adjusted reductions in maintenance funding since the base year.

Some deferred maintenance has been deemed critical. Such amounts and conditions are defined by the individual agencies with responsibility for the safekeeping of these assets. Low and high estimates are based on the materiality of the estimated cost of returning the asset to the acceptable condition versus the total value of the corresponding asset.

Deferred Maintenance as of September 30

| | Deferred Maintenance Cost Range | | | | Critical Maintenance | |
| | Low Estimate | | High Estimate | | | |
(In billions of dollars)	2005	2004	2005	2004	2005	2004
Asset Category:						
Buildings, structures, and facilities	23.2	13.4	33.7	25.2	11.4	7.6
Furniture, fixtures, and equipment	-	-	0.1	0.1	0.1	0.1
Other general property, plant, and equipment	1.1	-	1.1	-	-	-
Heritage assets...........................	1.7	-	2.9	0.1	0.1	-
Total deferred maintenance....	26.0	13.4	37.8	25.4	11.6	7.7

Unexpended Budget Authority

Unexpended budget authority is the sum of the unobligated and obligated, but unliquidated, budget authority. Unobligated budget authority, including amounts for trust funds, is the cumulative amount of budget authority that is not obligated and that remains available for obligation. In 1-year accounts, the unobligated balance is not available for new obligations after the end of the fiscal year. In multiyear accounts, the unobligated balance may be carried forward and remains available for obligation for the period specified. In no-year accounts, the unobligated balance is carried forward until specifically rescinded by law or until the purposes for which it was provided have been accomplished. The total unobligated budget authority amount balance for fiscal years 2005 and 2004 are $541.1 billion and $407.3 billion, respectively.

Obligated budget authority is the cumulative amount of budget authority that has been obligated but not liquidated. This balance can be carried forward for a maximum of 5 years after the appropriation has expired. The total obligated budget authority amount balance for fiscal years 2005 and 2004 are $927.6 billion and $863.8 billion, respectively.

The President's Budget with fiscal year 2005 actuals is expected to be published in February 2006. The amounts initially reported as balances for unexpended budget authority at the end of fiscal year 2004 were estimates from the President's Budget that was issued in February 2004.

Tax Burden

The Internal Revenue Code provides for progressive tax rates, whereby higher incomes are generally subject to higher tax rates. The tables present the latest available information on income tax and related income, deductions, and credit for individuals by income level and for corporations by size of assets.

Individual Income Tax Returns for Tax Year 2003

Adjusted Gross Income (AGI)	Number of Taxable Returns (In thousands)	AGI (In millions of dollars)	Total Income Tax (In millions of dollars)	Average AGI per Return (In whole dollars)	Average Income Tax per Return (In whole dollars)	Income Tax as a Percentage of AGI
Under $15,000	37,985	211,227	3,645	5,560	96	1.7%
$15,000 under $30,000	29,739	653,834	24,728	21,987	832	3.8%
$30,000 under $50,000	24,469	954,681	64,430	39,015	2,633	6.7%
$50,000 under $100,000	26,935	1,889,302	178,640	70,142	6,632	9.5%
$100,000 under $200,000	8,902	1,174,675	164,509	131,966	18,481	14.0%
$200,000 or more	2,541	1,329,254	314,073	523,154	123,610	23.6%
Total	130,571	6,212,973	750,025	-	-	-

Corporation Income Tax Returns for Tax Year 2002

Total Assets	Income Subject to Tax (In millions of dollars)	Total Income Tax after Credits (In millions of dollars)	Percentage of Income Tax after Credits to Taxable Income
Zero assets	8,045.0	2,311.0	28.7%
$1 under $500	8,072.0	1,453.0	18.0%
$500 under $1,000	3,745.0	843.0	22.5%
$1,000 under $5,000	11,750.0	3,377.0	28.7%
$5,000 under $10,000	6,413.0	2,073.0	32.3%
$10,000 under $25,000	9,358.0	3,007.0	32.1%
$25,000 under $50,000	8,640.0	2,774.0	32.1%
$50,000 under $100,000	10,090.0	3,198.0	31.7%
$100,000 under $250,000	21,072.0	6,524.0	31.0%
$250,000 or more	513,369.0	128,052.0	24.9%
Total	600,554.0	153,612.0	25.6%

Tax Gap

The tax gap is the aggregate amount of tax (i.e., excluding interest and penalties) that is imposed by the tax laws for any given tax year but is not paid voluntarily and timely. The Internal Revenue Service (IRS) currently projects that the annual Federal gross tax gap is somewhere between $312 billion and $353 billion. This estimate is based on the preliminary results of the National Research Program (NRP). The NRP was a study conducted to measure the compliance rate of the individual filers based on examination of a statistical sample of their filed returns for tax year 2001. The tax gap arises from three types of noncompliance: not filing timely tax returns (the nonfiling gap), underreporting the correct amount of tax on timely-filed returns (the underreporting gap), and not paying on time the full amount reported on timely-filed returns (the underpayment gap). Of these three components, only the underpayment gap is observed; the nonfiling gap and the underreporting gap must be estimated. Each instance of non-compliance by a taxpayer contributes to the tax gap, whether or not the IRS detects it, and whether or not the taxpayer is even aware of the noncompliance. The tax gap does not include under-payments by corporate taxpayers or include taxes that should have been paid on income from the illegal sector of the economy.

Underreporting of income tax, employment taxes, and other taxes represents 80 percent of the tax gap. The single largest sub-component of underreporting involves individuals understating their income, taking improper deductions, overstating business expenses, and erroneously claiming credits. Individual underre-porting represents about half of the total tax gap. Individual income tax also accounts for about half of all tax liabilities.

The collection gap is the cumulative amount of assessed tax, penalties, and interest that the IRS expects to remain uncol-lectible. In essence, it represents the difference between the total balance of unpaid assessments and the net taxes receivable reported on the IRS's balance sheet. The tax gap and the collection gap are related and overlapping concepts, but they have signifi-cant differences. The collection gap is a cumulative balance sheet concept for a particular point in time, while the tax gap is like an income statement item for a single year. Moreover, the tax gap estimates include all noncompliance, while the collection gap includes only amounts that have been assessed (a small portion of all noncompliance).

Other Claims for Refunds

Management has estimated amounts that may be paid out as other claims for tax refunds. This estimate represents an amount (principal and interest) that may be paid for claims pending judicial review by the Federal courts or, internally, by appeals. The total estimated payout (including principal and interest) for claims pending judicial review by the Federal courts is $12.0 billion and $1.7 billion for fiscal years 2005 and 2004, respectively. For those under appeal, the estimated payout is $11.1 billion and $6.7 billion for fiscal years 2005 and 2004, respectively. There are also unasserted claims for refunds of certain excise taxes. Although these refund claims have been deemed to be probable, they do not meet the criteria in SFFAS No. 5 for reporting the amounts in the balance sheets or for disclosure in the Notes to the Financial Statements. However, they meet the criteria in SFFAS No. 7 for inclusion as supplemental information. To the extent judgments against the Government for these claims prompt other similarly situated taxpayers to file similar refund claims, these amounts could become significantly greater.

Appendix: Significant Government Entities Included and Excluded from the Financial Statements

This *Financial Report* includes the executive branch with their corresponding departments and entities, the legislative and judicial branches, and other independent establishments and Government corporations. Excluded are privately owned Government-sponsored enterprises such as the Federal Home Loan Banks and the Federal National Mortgage Association. The Federal Reserve System is excluded because organizations and functions pertaining to monetary policy are traditionally separate from, and independent of, other central Government organizations and functions.

Significant Entities Included in these Statements:
(in Statement of Net Cost order):

Department of Defense (DOD)
  www.defenselink.mil
Department of Health and Human Services (HHS)
  www.hhs.gov
Social Security Administration (SSA)
  www.ssa.gov
Department of Veterans Affairs (VA)
  www.va.gov
Department of Agriculture (USDA)
  www.usda.gov
Department of the Treasury (Treasury)
  www.ustreas.gov
Department of Education (ED)
  www.ed.gov
Department of Homeland Security (DHS)
  www.dhs.gov
Department of Transportation (DOT)
  www.dot.gov
Department of Labor (DOL)
  www.dol.gov
Department of Energy (DOE)
  www.energy.gov
Department of Housing and Urban
  Development (HUD)
  www.hud.gov
Department of Justice (DOJ)
  www.usdoj.gov
Office of Personnel Management (OPM)
  www.opm.gov
National Aeronautics and Space Administration
  (NASA)
  www.nasa.gov
Department of the Interior (DOI)
  www.doi.gov
Department of State (State)
  www.state.gov
U.S. Agency for International Development
  (USAID)
  www.usaid.gov
Railroad Retirement Board (RRB)
  www.rrb.gov
Environmental Protection Agency (EPA)
  www.epa.gov
Department of Commerce (DOC)
  www.doc.gov
Federal Communications Commission (FCC)
  www.fcc.gov

National Science Foundation (NSF)
  www.nsf.gov
Federal Deposit Insurance Corporation (FDIC)
  www.fdic.gov
Small Business Administration (SBA)
  www.sba.gov
Pension Benefit Guaranty Corporation (PBGC)
  www.pbgc.gov
Nuclear Regulatory Commission (NRC)
  www.nrc.gov
Tennessee Valley Authority (TVA)
  www.tva.gov
National Credit Union Administration (NCUA)
  www.ncua.gov
General Services Administration (GSA)
  www.gsa.gov
Export-Import Bank of the United States
  (Ex-Im Bank)
  www.exim.gov
U.S. Postal Service (USPS)
  www.usps.gov
Farm Credit System Insurance Corporation
  (FCSIC)
  www.fcsic.gov
U.S. Securities and Exchange Commission (SEC)
  www.sec.gov
Smithsonian Institution
  www.si.edu

All Other Entities
Executive Office of the President
Federal Trade Commission (FTC)
  www.ftc.gov
Government Accountability Office (GAO)
  www.gao.gov
Government Printing Office (GPO)
  www.gpo.gov
Library of Congress (LC)
  www.loc.gov
National Archives and Records Administration
  (NARA)
  www.nara.gov
National Transportation Safety Board (NTSB)
  www.ntsb.gov
Office of Management and Budget(OMB)
  www.whitehouse.gov/omb

Significant Entities Excluded from these Statements:

Army and Air Force Exchange Service

Board of Governors of the Federal Reserve System (Including the Federal Reserve Banks)

Federal National Mortgage Association (Fannie Mae)

Farm Credit System

Federal Home Loan Banks

Federal Retirement Thrift Investment Board (Including the Thrift Savings Fund)

Financing Corporation

Federal Home Loan Mortgage Corporation (Freddie Mac)

Marine Corps Exchange

Navy Exchange Service Command

Resolution Funding Corporation

U.S.A. Education Inc. (Sallie Mae)

G A O
Accountability • Integrity • Reliability

United States Government Accountability Office
Washington, DC 20548

Comptroller General
of the United States

The President
The President of the Senate
The Speaker of the House of Representatives

The Secretary of the Treasury, in coordination with the Director of the Office of Management and Budget (OMB), is required annually to submit financial statements for the U.S. government to the President and the Congress. GAO is required to audit these statements.[1] This is our report on the accompanying U.S. government's consolidated financial statements for the fiscal years ended September 30, 2005 and 2004,[2] and our associated reports on internal control and compliance with significant laws and regulations.

The federal government is responsible for (1) preparing annual consolidated financial statements in conformity with U.S. generally accepted accounting principles (GAAP); (2) establishing, maintaining, and assessing internal control to provide reasonable assurance that the control objectives of the Federal Managers'

[1] The Government Management Reform Act of 1994 has required such reporting, covering the executive branch of government, beginning with financial statements prepared for fiscal year 1997. 31 U.S.C. 331(e). The federal government has elected to include certain financial information on the legislative and judicial branches in the consolidated financial statements as well.

[2] The consolidated financial statements for the fiscal years ended September 30, 2005 and 2004, consist of the Statements of Net Cost, Statements of Operations and Changes in Net Position, Reconciliations of Net Operating Cost and Unified Budget Deficit, Statements of Changes in Cash Balance from Unified Budget and Other Activities, and Balance Sheets, including the related notes to these financial statements.

Financial Integrity Act (FMFIA) are met;[3] and (3) complying with significant laws and regulations. Also, the 24 Chief Financial Officers (CFO) Act agencies[4] are responsible for implementing and maintaining financial management systems that substantially comply with Federal Financial Management Improvement Act of 1996 (FFMIA)[5] requirements. Our objective was to audit the consolidated financial statements for the fiscal years ended September 30, 2005 and 2004. Appendix I discusses the scope and methodology of our work.

A significant number of material weaknesses[6] related to financial systems, fundamental recordkeeping and financial reporting, and incomplete documentation continued to (1) hamper the federal government's ability to reliably report a significant portion of its assets, liabilities, costs, and other related information; (2) affect the federal government's ability to reliably measure the full cost as well as the financial and nonfinancial performance of certain pro-

---

[3] 31 U.S.C. 3512 (c), (d) (commonly referred to as FMFIA). This act requires agency heads to evaluate and report annually to the President on the adequacy of their internal control and accounting systems and on actions to correct significant problems.

[4] 31 U.S.C. 901(b). The Federal Emergency Management Agency (FEMA) was transferred to the new Department of Homeland Security (DHS) effective March 1, 2003. With this transfer, FEMA is no longer required to prepare and have audited stand-alone financial statements under the CFO Act, leaving 23 CFO Act agencies for fiscal year 2004. For fiscal year 2004, DHS was required to prepare and have audited financial statements under the Accountability of Tax Dollars Act of 2002, Pub. L. No. 107-289, 116 Stat. 2049 (Nov. 7, 2002). The DHS Financial Accountability Act, Pub. L. No. 108-330, 118 Stat.1275 (Oct. 16, 2004), added DHS to the list of CFO Act agencies and deleted FEMA, increasing the number of CFO Act agencies again to 24 for fiscal year 2005. With this designation, DHS is required to implement and maintain financial management systems that comply with FFMIA and its auditors are required to report on DHS's financial management systems' compliance with FFMIA beginning with fiscal year 2005. Also beginning in fiscal year 2005, the law requires that the Secretary of DHS include in its performance and accountability report an assertion on the internal control over financial reporting. DHS's auditors will be required to opine on such internal control beginning in fiscal year 2006.

[5] 31 U.S.C. 3512 note (Federal Financial Management Improvement Act).

[6] A material weakness is a condition that precludes the entity's internal control from providing reasonable assurance that misstatements, losses, or noncompliance material in relation to the financial statements or to stewardship information would be prevented or detected on a timely basis.

grams and activities; (3) impair the federal government's ability to adequately safeguard significant assets and properly record various transactions; and (4) hinder the federal government from having reliable financial information to operate in an economical, efficient, and effective manner. We found the following:

Material deficiencies in financial reporting (which also represent material weaknesses) and other limitations on the scope of our work resulted in conditions that continued to prevent us from expressing an opinion on the accompanying consolidated financial statements for the fiscal years ended September 30, 2005 and 2004.[7]

- The federal government did not maintain effective internal control over financial reporting (including safeguarding assets) and compliance with significant laws and regulations as of September 30, 2005.
- Our work to determine compliance with selected provisions of significant laws and regulations in fiscal year 2005 was limited by the material weaknesses and scope limitations discussed in this report.

DISCLAIMER OF OPINION ON THE CONSOLIDATED FINANCIAL STATEMENTS

Because of the federal government's inability to demonstrate the reliability of significant portions of the U.S. government's accompanying consolidated financial statements for fiscal years 2005 and 2004, principally resulting from the material deficiencies, and other limitations on the scope of our work, described in this

---

[7] We previously reported that material deficiencies prevented us from expressing an opinion on the consolidated financial statements of the U.S. government for fiscal years 1997 through 2004.

report, we are unable to, and we do not, express an opinion on such financial statements.

As a result of the material deficiencies in the federal government's systems, recordkeeping, documentation, and financial reporting and scope limitations, readers are cautioned that amounts reported in the consolidated financial statements and related notes may not be reliable. These material deficiencies and scope limitations also affect the reliability of certain information contained in the accompanying Management's Discussion and Analysis and other financial management information—including information used to manage the government day to day and budget information reported by federal agencies—that is taken from the same data sources as the consolidated financial statements.

We have not audited and do not express an opinion on the Management's Discussion and Analysis, Stewardship Information, Supplemental Information, or other information included in the accompanying fiscal year 2005 *Financial Report of the United States Government.*

Significant Matters of Emphasis

Before discussing the material deficiencies and the additional limitations on the scope of our work we identified, two significant matters require emphasis—the nation's fiscal imbalance and restatements of certain agencies' prior-year financial statements.

The Nation's Fiscal Imbalance

While we are unable to express an opinion on the U.S. government's consolidated financial statements, several key items deserve emphasis in order to put the information contained in the financial statements and the Management's Discussion and Analysis section of the *Financial Report of the United States Government* into context. First, while the reported $319 billion fiscal year 2005 unified budget deficit was significantly lower than the $412 billion unified budget deficit in fiscal year 2004, it was still very high given current economic growth rates and the overall composition of federal spending.[8] Furthermore, the federal government's reported net operating cost, which included expenses incurred during the year, increased to $760 billion in fiscal year 2005 from $616 billion in fiscal year 2004. Second, the U.S. government's total reported liabilities, net social insurance commitments[9] and other fiscal exposures continue to grow and now total more than $46 trillion, representing close to four times current GDP and up from about $20 trillion or two times GDP in 2000. Finally, while the nation's long-term fiscal imbalance continues to grow, the retirement of the "baby boom" generation is closer to becoming a reality with the first wave of boomers eligible for early retirement under Social Security in 2008. Given these and other factors, it seems clear that the nation's current fiscal path is unsustainable and that tough choices by the President and the Congress are necessary in order to address the nation's large and growing long-term fiscal imbalance.

---

[8] The reported on-budget deficits for fiscal years 2005 and 2004 were $494 billion and $567 billion, respectively. The transactions of the Postal Service and the Social Security trust funds are classified as off-budget. As such, their reported fiscal year 2005 and 2004 surpluses—$2 billion and $4 billion, respectively, for the Postal Service and $173 billion and $151 billion, respectively, for the Social Security trust funds—are excluded from the on-budget deficit but included in the unified budget deficit.

[9] These amounts are calculated based on the present value of net social insurance obligations for a 75 year period computed on an open group basis.

Potential Impact of Restatements

We continue to have concerns about the identification of mis-statements in federal agencies' prior year financial statements. At least 7[10] of the 24 CFO Act agencies restated certain of their fiscal year 2004 financial statements to correct errors. During fiscal year 2005, we reviewed the causes and nature of the restatements made by certain CFO Act agencies to their fiscal year 2003 financial statements and recommended improvements in internal controls and audit procedures to prevent or detect future similar errors. Frequent restatements to correct errors can undermine public trust and confidence in both the entity and all responsible parties. The material internal control weaknesses discussed in this report serve to increase the risk that additional errors may occur and not be identified on a timely basis by agency management or their auditors, resulting in further restatements.

Limitations on the Scope of Our Work

For fiscal year 2005, there were limitations on the scope of our work in addition to the material deficiencies. Specifically, Treasury was unable to provide us with complete and properly supported drafts of the U.S. government's consolidated financial statements in time for us to complete all of our planned auditing procedures related to the compilation of these financial statements.

Treasury and OMB depend on certain federal agencies' representations to provide their representations to us regarding the U.S.

---

[10] Three of these agencies had received an unqualified opinion on their originally issued fiscal year 2004 financial statements while the remaining four of the seven agencies had received a disclaimer of opinion on their financial statements. The auditor for one of the agencies withdrew the unqualified opinion that had been previously rendered on the agency's fiscal year 2004 financial statements and issued a qualified opinion on the restated financial statements.

government's consolidated financial statements. For fiscal year 2005, Treasury and OMB were unable to provide us with adequate representations regarding the U.S. government's consolidated financial statements primarily because of insufficient representations provided to them by two CFO Act agencies.

For fiscal year 2004, additional limitations on the scope of our work related to (1) the timing of receipt of the U.S. government's consolidated financial statements, (2) the availability of certain audit documentation for several federal agencies, and (3) the adequacy of management and legal representations.

Material Deficiencies

The federal government did not maintain adequate systems or have sufficient, reliable evidence to support certain material information reported in the accompanying consolidated financial statements, as briefly described below. These material deficiencies, which generally have existed for years, contributed to our disclaimer of opinion and also constitute material weaknesses in internal control. Appendix II describes the material deficiencies in more detail and highlights the primary effects of these material weaknesses on the accompanying consolidated financial statements and on the management of federal government operations. These material deficiencies were the federal government's inability to:

- satisfactorily determine that property, plant, and equipment and inventories and related property, primarily held by DOD, were properly reported in the consolidated financial statements;

- reasonably estimate or adequately support amounts reported for certain liabilities, such as environmental and disposal liabilities, or determine whether commitments and contingencies were complete and properly reported;
- support significant portions of the total net cost of operations, most notably related to DOD, and adequately reconcile disbursement activity at certain agencies;
- ensure that the federal government's consolidated financial statements were consistent with the underlying audited agency financial statements, balanced, and in conformity with GAAP;
- adequately account for and reconcile intragovernmental activity and balances between federal agencies; and
- resolve material differences that exist between the total net outlays reported in federal agencies' Statements of Budgetary Resources and the records used by Treasury to prepare the Statements of Changes in Cash Balance from Unified Budget and Other Activities.

Due to the material deficiencies and the additional limitations on the scope of our work discussed above, there may also be additional issues that could affect the consolidated financial statements that have not been identified.

ADVERSE OPINION ON INTERNAL CONTROL

Because of the effects of the material weaknesses discussed in this report, in our opinion, the federal government did not maintain effective internal control as of September 30, 2005, to meet the following objectives: (1) transactions are properly recorded, processed, and summarized to permit the preparation of the financial statements and stewardship information in conformity with GAAP, and assets are safeguarded against loss from unauthorized acquisition, use, or disposition; and (2) transactions are executed in accordance with laws governing the use of budget authority and with other significant laws and regulations that could have a direct and material effect on the financial statements and stewardship information. Consequently, the federal government's internal control did not provide reasonable assurance that misstatements, losses, or noncompliance material in relation to the financial statements or to stewardship information would be prevented or detected on a timely basis. Our adverse opinion on internal control over financial reporting and compliance is based upon the criteria established under FMFIA. Individual federal agency financial statement audit reports identify additional reportable conditions[11] in internal control, some of which were reported by agency auditors as being material weaknesses at the individual agency level. These additional reportable conditions do not represent material weaknesses at the governmentwide level. Also, due to the issues noted throughout this report, additional material weaknesses may exist that have not been reported.

In addition to the material weaknesses that represented material deficiencies, which were discussed above, we found the following four other material weaknesses in internal control as of September 30, 2005. These weaknesses are discussed in more detail in appen-

---

[11] Reportable conditions are matters coming to our attention that, in our judgment, should be communicated because they represent significant deficiencies in the design or operation of internal control that could adversely affect the federal government's ability to meet the internal control objectives described in this report.

dix III, including the primary effects of the material weaknesses on the accompanying consolidated financial statements and on the management of federal government operations. These material weaknesses were the federal government's inability to:

- implement effective processes and procedures for properly estimating the cost of certain lending programs, related loan guarantee liabilities, and value of direct loans;
- determine the extent to which improper payments exist;
- identify and resolve information security control weaknesses and manage information security risks on an ongoing basis; and
- effectively manage its tax collection activities.

COMPLIANCE WITH SIGNIFICANT LAWS AND REGULATIONS

Our work to determine compliance with selected provisions of significant laws and regulations related to financial reporting was limited by the material weaknesses and scope limitations discussed above. U.S. generally accepted government auditing standards and OMB guidance require auditors to report on the agency's compliance with significant laws and regulations. Certain individual agency audit reports contain instances of noncompliance. None of these instances were material to the accompanying consolidated financial statements.

We caution that other noncompliance may have occurred and not been detected. Further, the results of our limited procedures may not be sufficient for other purposes. Our objective was not to, and we do not, express an opinion on compliance with significant laws and regulations.

AGENCY FINANCIAL MANAGEMENT SYSTEMS

To achieve the financial management improvements envisioned by the CFO Act, FFMIA, and, more recently, the President's Management Agenda, federal agencies need to modernize their financial management systems to generate reliable, useful, and timely financial and performance information throughout the year and at year-end. As discussed throughout this report, serious financial management weaknesses have contributed significantly to our inability to determine the reliability of the consolidated financial statements. In this regard, for fiscal year 2005, auditors for the majority of the CFO Act agencies reported material weaknesses or other reportable conditions in internal control over financial reporting.

FFMIA requires auditors, as part of the CFO Act agencies' financial statement audits, to report whether agencies' financial management systems substantially comply with (1) federal financial management systems requirements, (2) applicable federal accounting standards, and (3) the federal government's *Standard General Ledger* at the transaction level. For fiscal year 2005, auditors for 19 of the 24 CFO Act agencies reported that the agencies' financial management systems did not substantially comply with one or more of these three FFMIA requirements, compared to 16 of 23 CFO Act agencies in fiscal year 2004. The DHS Financial Accountability Act added DHS to the list of CFO Act agencies, increasing the number of CFO Act agencies to 24 for fiscal year 2005. The auditors for DHS reported for fiscal year 2005 that the agency's financial management systems did not substantially comply with any of the three FFMIA requirements. In addition, auditors for the Department of Energy and the General Services

Administration reported that those agencies' financial management systems did not substantially comply with FFMIA requirements. The auditors had not reported any FFMIA compliance issues at those agencies in fiscal year 2004. As a result, the financial management systems at the majority of federal agencies are still unable to routinely produce reliable, useful, and timely financial information; and the federal government's capacity to manage with timely and objective data is limited, thereby hampering its ability to effectively administer and oversee its major programs.

- - - - -

We provided a draft of this report to Treasury and OMB officials, who provided technical comments, which have been incorporated as appropriate. Treasury and OMB officials expressed their continuing commitment to address the problems this report outlines.

David M. Walker
Comptroller General
of the United States

December 2, 2005

APPENDIX I

Objectives, Scope, and Methodology

The Government Management Reform Act of 1994 expanded the requirements of the Chief Financial Officers (CFO) Act by making the inspectors general of 24 major federal agencies[12] responsible for annual audits of agencywide financial statements prepared by these agencies and GAO responsible for the audit of the U.S. government's consolidated financial statements. The Accountability of Tax Dollars (ATD) Act of 2002[13] requires most other executive branch agencies to prepare and have audited annual financial statements. The Office of Management and Budget and the Department of the Treasury (Treasury) have identified 35 agencies[14] that are significant to the U.S. government's consolidated financial statements. Our work was performed in coordination and cooperation with the inspectors general and independent public accountants for these 35 agencies to achieve our joint audit objectives. Our audit approach focused primarily on determining the current status of the material deficiencies and the other material weaknesses affecting internal control that we had previously reported in our report on the consolidated financial statements for fiscal year 2004.[15] Our work included separately auditing the following significant federal agency components:

- We audited and expressed an unqualified opinion on the Internal Revenue Service's (IRS) fiscal years 2005 and 2004

---

[12] 31 U.S.C. 901(b), 3521(e); see footnote 4. The 1994 act authorized the Office of Management and Budget to designate agency components that also would receive a financial statement audit. 31 U.S.C. 3515(c); see footnote 1.

[13] Pub. L. No. 107-289, 116 Stat. 2049 (Nov. 7, 2002).

[14] See *Treasury Financial Manual*, volume I, part 2, chapter 4700, for a listing of the 35 agencies.

[15] For our report on the U.S. government's consolidated financial statements for fiscal year 2004, see U.S. Department of the Treasury, *Financial Report of the United States Government* (Washington, D.C. December 2004), pp. 33-53, which can be found on GAO's Internet site at www.gao.gov.

financial statements. In fiscal years 2005 and 2004, IRS collected about $2.3 trillion and $2.0 trillion, respectively, in tax payments and paid about $267 billion and $278 billion, respectively, in refunds to taxpayers.[16] In fiscal year 2005, we continued to report material internal control weaknesses, which resulted in ineffective internal control. Our tests of compliance with selected provisions of significant laws and regulations disclosed one area of noncompliance. We also found that IRS's financial management systems did not substantially comply with the requirements of the Federal Financial Management Improvement Act of 1996.

- We audited and expressed an unqualified opinion on the Schedules of Federal Debt managed by Treasury's Bureau of the Public Debt (BPD) for the fiscal years ended September 30, 2005 and 2004.[17] The schedules reported for these 2 fiscal years (1) approximately $4.6 trillion (2005) and $4.3 trillion (2004) of federal debt held by the public;[18] (2) about $3.3 trillion (2005) and $3.1 trillion (2004) of intragovernmental debt holdings;[19] and (3) about $181 billion (2005) and $158 billion (2004) of interest on federal debt held by the public. We reported that as of September 30, 2005, BPD had effective internal control over financial reporting and compliance with significant laws and regulations relevant to the Schedule of Federal Debt. Further, we reported that there was no reportable noncompliance in fiscal year 2005 with selected provisions of significant laws we tested.

---

[16] GAO, *Financial Audit: IRS's Fiscal Years 2005 and 2004 Financial Statements,* GAO-06-137 (Washington, D.C.: Nov. 10, 2005).

[17] GAO, *Financial Audit: Bureau of the Public Debt's Fiscal Years 2005 and 2004 Schedules of Federal Debt,* GAO-06-169 (Washington, D.C.: Nov. 7, 2005).

[18] The public holding federal debt is comprised of individuals, corporations, state and local governments, the Federal Reserve Banks, and foreign governments and central banks.

[19] Intragovernmental debt holdings represent federal debt issued by Treasury and held by certain federal government accounts such as the Social Security and Medicare trust funds.

- We audited and expressed unqualified opinions on the December 31, 2004 and 2003, financial statements of the funds administered by the Federal Deposit Insurance Corporation (FDIC), including the Bank Insurance Fund, the Savings Association Insurance Fund, and the FSLIC Resolution Fund.[20] We reported that as of December 31, 2004, FDIC had effective internal control over financial reporting and compliance with significant laws and regulations. In addition, we performed certain procedures and tests of internal control over certain material balances of the funds administered by FDIC as of September 30, 2005.

- We audited and expressed unqualified opinions on the fiscal years 2005 and 2004 financial statements of the United States Securities and Exchange Commission (SEC).[21] In fiscal year 2005, we continued to report material internal control weaknesses, which resulted in ineffective internal control over financial reporting. We reported that SEC had effective internal control over compliance with selected provisions of significant laws and regulations. Further, we reported that there was no reportable noncompliance with selected provisions of significant laws and regulations we tested.

We considered the CFO Act agencies' and certain other federal agencies' fiscal years 2005 and 2004 financial statements and the related auditors' reports prepared by the inspectors general or contracted independent public accountants. Financial statements and audit reports for these agencies provide information about the operations of each of these entities. We did not audit, and we do not express an opinion on, any of these individual federal agency financial statements.

---

[20] GAO, *Financial Audit: Federal Deposit Insurance Corporation Funds' 2004 and 2003 Financial Statements*, GAO-05-281 (Washington, D.C.: Feb. 11, 2005).

[21] GAO, *Financial Audit: Securities and Exchange Commission's Financial Statements for Fiscal Years 2005 and 2004*, GAO-06-239 (Washington, D.C.: Nov. 15, 2005).

We considered the Department of Defense's (DOD) assertion that DOD management prepared and submitted pursuant to the provisions of the National Defense Authorization Act for Fiscal Year 2002.[22] In accordance with section 1008 of this act, DOD reported that its fiscal year 2005 financial statements were not completely reliable. DOD cited deficiencies in several areas affecting its financial statements, including among others (1) property, plant, and equipment; (2) inventory and operating material and supplies; (3) environmental liabilities; (4) intragovernmental eliminations and related accounting adjustments; and (5) disbursement activity.

We performed sufficient audit work to provide this report on the consolidated financial statements, internal control, and the results of our assessment of compliance with selected provisions of significant laws and regulations. We considered the limitations on the scope of our work in forming our conclusions. Our work was performed in accordance with U.S. generally accepted government auditing standards.

---

[22] Pub. L. No. 107-107, §1008,115 Stat. 1012, 1204 (Dec. 28, 2001).

APPENDIX II

Material Deficiencies

The continuing material deficiencies discussed below contributed to our disclaimer of opinion on the federal government's consolidated financial statements. The federal government did not maintain adequate systems or have sufficient, reliable evidence to support information reported in the accompanying consolidated financial statements, as described below.

Property, Plant, and Equipment and Inventories and Related Property

The federal government could not satisfactorily determine that property, plant, and equipment (PP&E) and inventories and related property were properly reported in the consolidated financial statements. Most of the PP&E and inventories and related property are the responsibility of the Department of Defense (DOD). As in past years, DOD did not maintain adequate systems or have sufficient records to provide reliable information on these assets. Other agencies, most notably the National Aeronautics and Space Administration, reported continued weaknesses in internal control procedures and processes related to PP&E.

Without reliable asset information, the federal government does not fully know the assets it owns and their location and condition and cannot effectively (1) safeguard assets from physical deterioration, theft, or loss; (2) account for acquisitions and disposals of such assets; (3) ensure that the assets are available for use when needed; (4) prevent unnecessary storage and maintenance costs or purchase of assets already on hand; and (5) determine the full costs of programs that use these assets.

Liabilities and Commitments and Contingencies

The federal government could not reasonably estimate or adequately support amounts reported for certain liabilities. For example, DOD was not able to estimate with assurance key components of its environmental and disposal liabilities. In addition, DOD could not support a significant amount of its estimated military postretirement health benefits liabilities included in federal employee and veteran benefits payable. These unsupported amounts related to the cost of direct health care provided by DOD-managed military treatment facilities. Further, the federal government could not determine whether commitments and contingencies, including those related to treaties and other international agreements entered into to further the U.S. government's interests, were complete and properly reported.

Problems in accounting for liabilities affect the determination of the full cost of the federal government's current operations and the extent of its liabilities. Also, improperly stated environmental and disposal liabilities and weak internal control supporting the process for their estimation affect the federal government's ability to determine priorities for cleanup and disposal activities and to appropriately consider future budgetary resources needed to carry out these activities. In addition, when disclosures of commitments and contingencies are incomplete or incorrect, reliable information is not available about the extent of the federal government's obligations.

Cost of Government Operations and Disbursement Activity

The previously discussed material deficiencies in reporting assets and liabilities, material deficiencies in financial statement preparation, as discussed below, and the lack of adequate disbursement reconciliations at certain federal agencies affect reported net costs. As a result, the federal government was unable to support significant portions of the total net cost of operations, most notably related to DOD.

With respect to disbursements, DOD and certain other federal agencies reported continued weaknesses in reconciling disbursement activity. For fiscal years 2005 and 2004, there was unreconciled disbursement activity, including unreconciled differences between federal agencies' and the Department of the Treasury's records of disbursements and unsupported federal agency adjustments, totaling billions of dollars, which could also affect the balance sheet.

Unreliable cost information affects the federal government's ability to control and reduce costs, assess performance, evaluate programs, and set fees to recover costs where required. Improperly recorded disbursements could result in misstatements in the financial statements and in certain data provided by federal agencies for inclusion in the President's budget concerning obligations and outlays.

Preparation of Consolidated Financial Statements

Fiscal year 2005 was the second year that Treasury used its Governmentwide Financial Reporting System (GFRS) to collect agency financial statement information taken directly from federal agencies' audited financial statements. The goal of GFRS is to be able to directly link information from federal agencies' audited financial statements to amounts reported in the consolidated financial statements and resolve many of the weaknesses we previously identified in the process for preparing the consolidated financial statements. For both the fiscal year 2005 and 2004 reporting processes, GFRS was able to capture agency financial information, but GFRS was still not at the stage that it could be used to fully compile the consolidated financial statements from the information captured. Therefore, for fiscal year 2005 Treasury continued to primarily use manual procedures to prepare the consolidated financial statements. As discussed in our scope limitation section of this report, Treasury could not produce the fiscal year 2005 consolidated financial statements and supporting documentation in time for us to complete all of our planned auditing procedures. In addition, the federal government continued to have inadequate systems, controls, and procedures to ensure that the consolidated financial statements are consistent with the underlying audited agency financial statements, balanced, and in conformity with U.S. generally accepted accounting principles (GAAP). Specifically, during our fiscal year 2005 audit, we found the following:[23]

- Treasury's process for compiling the consolidated financial statements did not ensure that the information in all of the 5 principal financial statements and notes were fully consistent with the underlying information in federal agencies' audited financial statements and other financial data. Treasury made progress in demonstrating amounts in the Balance Sheet and the Statement of Net Cost were consistent with federal agencies' audited financial statements prior to eliminating intragovernmental activity and balances. However, about 25 percent of the significant federal agencies' auditors reported internal control weaknesses related to the processes the agencies perform to provide financial statement information to Treasury for preparing the consolidated financial statements.
- To make the fiscal years 2005 and 2004 consolidated financial statements balance, Treasury recorded a net $4.3 billion decrease and a net $3.4 billion increase, respectively, to net operating cost on the Statements of Operations and Changes in Net Position, which it labeled "Unreconciled Transactions Affecting the Change in Net Position."[24] An additional net $3.2 billion and $1.2 billion of unreconciled transactions were recorded in the Statement of Net Cost for fiscal years 2005 and 2004, respectively. Treasury is unable to fully identify and quantify all components of these unreconciled activities.

---

[23] Most of the issues we identified in fiscal year 2005 existed in fiscal year 2004, and many have existed for a number of years. In May 2005, we reported in greater detail on the issues we identified in GAO, *Financial Audit: Process for Preparing the Consolidated Financial Statements of the U.S. Government Continues to Need Improvement*, GAO-05-407 (Washington, D.C.: May 4, 2005). This report includes numerous recommendations to Treasury and OMB.

[24] Although Treasury was unable to determine how much of the unreconciled transactions, if any, relate to operations, it reported unreconciled transactions as a component of net operating cost in the accompanying consolidated financial statements.

- The federal government did not have an adequate process to identify and report items needed to reconcile the operating results, which for fiscal year 2005 showed a net operating cost of $760 billion, to the budget results, which for the same period showed a unified budget deficit of $318.5 billion. In addition, a net $13.2 billion "net amount of all other differences" was needed to force this statement into balance.

- Treasury's ability to eliminate certain intragovernmental activity and balances continues to be impaired by the federal agencies' problems in handling their intragovernmental transactions. As discussed below, amounts reported for federal agency trading partners[25] for certain intragovernmental accounts were significantly out of balance, resulting in the need for unsupported intragovernmental elimination entries in order to force the Statement of Operations and Changes in Net Position into balance. In addition, significant differences in other intragovernmental accounts, primarily related to transactions with the General Fund, have not been reconciled and still remain unresolved. Therefore, the federal government continues to be unable to determine the impact of unreconciled intragovernmental activity and balances to the consolidated financial statements.

- Treasury lacked a process to ensure that fiscal years 2005 and 2004 consolidated financial statements and notes were comparable. Certain information reported for fiscal 2004 may require reclassification to be comparable to the fiscal year 2005 amounts. However, Treasury did not analyze this information or reclassify amounts within various financial statement line items and notes to enhance comparability. For example, the Reconciliations of Net Operating Cost and Unified Budget Deficit showed $47.8 billion and $.2 billion for property,

---

[25] Trading partners are U.S. government agencies, departments, or other components included in the consolidated financial statements that do business with each other.

plant and equipment disposals and revaluations for fiscal years 2005 and 2004, respectively. However, based on the financial information provided by agencies to Treasury in GFRS, the fiscal year 2004 amount would be $25.4 billion. The difference would be reclassified from the net amount of all other differences line item on the Reconciliations of Net Operating Cost and Unified Budget Deficit.

- Treasury did not have an adequate process to ensure that the financial statements, related notes, Stewardship Information, and Supplemental Information are presented in conformity with GAAP. For example, we found that certain financial information required by GAAP was not disclosed in the consolidated financial statements. Treasury submitted a proposal to the Federal Accounting Standards Advisory Board (FASAB) seeking to amend previously issued standards and eliminate or lessen the disclosure requirements for the consolidated financial statements so that GAAP would no longer require certain of the information that Treasury has not been reporting. An exposure draft of a proposed FASAB standard, based on the Treasury proposal, is currently out for comment. Treasury stated that it is waiting for FASAB approval and issuance of this proposed standard to determine the disclosures that will be required in future consolidated financial statements. As a result of Treasury not providing us with adequate documentation of its rationale for excluding the currently required information and certain of the material deficiencies noted above, we were unable again to determine if the missing information was material to the consolidated financial statements.

- Information system weaknesses existed within the segments of GFRS that were used during the fiscal years 2005 and 2004 reporting processes. We found that the GFRS database (1) was not configured to prevent the alteration of data submitted by federal agencies and (2) was used for both production and testing during the reporting processes. Therefore, information submitted by federal agencies within GFRS is not adequately protected against unauthorized modification or loss. In addition, Treasury was unable to explain why numerous GFRS users appeared to have inappropriate access with GFRS agency information or demonstrate the appropriate segregation of duties exist.

- Although Treasury made progress in addressing them, certain other internal control weaknesses in its process for preparing the consolidated financial statements continued to exist and involved a lack of (1) appropriate documentation of certain policies and procedures for preparing the consolidated financial statements, (2) adequate supporting documentation for certain adjustments made to the consolidated financial statements, and (3) necessary management reviews.
- The consolidated financial statements include financial information for the executive, legislative, and judicial branches, to the extent that federal agencies within those branches have provided Treasury such information. However, there are undetermined amounts of assets, liabilities, costs, and revenues that are not included, and the federal government did not provide evidence or disclose in the consolidated financial statements that the excluded financial information was immaterial.
- Treasury did not have the infrastructure to address the magnitude of the fiscal year 2005 financial reporting challenges it was faced with, such as an incomplete financial reporting system, compressed time frames for compiling the financial information, and lack of adequate internal control over the financial statement preparation process. We found that personnel at Treasury's Financial Management Service had excessive workloads that required an extraordinary amount of effort and dedication to compile the consolidated financial statements; however, there were not enough personnel with specialized financial reporting

experience to ensure reliable financial reporting by the
reporting date.
- Treasury, in coordination with OMB, had not provided us with
adequate documentation evidencing an executable plan of
action and milestones for short-term and long range solutions
for certain internal control weaknesses we have previously
reported regarding the process for preparing the consolidated
financial statements.

Accounting for and Reconciliation of Intragovernmental Activity and Balances

Federal agencies are unable to adequately account for and reconcile
intragovernmental activity and balances. The Office of Management
and Budget (OMB) and Treasury require the chief financial officers
(CFO) of 35 executive departments and agencies to reconcile, on a quarterly basis, selected intragovernmental activity and balances with their
trading partners. In addition, these agencies are required to report to
Treasury, the agency's inspector general, and GAO on the extent and
results of intragovernmental activity and balances reconciliation efforts
as of the end of the fiscal year.

A substantial number of the agencies did not fully perform the required
reconciliations for fiscal years 2005 and 2004. For these fiscal years,
based on trading partner information provided in GFRS, Treasury produced a "Material Difference Report" for each agency showing amounts
for certain intragovernmental activity and balances that significantly
differed from those of its corresponding trading partners. After analysis
of the "Material Difference Reports" for fiscal year 2005, we noted a significant number of CFOs were still unable to explain the differences
with their trading partners. For both fiscal years 2005 and 2004,
amounts reported by federal agency trading partners for certain
intragovernmental accounts were significantly out of balance. In addition, about 25 percent of the significant federal agencies reported internal control weaknesses regarding reconciliations of intragovernmental

activity and balances. As a result, the federal government's ability to determine the impact of these differences on the amounts reported in the consolidated financial statements is impaired. Resolving the intra-governmental transactions problem remains a difficult challenge and will require a commitment by federal agencies and strong leadership and oversight by OMB.

Net Outlays—A Component of the Budget Deficit

OMB Circular A-136, *Financial Reporting Requirements*, which incorporated and updated OMB Bulletin No. 01-09, *Form and Content of Agency Financial Statements*, states that outlays in federal agencies' Statement of Budgetary Resources (SBR) should agree with the net outlays reported in the budget of the U.S. government. In addition, Statement of Federal Financial Accounting Standards No. 7, *Accounting for Revenue and Other Financing Sources and Concepts for Reconciling Budgetary and Financial Accounting*, requires explanation of any material differences between the information required to be disclosed (including net outlays) in the financial statements and the amounts described as "actual" in the budget of the U.S. government.

The federal government reported in the Statement of Changes in Cash Balance from Unified Budget and Other Activities (Statement of Changes in Cash Balance) and the Reconciliations of Net Operating Cost and Unified Budget Deficit (Reconciliation Statement) budget deficits for fiscal years 2005 and 2004 of $318.5 billion and $412.3 billion, respectively. The budget deficit is calculated by subtracting actual budget outlays from actual budget receipts.[26] As we have reported since

---

[26] In previous years, the Statement of Changes in Cash Balance reported actual budget outlays and actual budget receipts; however, beginning in fiscal year 2004, the federal government chose not to disclose budget outlays and budget receipts in this financial statement and only included the budget deficit. Receipts and net outlays (unified budget amounts) are also reported in governmentwide reports—specifically, in the President's Budget (annually); Treasury's Final Monthly Treasury Statement, as part of leading economic indicators on federal finances (quarterly); and Treasury's annual *Combined Statement of Receipts, Outlays, and Balances of the United States Government*.

fiscal year 2003, we found material unreconciled differences between the total net outlays reported in selected federal agencies' SBRs and Treasury's central accounting records, which it uses to prepare the Statement of Changes in Cash Balance. Treasury's processes for preparing the Statement of Changes in Cash Balance do not include procedures for identifying and resolving differences between its central accounting records and net outlay amounts reported in agencies' SBRs.

In fiscal year 2004, we noted reported internal control weaknesses regarding certain agencies' SBRs. In fiscal year 2005, several agencies' auditors reported internal control weaknesses (1) affecting the agencies' SBRs, and (2) relating to monitoring, accounting and reporting of budgetary transactions. These weaknesses could affect the reporting and calculation of the net outlay amounts in the agencies' SBRs. In addition, such weaknesses transcend to agencies' ability to also report reliable budgetary information to Treasury and OMB and may affect the unified budget outlays reported by Treasury in its *Combined Statement of Receipts, Outlays, and Balances*,[27] and certain amounts reported in the President's Budget.

OMB has been working with agencies to reduce the differences between the total net outlays reported in the federal agencies' SBRs and the Statement of Changes in Cash Balance. In June 2005, OMB issued its *Differences Between FY 2004 Budget Execution Reports and Financial Statements for CFO Act Agencies* report that discusses various types of differences in federal agency financial statements and budget execution reports, including net outlays and makes recommendations for OMB and federal agencies to consider in improving both sets of reports in the future.

---

[27] Treasury's *Combined Statement of Receipts, Outlays, and Balances* presents budget results and cash related assets and liabilities of the federal government with supporting details. Treasury represents this report as the recognized official publication of receipts and outlays of the federal government based on agency reporting.

Until the material differences between the total net outlays reported in the federal agencies' SBRs and the records used to prepare the Statement of Changes in Cash Balance are timely reconciled, the effect of these differences on the U.S. government's consolidated financial statements will be unknown.

APPENDIX III

Other Material Weaknesses

The federal government did not maintain effective internal control over financial reporting (including safeguarding assets) and compliance with significant laws and regulations as of September 30, 2005. In addition to the material deficiencies discussed in appendix II, we found the following four other material weaknesses in internal control.

Loans Receivable and Loan Guarantee Liabilities

Federal agencies continue to have material weaknesses and reportable conditions related to their lending activities. The Department of Housing and Urban Development lacked adequate management reviews of underlying data and cost estimation methodologies that resulted in material errors being undetected, and significant adjustments were needed. In addition, the Department of Education's processes do not provide for a robust budget-to-actual cost comparison or facilitate assessments of the validity of its lending program cost estimates. While the Small Business Administration made substantial progress to improve its cost estimation processes, additional improvements are still needed to ensure that year end reporting is accurate. These deficiencies plus others at the Department of Agriculture relating to the processes and procedures for estimating program costs, continue to adversely affect the federal government's ability to support annual budget requests for these programs, making future budgetary decisions, manage program costs, and measure the performance of lending activities. Further, these weaknesses and the complexities associated with estimating the costs of lending activities greatly increase the risk that significant errors in agency and governmentwide financial statements could occur and go undetected.

Improper Payments

While agencies have made progress in implementing processes and controls to identify, estimate, and reduce improper payments,[28] such improper payments are a longstanding, widespread, and significant problem in the federal government. Congress acknowledged this problem by passing the Improper Payment Information Act (IPIA)[29] in 2002. The IPIA requires agencies to review all programs and activities, identify those that may be susceptible to significant improper payments,[30] estimate and report the annual amount of improper payments for those programs, and implement actions to cost-effectively reduce improper payments. Further, in fiscal year 2005, OMB began to separately track the elimination of improper payments under the President's Management Agenda.

Significant challenges remain to effectively achieve the goals of the IPIA. From our review of agencies' fiscal year 2005 Performance and Accountability Reports (PARs), we noted that some agencies still have not instituted a systematic method of reviewing all programs and activities, have not identified all programs susceptible to significant improper payments, and/or have not annually estimated improper payments for its high risk programs. For example, 7 major agency programs with outlays totaling about $280 billion, including Medicaid and the Temporary Assistance For Needy Families programs, still cannot annually estimate improper payments, even though they were required by OMB to report such information beginning with their fiscal year 2003 budget submissions. In addition, two agency auditors that tested

---

[28] Improper payments include inadvertent errors, such as duplicate payments and miscalculations, payments for unsupported or inadequately supported claims, payments for services not rendered, payments to ineligible beneficiaries, and payments resulting from fraud and abuse by program participants and/or federal employees.

[29] Pub. L. No. 107-300, 116 Stat. 2350 (Nov. 26, 2002).

[30] OMB defines the term "significant improper payments" as "annual erroneous payments in the program exceeding both 2.5 percent of program payments and $10 million."

compliance with IPIA cited agency noncompliance with the act in their annual audit reports.

Federal agencies' estimates of improper payments, based on available information, for fiscal year 2005 exceeded $38 billion, a net decrease of about $7 billion, or 16 percent, from the prior year improper payment estimate of $45 billion.[31] This decrease was attributable to the following factors. In fiscal year 2005, the Department of Health and Human Services reported a $9.6 billion decrease in its Medicare program improper payment estimate, principally due to improvements in its due diligence with providers to ensure the necessary documentation is in place to support payment claims. However, in fiscal year 2005, this decrease was partially offset as a result of more programs reporting estimates of improper payments.

Information Security

Although progress has been made, serious and widespread information security control weaknesses continue to place federal assets at risk of inadvertent or deliberate misuse, financial information at risk of unauthorized modification or destruction, sensitive information at risk of inappropriate disclosure, and critical operations at risk of disruption. GAO has reported information security as a high-risk area across government since February 1997. Such information security control weaknesses could result in compromising the reliability and availability of data that are recorded in or transmitted by federal financial management systems. A primary reason for these weaknesses is that federal agencies have not yet fully institutionalized comprehensive security management programs, which are critical to identifying information security control weaknesses, resolving information security problems, and managing information security risks on an ongoing basis. The

---

[31] In their fiscal year 2005 PARs, selected agencies updated their fiscal year 2004 improper payment estimates to reflect changes since issuance of their fiscal year 2004 PARs. These updates increased the governmentwide improper payment estimate for fiscal year 2004 from $45 billion to $46 billion.

Congress has shown continuing interest in addressing these risks, as evidenced with hearings on Federal Information Security Management Act of 2002[32] implementation and information security. In addition, the administration has taken important actions to improve information security, such as revising agency internal control requirements in OMB Circular A-123[33] and issuing extensive guidance on information security.

Tax Collection Activities

Material internal control weaknesses and systems deficiencies continue to affect the federal government's ability to effectively manage its tax collection activities,[34] an issue that has been reported in our financial statement audit reports for the past 8 years. Due to errors and delays in recording taxpayer information, payments, and other activities, taxpayers were not always credited for payments made on their taxes owed, which could result in undue taxpayer burden. In addition, the federal government did not always follow up on potential unreported or underreported taxes and did not always pursue collection efforts against taxpayers owing taxes to the federal government.

Weaknesses in controls over tax collection activities continue to affect the federal government's ability to efficiently and effectively account for and collect revenue. Additionally, weaknesses in financial reporting of revenues affect the federal government's ability to make informed decisions about collection efforts. As a result, the federal government is vulnerable to loss of tax revenue and exposed to potentially billions of dollars in losses due to inappropriate refund disbursements.

(198319)

---

[32] Title III of the E-Government Act of 2002, Pub. L. No. 107-347, 116 Stat. 2899, 2946 (Dec. 17, 2002).

[33] OMB Circular No. A-123, *Management's Responsibility for Internal Control*, (Revised December 21, 2004).

[34] GAO, *Financial Audit: IRS's Fiscal Years 2005 and 2004 Financial Statements*, GAO-06-137 (Washington, D.C.: Nov. 10, 2005).